$69.95

THE SUPREME COURT OF OHIO ON CRIMINAL LAW

2017 EDITION

(Contains Decisions to December 31, 2016)

BY GARY A. POTTS, J.D.

FORMER MASTER COMMISSIONER OF CRIMINAL LAW FOR THE SUPREME COURT OF OHIO.

North American Legal Publishing

2017

NORTH AMERICAN LEGAL PUBLISHING
440-804-4592

Gpotts49@aol.com

ISBN:

INTRODUCTION

While Master Commissioner of Criminal Law and the Death Penalty with the Supreme Court of Ohio, I kept a journal of significant rulings of the Court.

This book grew out of that journal. It contains summaries and analyses of major decisions of the Supreme Court of Ohio on criminal law. It is my intention to provide the practitioner with the most significant rulings of the highest court of Ohio.

About Author:

Gary A. Potts received his undergraduate degree from Case-Western Reserve University, and his Juris Doctor degree from The Ohio State University College of Law.

He served as Master Commissioner of Criminal Law and Death Penalty Appeals with the Supreme Court of Ohio. He was also a special prosecutor for the FBI in organized crime and political corruption prosecutions. He has served as both a prosecutor for the State of Ohio and as a defense attorney. He has tried over seventy felony jury trials including death penalty prosecutions.

Other Works by Mr. Potts:

□ *Handling the Defense in a Bribery Prosecution*, 37 Am Jur Model Trials 273.

□ Book reviews for *Champion Magazine* (the publication of the National Association of Criminal Defense Lawyers).

Table of Contents

PART ONE: PRETRIAL ISSUES

CHAPTER 1

ARREST

1. Arrest Defined.
2. Minor Misdemeanors.
3. Arrest for Minor Misdemeanor.
4. Warrantless Arrest for Minor Misdemeanor.
5. Extra-Jurisdictional Arrest.
6. Warrantless Arrest for Felony.
7. Warrantless Arrest based on Prior knowledge.
8. Offenses of Violence.
9. Knowledge of Warrant for Felony.
10. Legal Warrantless Arrest.
11. A Stop Is Not an Arrest.
12. Custodial Search after Misdemeanor Arrest
13. Arrestee Improperly Removed from County.
14 Waiver of Miranda Rights Must Be Clear.
15. Implied Consent and the right to Counsel.
16. Providing Communication Facilities to Arrestee.
17 Eavesdropping Police Officer.
18. Common Investigation Arrest.
19. Radio Communication Arrest
20. Warrant Issued by a Non-Judicial Clerk.
21. Extraterritorial Arrest.

22. Commencement of Prosecution, Warrant or Summons not required.

1. Arrest, Defined.

An arrest consists of:
An intent to arrest,
Under a real or pretended authority,
Accompanied by an actual or constructive seizure or detention of the person,
Which is so understood by the person arrested."[1]

The decisions of the Supreme Court of Ohio on "arrests" focus on whether the arrest is with a warrant or is warrantless; the legality of the arrest, that is, whether the arrest is violative of a statute and, if so, whether that violation arises to the level of a Constitutional Fourth Amendment violation or a violation of the Ohio Constitution requiring suppression of any evidence seized incidental to the arrest.

2. Minor Misdemeanors.

A minor misdemeanor is an offense for which there is no possible term of incarceration, and where the penalty does not exceed a fine of one hundred and fifty dollars and optional community service. R.C. 2901.02 (G)(2).

Under R.C. 2935.26, a substantive right of freedom from arrest was created for one charged with a minor misdemeanor,[2]

---

[1] *State v. Barker*, 53 Ohio St. 2d 135, 372 N.E. 2d 1324 (1978).

The remaining misdemeanors are classified as misdemeanors of the first, second, third, fourth degree, and "unclassified misdemeanors.

"* * * where a law enforcement officer is otherwise authorized to arrest a person for a minor misdemeanor, the officer shall not arrest the person, but shall issue a citation * * *." This statute, however, contains exceptions that authorize an arrest for a minor misdemeanor [3] (See following section).

3. Arrest for Minor Misdemeanor.

The United States Supreme Court in *Atwater v. Lago Vista*,[4] held that a police officer may, with probable cause, arrest a person for a minor criminal offense committed in his presence without violating the Fourth Amendment. The Supreme Court of Ohio has determined that the Ohio Constitution provides greater protection for one who commits a minor misdemeanor than does the Fourth Amendment.[5]

Accordingly, a full custodial arrest for a minor misdemeanor, under most circumstances, is violative of the Ohio Constitution.[6] In recognizing the conditions under which an arrest for a minor misdemeanor is authorized, the *Jones* court held: "(A) Notwithstanding any other provision of the Revised Code, when a law enforcement officer is otherwise authorized to arrest a person for the commission of a minor misdemeanor, the officer shall not arrest the person, but shall issue a citation, unless one of the following applies:

"(1) The offender requires medical care or is unable to provide for his own safety.

"(2) The offender cannot or will not offer satisfactory evidence of his identity.

---

[3] *State v. Slatter,* 66 Ohio St. 2d 452, 423 N.E. 2d 100 (1981).

[4] *Atwater v. Lago Vista,* 532 U.S. 318, 121 S. Ct. 1536, 149 L.Ed. 2d 549 (2001).

[5] *State v. Brown*, 99 Ohio St. 3d 323, 792 N.E. 2d 175 (2003).

[6] *State v. Jones*, 88 Ohio St.3d 430, 727 N.E.2d 886 (2000).

"(3) The offender refuses to sign the citation.
"(4) The offender has previously been issued a citation for the commission of that misdemeanor and has failed to do one of the following:
"(a) Appear at the time and place stated in the citation;
"(b) Comply with division (C) of this section." (Division [C] provides a means of pleading guilty and paying the fine without a court appearance.) R.C. 2935.26.

CHECKLIST

- ☐ The police officer shall not arrest the offender unless one of the following occurs:
    - The offender requires medical care.
    - The offender cannot prove identity.
    - The offender refuses to sign the citation.
    - The offender failed to appear previously in court pursuant to a citation.
    - The offender has failed to waived appearance previously and has failed to appear in court.

4. Warrantless Arrest for Misdemeanor.

A municipal police officer does not have authority to arrest a person without a warrant for misdemeanors observed outside of the municipal limits of the police department. This is so notwithstanding R. C. 2935.03, which gives the police officer general authority to arrest and detain a person in violation of the laws of the state.[7] [It should be noted that in *Cincinnati*, the state conceded in its brief that if the arrest was found to be illegal the evidence should be suppressed].

As a result, the evidence was suppressed because the arrest was illegal under Ohio Law. The Court did not decide whether the evidence was nevertheless admissible based on a non-constitutional violation. Had the state argued admissibility based on a non-constitutional violation, the evidence would have probably been admitted. [8] See following sections.

CHECKLIST

- ☐ Arrest outside police officer's municipality for observed misdemeanors.
    - o Was the arrest without a warrant?
- ▪ If so, it is an illegal arrest. (An illegal arrest does not necessarily prohibit the introduction of seized evidence. See following section.)

5. Extra-jurisdictional Arrest.

R.C. 2935.03 delineates the territorial jurisdiction of law enforcement officers. It should be kept in mind that a violation of state law in regard to arrests made outside an officer's jurisdiction does not necessarily rise to the level of a Fourth Amendment violation requiring suppression of seized evidence.

For instance, in the case of an intoxicated driver, a police officer located outside of his jurisdiction may stop and detain the suspect without violating the Fourth Amendment and thereby triggering the exclusionary rule.

---

[7] *Cincinnati v. Alexander*, 54 Ohio St.2d 248, 375 N.E.2d 1241 (1978).

[8] See *State v. Lindway,*131 Ohio St. 166, 2 N.E.2d 490 (1936).

"Where a law enforcement officer, acting outside the officer's statutory territorial jurisdiction, stops and detains a motorist for an offense committed and observed outside the officer's jurisdiction, the seizure of the motorist by the officer is not unreasonable *per se* under the Fourth Amendment." [9]

The Court in *Weideman* balanced the interest of public safety with the right of a dangerous person to drive unhindered. Because the officer had *probable cause* to stop the vehicle, there was no Fourth Amendment Violation.[10]

In *Weideman*, the police officer, outside of his jurisdiction, stopped the driver after having observed her driving left of center several times. A strong odor of alcohol was detected. The officer called the Highway patrol to assist. Although he did not arrest her, the officer gave her a field sobriety test that was later repeated by the arresting officer. The motion to suppress alleged that the officer had no lawful cause to arrest her. The Court, in overruling the motion reiterated its previous holding that a state law violation, in this case an extraterritorial arrest, is not per se violative of the Fourth Amendment. See also, *Kettering v. Hollen*. [11]

6. Warrantless Arrest for Felony.

(Exigent Circumstances)

Pursuant to R.C. 2935.04, anyone may arrest any person without a warrant where there is reasonable cause to believe a felony has been

---

[9] *State v. Weideman*, 94 Ohio St.3d 501, 764 N.E.2d 997 (2002).

[10] See also, *State v.Jones,* 121 Ohio St. 3d 103, 2009-Ohio-316

[11] *Kettering v. Hollen*, .64 Ohio St.2d 232, 416 N.E.2d 598 (1980).

committed and that the arrested person is guilty of the felony. The arrested person can be detained until a warrant can be obtained.

This principal also applies to warrantless arrests due to exigent circumstances. A valid arrest due to exigent circumstances is not a violation of the Fourth amendment, and any evidence seized as a result is not excludible.

In *State v. Williams*,[12] the defendant was arrested in his home after police officers received information from co-defendants that the defendant was involved in a murder. Because it was likely the defendant would have discovered that the police were seeking him, it was necessary to apprehend him immediately without waiting for a warrant. Incriminating evidence was discovered in his home. In upholding the validity of the arrest, and the admission of the incriminating evidence, the court held: "* * * warrantless arrests are not *per se* illegal. An otherwise unlawful arrest may be valid if exigent circumstances necessitated the warrantless seizure or if the arresting officers were acting in good faith and in compliance with then permissible standards of conduct." [13]

CHECKLIST

- ☐ Was there reasonable cause to believe the arrested person committed a felony?
- ☐ If so, any person may arrest.
- ☐ In addition, the arrested person may be detained until a warrant is obtained.

☐ Exigent Circumstances

- ☐ Were there exigent circumstances?
- ☐ If so, the arresting officer must have acted in good faith and within permissible standards of conduct.

---

[12]*State v. Williams,* 6 Ohio St.3d 281, 452 N.E.2d 1323 (1983).

[13] *Williams*, *supra.*, at 283.

7. Warrantless Arrest for Felony Based on Prior Knowledge of Criminal History.

A warrantless arrest for a felony can be based on a police officer's knowledge of the criminal convictions of the arrestee. For instance, what would otherwise possibly be an illegal warrantless arrest for a misdemeanor can be a legal arrest if the arresting officer has knowledge of the arrestee' s prior misdemeanor conviction which has the effect of causing the new observed offense to be a felony.[14] The "reasonable cause to believe a felony has been committed" language of R.C. 2935.04 includes the above scenario.

In *Wac*, a prior gambling misdemeanor conviction within the knowledge of the arresting officer elevated the new charge to one in which a felony arrest was proper.

CHECKLIST

- Is the arrest warrantless?
- Did the police officer have prior knowledge of the arrested person's criminal record?
- Does this prior knowledge in light of the observed misdemeanor cause the crime to be a felony?
  - If, so a warrantless arrest is proper.

8. Offenses of Violence.

R.C. 2935.03 (B)(1) provides: "[w]hen there is reasonable ground to believe that an offense of violence * * * has been committed within the limits of the political subdivision * * * in which the peace officer is * * * employed * * * a peace officer * * * may arrest and detain * * * any person whom the peace officer has reasonable cause to believe is guilty of the violation." [15]

---

[14] *State v. Wac,* 68 Ohio St. 2d 84, 428 N.E.2d 428 (1981).

CHECKLIST:

- ☐ Are there reasonable grounds to believe an offense of violence has occurred?
- ☐ Did the crime occur within the officer's political subdivision?
    - o If so, the offender may be detained and arrested.

9. Knowledge of a Warrant not enough unless for a Felony.

Mere knowledge, by itself, of an outstanding warrant for the arrest of a person on the part of an arresting officer is not enough to satisfy the statute. It must be established that the arrested person was wanted in connection with the commission of a *felony*, pursuant to R.C. 2935.04,[16] or, there was otherwise *probable cause* for the arrest.

In State v. Timson the arresting officer received an oral communication from a U.S. Marshall of an outstanding warrant for the arrested person. (Timson). The arresting officer was given no information that Timson was wanted for a *felony*. The warrant turned out to be a shown cause order for contempt of court. As a result, a handgun found on the defendant was excluded from evidence.

The key to the *Timson* holding is that the arresting officer did not have *probable cause* to make the arrest. "To have probable cause, the arresting officer must have sufficient information derived from a reasonably trustworthy source to warrant a prudent man in believing a

---

[15] *State v. Mesa*, 87 Ohio St.3d 105, 717 N.E.2d 329 (1999).

[16] *State v. Timson*, 38 Ohio St. 2d 122, 311 N.E. 2d 16 (1974).

felony has been committed and that it has been committed by the accused." Paragraph 1 of the syllabus.

CHECKLIST

- Was there a communication of a warrant for arrest?
- Was the warrant for a felony?
- If not, was there otherwise probable cause for arrest?
- If not, the arrest is in violation of R.C. 2935.04.

An improper seizure of a person and the subsequent discovery of contraband cannot be justified by the existence of an arrest warrant of which the police were unaware.[17]

10. Legal Warrantless Arrest.

Under R.C. 2935.26, a police officer is not normally permitted to arrest for a misdemeanor not committed in his presence. However, the officer is permitted to "reasonably conclude" that the arrested person has committed the offense.

To illustrate, in the case of a traffic violation it is not necessary that the arresting officer observe the defendant's operation of the motor vehicle. The circumstances surrounding the scene can provide the basis for a reasonable conclusion on the part of the arresting officer of the arrestees' operation of the vehicle. "After viewing the scene of the accident, and hearing appellant's admissions on a first-hand basis, the officers could reasonably conclude that he had been operating his vehicle shortly before the officers arrived."[18]

---

[17] *State v. Gardner*, 135 Ohio St.3d 99, 2012-Ohio-5683.

[18] *Oregon v. Szakovitz*, 32 Ohio St. 2d 271, 291 N.E. 2d 742 (1972).

CHECKLIST

- ☐ Is the arrest warrantless?
- ☐ Is there a basis for a reasonable conclusion that the arrested person committed the crime?
    - o If so, the arrest is proper.

11. A Stop is not Equivalent to an Arrest.

A truck driver is not unlawfully arrested for a misdemeanor not committed in the presence of the officer where the trucker fails to stop his vehicle to be weighed, and a worker at the weigh station observes his failure to stop and notifies the officer, who then stops the vehicle.

The stop of the vehicle and the issuance of the citation is not an arrest because an arrest constitutes restraint of the person in order to formally charge him with a crime. There was no arrest here because the officer who stopped the trucker had no intent to take the driver into custody, the confrontation was brief and presumably, he was allowed to proceed after being issued the citation.[19]

Where a police officer stops a vehicle pursuant to a radio dispatch in which he is informed that the driver of the vehicle is armed and suicidal, and the defendant after the stop makes incriminating statements without having received Miranda warnings, the statement is nevertheless admissible because the officer was acting under the community-caretaking/emergency-aid exception to the Fourth Amendment.

"The community-caretaking/emergency-aid exception to the Fourth Amendment warrant requirement allows a law-enforcement officer with objectively reasonable grounds to believe that there is an immediate need

---

[19] *State v. Darrah*, 64 Ohio St. 2d 22, 412 N.E. 2d 1328 (1980).

for his or her assistance to protect life or prevent serious injury to effect a community caretaking/emergency-aid stop."[20]

12. Custodial Search after Misdemeanor Arrest.

"A custodial search of the handbag of one lawfully arrested for a misdemeanor committed in the presence of a police officer is a reasonable search under the Fourth Amendment to the United States Constitution, and evidence so obtained is properly admissible in a criminal action."[21]

However, an unauthorized traffic stop for a minor misdemeanor by a township police officer outside of his jurisdiction is unreasonable and evidence found as a result is not admissible as being a violation of Article I, Section 14 of the Ohio Constitution. The authority to enforce traffic laws on state highways is not provided to all police officers. R.C. 4513.39(A).[22]

13. Arrestee Improperly Removed from County.

R.C. 2935.14 prohibits law enforcement officers from removing an arrestee from the county in which he was arrested until he is permitted to communicate with an attorney, a relative, or another person for the purpose of obtaining counsel.

Notwithstanding this prohibition, a confession will not be suppressed as violative of the Exclusionary Rule where the arrestee was transported from the county of his arrest to another county in violation of

---

[20] *State v. Dunn*, 131 Ohio St.3d 325, 2012-Ohio-1008

[21] *State v. Matthews,* 46 Ohio St 2d 72, 346 N.E. 2d 151 (1976).

[22] State v. Brown, 143 Ohio St. 3d 444, 2015-Ohio-2438.

R.C. 2935. This is so because the Exclusionary Rule has been invoked only for constitutional violations, not statutory violations that do not have constitutional implications.

CHECKLIST

- ☐ Was the arrestee removed from the county of arrest?
- ☐ Was the arrestee permitted to communicate with an attorney or other person to obtain counsel?
- ☐ If not, the arrestee was improperly removed from the county of arrest in violation of R.C. 2935. (This improper removal does not prevent the admission of a statement of the arrestee)

MIRANDA RIGHTS

AN ARRESTED PERSON MUST BE GIVEN MIRANDA RIGHTS WHETHER ARRESTED FOR A FELONY OR A MISDEMEANOR. THE FIFTH AMENDMENT RIGHT AGAINST SELF-INCRIMINATION SHOULD BE CONTRASTED WITH THE SIXTH AMENDMENT RIGHT TO COUNSEL IN THAT THERE IS NO RIGHT TO APPOINTED COUNSEL WHERE THE CRIME DOES NOT CARRY POSSIBLE IMPRISONMENT AS IN THE CASE OF A MINOR MISDEMEANOR.[23]

---

[20] *State v. Buchholz*, 11 Ohio St. 3d 24, 462 N.E. 2d 122 (1984).

14. Waiver of Miranda Rights must be clear.

To introduce custodial statements of a defendant at trial, it must be clear he has waived his Miranda Rights. In Jones, the court excluded the statements of the defendant because it was possible he misunderstood what constituted a statement for these purposes. There was some evidence that the arrestee believed only written statements and written notes of the interrogating officer could be used against him:

"What we do require, however, is that when a defendant subsequently acts in such a way as to reasonably alert an interrogating officer that the warnings given have been misapprehended, the officer must, before any further questioning, insure that the defendant fully and correctly understands his Fifth Amendment rights. This was not done by Detective Powell, and the trial court, therefore, erred in failing to suppress appellant's statement to the officer." *Jones* at 27, 28.

---

[21]*State v. Jones*, 37 Ohio St.2d 21, 306 N.E.2d 409 (1974).

CHECKLIST:

- Is the introduction of the statement pursuant to a waiver of Miranda Rights?
- If so, is it clear that a waiver has been made?
- Is it possible there was a misunderstanding as to the definition of a statement? Is it possible that the arrestee believed only written statements could be used against him?

R.C. 2933.81(B) is unconstitutional. It provides a presumption of voluntariness to a custodial statement if it was recorded. When a defendant makes a voluntary statement, it does not necessarily mean there was also a knowingly, voluntary and intelligent waiver of his Miranda rights. The burden remains on the state to prove the existence of a knowingly, voluntary and intelligent waiver.

In regard to juveniles, R.C. 2933.81(B) is a violation of due process and one must consider the totality of circumstances test when considering whether the statement was a knowingly and voluntary and intelligent waiver.[24]

15. Implied Consent and the Right to Counsel.

A violation of the right to counsel provided in R.C. 2935.20 does not impact the implied consent statute, and a request to speak to an attorney before submitting to a blood alcohol test is a refusal to take the test. The one-year administrative license suspension based on a refusal to take the blood alcohol test will go into effect. It should be noted that the ALS suspension is civil in nature.

---

[24] State v, Baker, Slip Opinion No. 2016-Ohio-2708.

By refusing to submit to the test "contingent on receiving the advice of counsel, the arrestee has, for the purposes of the implied consent statute, R.C. 4511.191'refused' to take the chemical alcohol test." [25]

CHECKLIST:

- Did the arrestee state that he wanted to speak with an attorney before submitting to the blood alcohol test?
- If so, this is a refusal to take the test pursuant to the implied consent statute.

16. Providing Communication Facilities to Arrestee.

R.C. 2935.20 requires law enforcement officials to permit a person taken into custody an opportunity to communicate with any person for the purpose of obtaining counsel.

However, it is not required that the arrested person personally communicate with an attorney or relative, it is sufficient that the person who the defendant intends to contact is contacted.

Therefore, a police communication to a family member of the arrested person is sufficient to comply with the requirement that the arrested person be furnished facilities to communicate with an attorney, relative, or another person.

[25] *Dobbins v. Ohio Bur. of Motor Vehicles*, 75 Ohio St.3d 533, 664 N.E.2d 908 (1996).

[26] *Toledo v. Dietz*, Ohio St. 2d 30, 209 N.E. 2d 127 (1965).

Therefore, where the arresting officer called appellant's brother to inform him of the arrest, "* * * it may be assumed that the brother would take appropriate steps on behalf of appellant." [26]

CHECKLIST:

- Was the arrestee allowed to personally contact anyone for the purpose of communicating with an attorney?
- If not, was a police communication made to a family member for this purpose?
- If so, the police communication complies with R.C. 2935.20.

17. Right to Communicate with Counsel, Eavesdropping Police Officer.

Where communication facilities are provided to an arrested person who calls his attorney, the right to effective counsel prohibits a police officer present in the room from eavesdropping and testifying as to the statements the arrested person makes to his attorney. However, the officer is permitted to testify as to the arrested person's demeanor, his "mumbled" speech, and his inability to remember his phone number, accordingly, there is no denial of right to effective counsel where the testimony was limited to the observation of the officer, and not the content of the conversation.[27]

---

[27] *State v. Sargent*, 41 Ohio St. 2d 85, 322 N.E. 2d 634 (1965).

CHECKLIST

- ☐ Did the police officer eavesdrop as to the statements the arrestee made to his attorney?
- ☐ If so, did the police officer testify as to the statements?
    - o If so, the statement is inadmissible.
- ☐ Did the police officer testify as to the arrestee's demeanor, his way of speaking, and his inability to remember common things?
    - o If so, the police officer's testimony is properly admitted.

18. Probable Cause for Arrest Resulting from a Common Investigation.

Where police officers from different agencies are engaged in a common investigation, information furnished by officers other than the arresting officers may be used to establish probable cause for arrest.

Accordingly, where the arresting officer has received information from another officer that the defendant was driving in an erratic manner, this information, pursuant to *United States v. Ventresca,*[28] can establish probable cause for a warrantless arrest based on the other police officer's observation. "If we were to hold otherwise, a police officer could never legally arrest a fleeing misdemeanant in response to a call for help from a fellow officer who saw the offense take place." [29]

---

[28] *United States v. Ventresca* 380 U.S. 102 (1965).

[29] *State v.Henderson*, 51 Ohio St. 3d 54, 554 N.E. 2d 104 (1990).

CHECKLIST

- ☐ Did the arresting officer receive information from another police officer describing illegal acts of the arrestee?
- ☐ Was a warrantless arrest made as a result of this information?
- ☐ If so, probable cause for the arrest can be established as a result.

19. Arrest as a Result of a Radio Communication.

In the case of a felony warrantless arrest where the arresting police officer received information over the radio sufficient to cause him to *reasonably believe* a felony has been committed he, as a result thereof, has probable cause to believe a felony was committed. "Information received on a police broadcast is in the nature of an official trustworthy source of information." Here, information received was sufficient to give the officer reason to believe a felony was committed because the officer learned that appellant had used a firearm in an assault. [30]

20. Warrant Issued by a Non-Judicial Clerk.

R.C. 2935.08 authorizes a court clerk to issue an arrest warrant. Accordingly, there is no Fourth Amendment violation where a non-judicial clerk issues an arrest warrant. As the United States Supreme Court held in *Shadwick v. Tampa*,[31] a city charter that authorizes a court clerk to issue an arrest warrant complies with the Fourth Amendment. The court

---

[30] *State v.Fultz*, Ohio St. 2d 79, 234 N.E. 2d 593 (1974).

[31] *Shadwick v. Tampa* 407 U.S. 345, 32 L. Ed. 783 (1972).

reasoned that laymen were qualified to determine probable cause as can be seen in the case of the grand jury where laymen are permitted to determine probable cause. In *State v. Fairbanks,*[32] the court adopted the reasoning of the *Shadwick* court and sustained the warrant.

Crim. R. 4(A) requires a neutral magistrate to issue an arrest warrant. However, those magistrates who have dual roles, for instance, where one role is as a law enforcement officer and the other as an issuing magistrate, are not qualified to issue the arrest warrant. Such a situation results in an improper conflict causing the arrest to be illegal.

It must be kept in mind that an illegal arrest does not prevent a prosecution. An illegal arrest, without more, has never been "viewed as a bar to subsequent prosecution, nor as a defense to a valid conviction." United States v. Crews, 445 U.S. 463, 474, 100 S.Ct. 1244, 63 L.Ed.2d 537. [33]

A warrant for arrest must contain probable cause and not a mere allegation that the crime has been committed. The underlying circumstances must be presented to the magistrate. However, where there has been a previously established routine as to the minimum requirements for a warrant in which mere allegations have been the practice, there is a good faith factor that must be considered, such as where such practice has been previously approved by an appellate court.[34]

21. Extraterritorial Arrest.

The common-law rule that a municipal officer may not make an arrest outside of his territory has been changed by R.C. 2935.02. Though R.C. 2935.02 speaks of the limits of a county, the statute does not limit the type of law enforcement officer who may make arrests, therefore since an officer may make arrests outside of the county, he can also

---

[32] *State v. Fairbanks* 32 Ohio St. 2d 34, 289 N.E. 2d 352 (1972).

[33] *State v. Hobbs*, 133 Ohio St.3d 43, 2012-Ohio-3886

[34] *State v. Hoffman*, Slip Opinion No. 2014-Ohio-4795.

make arrests outside of the geographical limits of the municipality if the area is within the jurisdictional limits of the municipal court. Therefore, the arrest was upheld in *Fairbanks v. Munkins*, where the arresting officers left their municipal limits to arrest the defendant on a warrant. If such arrest was not permitted, a person could place himself outside of the municipal limits, and not be subject to arrest since under R.C. 2935.03, a warrant has to be directed to an officer of the municipal corporation. [35]

CHECKLIST

- ☐ Was the arrest made outside of the county of the police officer's jurisdiction?
- ☐ If so, R.C. 2935.02 permits the police officer to make the arrest with a warrant.

22. Warrant or Summons not necessary to Commence Prosecution.

It is not necessary that a warrant or summons issue in order to commence a prosecution, notwithstanding R.C. 2935.10, where the offense charged is a misdemeanor, it is not necessary that a warrant or summons issue in order to notify the offender of the charges against him. "* * * the filing of the affidavit is sufficient to cause the prosecution of one who is alleged to have committed a misdemeanor. [36]

---

[35] *Fairbanks v. Munkins* 28 Ohio St. 207, 277 N.E. 2d 227 (1971).

[36] *State v. Hooper*, 25 Ohio St. 2d 59, 267 N.E. 285 (1971).

Where a private citizen signs an affidavit and complaint that initiates a prosecution pursuant to R.C. 2935.09 but where a proper reviewing authority does not review the complaint, the trial court nevertheless has jurisdiction to try the case where there is no objection to jurisdiction pursuant to Crim. R. 12 (C). [37]

[37] *State v. Mbodji*, 129 Ohio St. 3d 325, 2011-Ohio-2880.

CHAPTER 2

Venue

1. Change of Venue Due to Pretrial Publicity.
2. Venue as Established by a Course of Conduct.
3. Cost of Transfer.

"The trial of a criminal case in this state shall be held in a court having jurisdiction of the subject matter, and in the territory of which the offense or any element of the offense was committed." R.C. 2901.12 (A).

Venue must be proven in all criminal prosecutions unless it is waived. "In a criminal case, it is not essential that the venue of a crime be proved in express terms, provided it be established by all the facts and circumstances, beyond a reasonable doubt, that the crime was committed in the county and state as alleged in the affidavit."[38] See also *State v. Nevius.* [39]

In *State v. Headley,* [40] no venue was established where the defendant planned a drug transaction and was headed toward, but never entered the county at the time of his arrest.

---

[38] *State v. Gibble*, 24 Ohio St. 2d 85, 263 N.E. 2d 904 (1970).

[39] *State v. Nevius* 147 Ohio St. 263, 71 N.E. 2d 258 (1947).

[40] *State v. Headley* 6 Ohio St. 3d 475, 453 N.E. 2d 716 (1983).

1. Venue as Established by a Course of Conduct.

In *State v. Bueke*,[41] venue was found as to a course of conduct. The court focused on R.C. 2901.12 (A) and its "any element" language. "Where offender commits an offense in different jurisdictions as part of course of criminal conduct, venue lies for all offenses in any jurisdiction in which offender committed one of offenses or any element thereof."

Where the defendant did not live in the county of indictment (Franklin), but where he nevertheless, was required to submit daily reports to his supervisor in Franklin County, and was further required to call his supervisor every two or three days, sufficient nexus with Franklin County was found, and that nexus fulfilled the "any element" requirement of the statute. *State v. Draggo* [42]

CHECKLIST:

- ☐ Has any element of the crime occurred in the county of prosecution?
- ☐ If so, venue is proper.
- ☐ Was the only contact with the county through telephone calls?
- ☐ If so, this is sufficient contact to establish venue.

2. Change of Venue Due to Pretrial Publicity.

"* * * [W]here there is a reasonable likelihood that prejudicial news prior to trial will prevent a fair trial, the judge should continue the case until the threat abates or transfer it to another county not so permeated with publicity. *Sheppard v. Maxwell.* [43] (This is the famous Dr. Sam

---

[41] *State v. Bueke,* 8 Ohio St. 3d 29, 526, N. E. 2d 274 (1988).

[42] *State v. Draggo,* 65 Ohio St. 2d 88, 418 N.E. 2d 1343 (1981).

[43] *Sheppard v. Maxwell.* 384 U.S. 337 (1966).

Sheppard murder trial on federal *habeas corpus*, this case is illustrative of over-the-top adverse pretrial publicity).

Crim. R. 18 (B) permits "the trial court to transfer a pending criminal case to any court having jurisdiction outside of the county where it appears that an impartial jury cannot be seated. See also R.C. 2931.29.

Often due to pretrial publicity, a jury pool can be so tainted that it may be difficult to seat a fair and impartial jury. The defendant, or the state, may move for a change of venue. Further, the trial judge may, on its own motion, transfer the trial to any other county having jurisdiction. The rule does not limit the amount of transfers, so that if it is determined that the new county cannot seat a fair and impartial jury, the trial can be transferred again until a satisfactory jury is seated.

The key factors to be considered in appellate review of a failure to transfer venue due to pretrial publicity are: (1) Whether the trial court abused its discretion in ruling that the trial should not be transferred, and (2) Whether an effective voir dire has been accomplished.

In regard to (1) Abuse of discretion, "The meaning of the term 'abuse of discretion' * * * connotes more than an error of law or judgment; it implied an unreasonable, arbitrary, or unconscionable attitude * * *"[44]

The second element is the voir dire itself. The most reliable method to insure a fair and impartial jury is to question the veniremen during voir dire: "* * * where it appears that the examination of jurors on their voir dire affords the best test as to whether or not prejudice exists in the community against the defendant; and where it appears that the opinion as to guilt of the defendant of those called for examination for jurors are * * * not fixed but would yield readily to evidence, it is not error to overrule an application for a change of venue." [45]

In *Swiger*, the defendant filed a motion for a change of venue due to pretrial publicity. "[News of a] factual nature and without distortion, or

---

[44] *Steiner v. Custer,* 137 Ohio St. 448, 31 N.E. 2d 855 (1940).

[45] *State v.* Swiger, 5 Ohio St. 2d 151, 214 N.E. 2d 417 (1966).

which are non-inflammatory in character, do not establish the impossibility of a defendant to have a fair and impartial trial where jurors have not read or heard the reports or such prospective veniremen have testified on voir dire that they will judge the defendant solely on the law and evidence."

In *State v. Fairbanks*, there was a newspaper article and a few radio broadcasts: "which stated that the defendant had the gun used in the crime in his possession at the time of arrest he had been charged with the killing and has other convictions, that the weapon found in his possession had been used in the shooting of another person. Nearly all the veniremen disclaimed knowledge of these reports and affirmed during an extensive voir dire that they would judge the defendant only on the law and facts presented at trial. This is not a case in which there exists a reasonable likelihood that the defendant would not receive a fair trial." [46]

The reasonable likelihood test is derived from Sheppard *v. Maxwell*, *supra.*

"In assessing whether a fair and impartial trial can be obtained in the county where the trial has been instituted, the judge may take judicial notice of the general demeanor and prejudice of the community, of the effectiveness of procedural employed at trial - such as sequestration of the jury and holding of simultaneous trials - and the prospect of obtaining jurors who are fair, impartial and not prejudiced."[47]

3. Cost of Transfer.

If the trial court concludes that a fair trial cannot be had in the county, it should transfer the case regardless of the cost of transporting the witnesses to and from the trial and the cost of taking the jurors to view the crime scene.[48]

---

[46] *State v. Fairbanks* 32 Ohio St. 2d 34, 289 N.E. 2d 352 (1972).

[47] *State v. Johnson,* 31 Ohio St. 2d 106, 285 N.E. 2d 751 (1972).

CHAPTER 3

SEARCH WARRANTS

1. Good Faith and the Totality of the Circumstances Test.
2. Particularity.
3. The Plain View Doctrine.
4. Affidavit for Search Warrant not Signed by Issuing Magistrate.
5. Searches for Intangible Objects.
6. Challenging the Veracity of the Affidavit.
7. Challenge of Warrant Based on Perjured Evidence.
8. Search of Automobile not Specified in Warrant.
9. Failure to Properly Return a Search Warrant.
10. Warrantless Searches by Private Persons.
11. Generalized Searches.
12. Search Incident to Arrest.
13. Warrantless Entry of Land by Wildlife Officers.
14. Search of Cell Phone without Warrant.
15. Abandoned Property.
16. DNA.
17. Planting a GPS Device on an Automobile.
18. Trash Pull Evidence.
19. Warrant Issued by a Probate Judge.
20. Warrantless Search Based on mistaken Belief

---

[48] *State ex rel Dayton Newspapers v. Phillips*, 46 Ohio St.2d 457, 351 N.E. 2d 127(1976).

1. Good Faith and the Totality of the Circumstances Test.

Where a law enforcement officer states in the affidavit for a search warrant that he or she has good cause to believe a house contained marijuana and other drug paraphernalia based on an observation of marijuana plants seen through a fence, even though the affidavit may be deficient, it may fall under the "good faith" exception to the exclusionary rule.[49] The two-prong test of *Aquilar v. Texas*, and *Spinelli v. United States* was abandoned by the United States Supreme Court in *Illinois v. Gates*, and replaced it with the "totality of the circumstances" test.[50]

Accordingly, the Supreme Court of Ohio held: "* * *reviewing courts may not substitute their own judgment for that of the issuing magistrate by conducting a *de novo* determination as to whether the affidavit contains probable cause * * * and doubtful or marginal cases * * * should be resolved in favor or upholding the warrant" A reviewing court includes the trial court conducting a suppression hearing. *State v. George*. [51]

Under the totality of circumstances test it must be determined whether the affidavit provided a substantial basis for the magistrate's conclusion that there was a probability that marijuana or related paraphernalia would be found in the defendant's residence. The court found there was a substantial basis to conclude that the drugs would be found because the plants were observed by a law enforcement officer trained in the recognition of growing marijuana plants. As a result, it cannot be said that the magistrate had no substantial basis for

---

[49] *United States v. Leon,* 468 U.S. 897 (1984).

[50] See *also Massachusetts v. Upton*, 466 U.S. 727 (1984).

[51] *State v. George*, 45 Ohio St. 3d 325, 544 N.E. 2d 640. (1989).

concluding there was a fair probability that marijuana or paraphernalia would be found in the house.

Even if the affidavit was insufficient, in that it did not provide a substantial basis to conclude there were plants in the house, the *good faith exception* to the exclusionary rule, *Leon, supra.,* would apply. That is, if the officer is acting on an objectively reasonable reliance on the warrant even though the warrant lacked probable cause, the search will be upheld.

The good faith exception points to the reason for excluding illegal searches: to curb improper police conduct. Where there is good faith reliance on the warrant, there is no improper police conduct to deter. *George, supra.*

CHECKLIST

- ☐ Was the affidavit insufficient in that it did not provide a substantial basis for one to conclude there was contraband in the dwelling?
- ☐ Did the officer act on good faith in relying on the warrant?
    - If so, the good faith exception to the exclusionary may apply.

2. Particularity.

In *State v. Benner,*[52] the warrant to search for "fibers and hairs and other trace evidence for comparison was upheld." The specificity necessary for the warrant will vary with the nature of the items sought. The police could not have described the items more precisely because, until the search, the officers could not have known what item in the residence would contain relevant evidence. The warrant was not for a

---

[52] *State v. Benner,* 40 Ohio St. 3d 301, 533 N.E. 2d 701 (1988).

general exploratory search, but was limited to items that could be sources of the fibers and hairs including "other trace evidence."

CHECKLIST

- ☐ Was the warrant for a general exploratory search?
  - o If so, it probably will not be upheld.
- ☐ Was warrant properly limited to relevant evidence depending on the nature of the items sought?
  - o If so, the warrant may contain sufficient particularity to be upheld.

3. The Plain View Doctrine.

Items seized under the plain view doctrine, are properly seized if (1) the intrusion was lawful, (2) it was immediately apparent to the officers that the items were incriminating, (3) their discovery was inadvertent. *State v. Williams.*[53]

The lack of probable cause to search for the items is the key to understanding the plain view doctrine. If the law enforcement officers did not have a search warrant, and they knew the evidence was there, it could not be seized under plain view, this prior knowledge would have required a warrant. See also *State v. Bayless.* [54]

---

[53] *State v. Williams* 55 Ohio St. 2d 82, 77 N.E. 2d 1013 (1978), Cooledge v. New Hampshire, 403 U.S. 443 (1971).

[54] *State v. Bayless* 48 Ohio St. 2d 73, 357 N.E. 2d 1033 (1978).

CHECKLIST

- ☐ Were the police officers lawfully in the area where the seized properly was found?
- ☐ Was criminal nature of the property immediately apparent?
- ☐ Was the discovery inadvertent?
    - o If so, the plain view doctrine is applicable and the seized items are properly admissible.

4. Affidavit for Search Warrant Not Signed by Issuing Magistrate.

Where the search warrant was not signed by a judge or magistrate, any evidence recovered as a result of the search is inadmissible. The warrant is void *ab initio* if it is not signed. R.C. 2933.21, Crim. R. 41 and, R.C. 2933.25 together specify the form of the warrant, including the requirement for the judge's signature.

5. Searches for Intangible Objects.

A judge is authorized to sign a search warrant for intangible objects since evidence of the commission of a crime can include intangible as well as tangible objects. Accordingly, a court may properly issue an order to a telephone company to assist law enforcement officers in installing a pen register that records telephone numbers dialed by that telephone. Further, in regard to phone companies and crimes that are committed over the phone, the phone company has a duty to assist law

---

[55] *State ex rel. Ohio Bell v. Williams*, 63 Ohio St. 2d 51, 407 N.E. 2d 2 (1980).

enforcement when it believes its facilities are being used in support of a crime such as gambling per Ohio Adm. Code. 4901:13-12(B).[55]

6. Challenging the Veracity of the Affidavit.

Where the veracity of a search warrant is challenged, an affidavit must be accompanied by an offer of proof specifying the portions of the affidavit that are claimed to be false with supplied reasons supporting the claim.[56] The *Franks* court did hold however, that a hearing to review the validity of the warrant is not required if, after the allegedly false parts are excluded, there remains sufficient evidence to support probable cause.

Where an affidavit for a search warrant incorrectly lists a person as a victim, this fact standing alone does not invalidate the remainder of the affidavit and authorize a suppression of the evidence seized. Oftentimes non-lawyers are affiants and courts must take this into account when reviewing a search warrant affidavit. In addition, the principal must be kept in mind that if one part of the affidavit proves to be invalid the court must look to the whole affidavit to determine whether the remaining part is sufficient for its validation.[57]

When presenting a search warrant affidavit to an issuing magistrate. evidentiary inferences are permitted by the magistrate. However, where the affiant presents undisclosed evidentiary inferences as empirical facts which cause the magistrate to the issue the search warrant, the affidavit is flawed.

Here the detective assumed that a computer was used in a search by the defendant where there was no evidence that a computer was used.

---

[56] *Franks v. Delaware*, 438 U.S. 154 (1978).

[57] *State v. Dibble*, Slip Opinion No. 2012-Ohio-4630

As a result of the search of defendant's computer, child pornography photographs were discovered. This court suppressed this evidence because of insufficient particularity.

"Particularity in regard to the search of a computer must be directed to the precise need of the search an overly broad particularity may result in the suppression of other evidence found."[58]

7. Challenge of Warrant Based on Perjured Evidence.

In the case of a warrant based on perjured evidence the "good faith exception" will not prevent the exclusion of the evidence. *Leon, supra*.

However, the false statement in the affidavit must have been knowingly and intentionally made. "Proof of these inaccuracies alone, however, obtained primarily by way of cross-examination, did not sustain the defendant's burden of making a substantial preliminary showing that a false statement was knowingly and intentionally made by the affiant in the warrant affidavit." [59]

CHECKLIST

- ☐ Was the warrant based on perjured evidence?
- ☐ If so, has it been established that the false statement was knowingly and intentionally made?
- ☐ If so, the good faith exception is not applicable and the evidence should be excluded.

---

[58] State v. Castagnola, 2015-Ohio-1565.

[59] *State v. Roberts*, 62 Ohio St. 2d 170, 405 N.E. 2d 247 (1980).

8. Search of Automobile Not Specified in Warrant.

Where a car is seized through a valid search warrant and is properly in the custody of the police, the search of the vehicle is reasonable even though the warrant did not state that it should be searched. "It would be unreasonable to hold that the defendant's garage, bedroom [etc.] could be searched for the weapon used in the homicide, but that the automobile parked adjacent to his residence could not be searched, without being specifically named as a place to be searched even though [it] was listed on the warrant * * *" [60]

See also *California v. Cooper,* 386 U.S.58 (1987).

CHECKLIST

- ☐ Was the vehicle seized pursuant to a valid search warrant?
- ☐ If so, the vehicle may be searched even though the warrant did not state it should be searched.

9. Failure to Properly Return a Search Warrant.

Where the sheriff failed to return a search warrant in accordance with Crim. R. 41(D) and Crim. R. 41 (E), this failure is an administrative error, not a constitutional error requiring suppression of the seized evidence. There must be a showing of prejudice to the rights of the defendant. Moreover, where the sheriff returned the warrant to the clerk of courts instead of the judge, there is similarly no prejudice. [61]

---

[60] *State v. Curtis***,** 54 Ohio St.2d 128, 375 N.E.2d 52 (1978).

[61] *State v. Downs*, 51 Ohio St 2d. 47, 363 N.E. 2d 1140 (1977).

10. Warrantless Searches by Private Persons.

Warrantless searches by private persons are valid where the only police participation was to protect the public and not to gather evidence of a crime. Such a search is not in violation of the Fourth Amendment, and plain view evidence is admissible at trial. Therefore, where a baggage handler at a railroad terminal became suspicious of a suitcase left by a nervous person and opened the suitcase in the presence of the police, the contraband was property seized. The employees of the terminal had a right to open the baggage to protect the property of the company and the passengers and the physical safety of others. Although the police were called to unlock the suitcase, there was no evidence that they knew of the existence of contraband. [62]

CHECKLIST

- ☐ Did a private person conduct the search?
- ☐ Was any police participation only for public safety and did the police not know of the existence of contraband.
- ☐ If so this warrantless search by private persons is not a Fourth Amendment violation.

11. Generalized Searches.

After executing a search warrant in which specific vehicles and certain automobiles parts are listed, and where the rest of the vehicles on the premises were searched with the assistance of a car theft expert,

---

[62] State v. Morris, 42 Ohio St. 2d 307, 329 N.E. 2d 85 (1975).

it could not be claimed by the police that the other vehicles were in plain view and were not required to be listed on the search warrant.

State v. Wilmoth, [63] illustrates the principal that the plain view doctrine as stated in *Williams*, supra., that a "generalized suspicion" will not support a warrantless seizure under the plain view doctrine. The cars searched were shown not be stolen from a computer search of their Vehicle Identification Numbers (VIN) numbers, and as such, it was not immediately apparent that the evidence was incriminating until the vehicles were searched.

However, the holdings in *Williams* and *Wilmoth* were modified in *State v. Halczyszak*. Where it was held that the police can have a generalized expectation of contraband that does not prevent the discovery of contraband from being inadvertent [64]

CHECKLIST

- ☐ The plain view doctrine can in some instances be invoked even though there was a *generalized* expectation of contraband.

12. Search incident to Arrest.

In the past, in defining the proper scope of a search incident to arrest, the court held that an arrest for a traffic violation does not automatically allow the police to conduct a detailed search of the automobile. [65]

---

[63] *State v. Wilmoth,* 1 Ohio St. 3d 118, 438 N.E. 2d 105 (1982).

[64] *State v. Halczyszak,* 25 Ohio St. 3d 301, 496 N.E. 2d 925 (1986).

[65] *State v. Brown*, 63 Ohio St.3d 349, 588 N.E. 2d 113 (1992).

In *Brown*, there was no probable cause to believe the automobile contained contraband. *Carroll v. United States* (1925), 267 U.S. 132, 69 L.Ed. 543, 45 S.Ct. 280; there was no inventory, *South Dakota v. Opperman* (1976), 428 U.S. 364, 96 S.Ct. 3092,49 L. Ed 1000; or plain view contraband, *Texas v. Brown* (1983), 460 U.S. 730, 75 L. Ed. 2d 502, 103 S.Ct. 1535.

The court focused on the only possible rationale for the warrantless search: to protect the officer from any nearby weapon, *Chemel v. California* (1969), 395 U.S. 752, 23 L.Ed. 2d 685, 89 S.Ct. 2034.

To this issue, because the defendant had been placed in the police car and had no opportunity to secure a weapon from the car, the contents of the car were no longer within the defendant's immediate control and no search of the glove compartment was justified.

"A police officer may not open a small, closed container found inside an automobile's glove compartment solely as a search incident to arrest for a traffic violation, after the officer has the suspect and sole occupant of the vehicle - under control in the police cruiser." *Brown, supra.*

State v. Brown was overruled in *State v. Murrell.* The law now states that when a police officer "has made a lawful custodial arrest of the occupant of an automobile, the officer may, as a contemporaneous incident of that arrest, search the passenger compartment of that automobile." [66] But see, the following from the syllabus of the United States Supreme Court's opinion in *Arizona v. Gant:*

"After Rodney Gant was arrested for driving with a suspended license, handcuffed, and locked in the back of a patrol car, police officers searched his car and discovered cocaine in the pocket of a jacket on the backseat. Because Gant could not have accessed his car to retrieve

---

[66] *State v. Murrell* ,94 Ohio St.3d 489, 764 N.E.2d 986 (2002)

weapons or evidence at the time of the search, the Arizona Supreme Court held that the search-incident-to-arrest exception to the Fourth Amendment's warrant requirement, as defined in Chimel v. California, 395 U.S. 752, 89 S.Ct. 2034, 23 L.Ed.2d 685 (1969), and applied to vehicle searches in New York v. Belton, 453 U.S. 454, 101 S.Ct. 2860, 69 L.Ed.2d 768 (1981), did not justify the search in this case. We agree with that conclusion." [67]

CHECKLIST

- ☐ Was there a lawful custodial arrest?
- ☐ If so, did the defendant have access to a weapon or evidence of the crime for which he was stopped?
- ☐ If not, a further search is not justified.

13. Warrantless Entry of Land by Wildlife Officers.

There are two statues that concern the right of a Wildlife officer to enter the land of another. R.C. 1531.14 and R.C. 1531.13. R.C. 1531.14 only requires that the officer be engaged in his normal enforcement of the game and fish laws. R. C. 1531.13 requires the establishment of good cause to enter the land because of a belief that the fish and game laws have been violated.

Therefore, where a wildlife officer observes hunters on private land he may enter the land to ensure that the wildlife laws are not being violated such as bag limits and proper licenses for those who do not own the land. This entry does not require good cause because it is done according to R.C. 1531.14[68]

---

[67] *Arizona v. Gant*, 556 U.S. ___ (2009), 129 S. Ct. 1982, 77 USLW 3631.

[68] *State v. Coburn*, 121 Ohio St. 3d 310, 2009-Ohio-834.

14. Search of Cell phone without Warrant.

Search of a cell phone's contents without exigent circumstances is violative of the 4th amendment. A cell phone is not a container and does not give the police the same rights they have to search containers. Once the cell phone is in custody a warrant can be obtained.[69]

15. Abandoned Property.

There is no violation of the 4th amendment rule against illegal searches where there is an abandonment of the property in question. An abandonment can occur where the owner of the property leaves the property in the hands of another person for safekeeping if a sufficient period of time passes wherein the owner shows no interest in the property. [70]

16. DNA

There is no 4th Amendment privacy interest in a defendant's dna profile that was acquired as a result of a search warrant. Therefore, where a dna sample is retained by law enforcement and used in a subsequent unrelated prosecution the defendant does not have standing to challenge its use.[71]

---

[69] State v. Smith, 2009-Ohio-6426.

[70] *State v. Gould*, 131 Ohio St.3d 179, 2012-Ohio-71

[71] *State v. Emerson*, Slip Opinion No. 2012-Ohio-5047

17. Planting a gps device on an automobile.

Planting a gps device on an automobile is a search. (cite Sp ct case) However if the device was planted before the decision, a police officer properly relied on the law at the time of the plant and the evidence was properly admitted. [72]

18. Trash Pull Evidence.

Trash pull evidence and probable cause.

The totality-of-the-circumstances test must be used when determining whether a search warrant based, in part, on trash pull evidence has been authorized with sufficient probable cause. The court of appeals incorrectly determined that trash pull evidence must be viewed in isolation. This view is a misinterpretation of the holding of State v. Weimer, 2009-Ohio-4983. This court viewed the evidence in Weimer in isolation because the corroborating evidence was flawed and all that was left to consider was the actual trash pull evidence the result of which required an examination of the probable cause in light of only the trash pull evidence.

Here the trash pull evidence was buttressed by other evidence, i.e. Information provided by a confidential informant, personal observations by the police of the defendant sitting next to a known methamphetamine trafficker and the fact that the trash revealed that the defendant was receiving mail at the address. [73]

---

[72] State v. Johnson, Slip Opinion No. 2014-Ohio-5021.

[73] State v, Jones, 143 Ohio St. 3d 266, 2015-Ohio-483.

19. Warrant Issued by a Probate Judge.

Probate judges do not have authority to issue search warrants absent a temporary assignment by the Chief Justice for the probate judge to temporarily sit in another division of the court of common pleas.

However, a good faith exception was found by the court of appeals and was not appealed to this court.[74] Keep in mind that the exclusionary rule is to target improper police conduct and where there is reasonable reliance on a search warrant the good-faith exception as articulated in United States v. Leon, 468 U.S. 897, will apply.

20. Warrantless Search Based on Mistaken Belief.

Where a passenger of a legally parked car is arrested because of an outstanding warrant and where the vehicle is searched, the search is unreasonable and is a violation of the 4th Amendment and Article I. Section 14 of the Ohio Constitution where the arresting officer has no knowledge that the arrested person is the owner of the vehicle and that the car contained evidence of the offense of the arrest. This search does not fall under the holding in Gant.[75]

---

[74] State v. Brown, 142 Ohio St. 3d 92, 2015-Ohio-486.

[75] State v. Leak, 145 Ohio St. 3d 165, 2016-Ohio-154.

CHAPTER 4

Preliminary Hearing Testimony

(Admission at Trial)

The decisions of this court and the most recent decision in this regard by the United States Supreme Court are as follows:

The Supreme Court of Ohio has held where a crime victim testifies at a preliminary hearing, but is later unable to be located for trial, that victim's testimony at the preliminary hearing is admissible at trial if: (1) it can be shown that the witness was unavailable, and there was a good faith effort on the part of the state to secure the witness. And, (2) there was an opportunity for cross-examination, so that the right to confrontation is satisfied.

A witness' unavailability has been established as a result of a good faith effort on the part of the prosecution where: (1) The witness was subpoenaed and the police visited his last known address, his employer had not seen him for a long time, a paycheck was waiting for him, a nationwide bulletin was posted to find him; (2) In regard to the opportunity for cross-examination, the record showed that the victim was under oath at the preliminary hearing, appellant had the same attorney, appellant had the opportunity to cross-examine the witness, the preliminary hearing was properly recorded and was held before a judicial officer.[76] See the following section for the changes this principal has received.

---

[76] *State v. Madison,* 64 Ohio St. 2d 322, 415 N.E. 2d 272 (1980).

1. Establishment of Unavailability. (Personal Knowledge Required)

Where the state seeks to use the preliminary hearing testimony of a victim at trial because the victim has become unavailable, the evidence of unavailability must be shown by the *personal knowledge* of the witnesses. Unavailability cannot be established where the prosecutor merely states to the court that the police have not been able to locate the witness. Such hearsay evidence is insufficient to establish witness unavailability.[77]

The court had established what is known as the *Roberts Rule*, [78] where preliminary hearing testimony was inadmissible where there was no cross examination of the witness, or if there is ineffective cross examination. See R.C. 2945.49.

The United States Supreme Court in *Roberts v. Ohio* reversed *Roberts* on 6th amendment grounds. [79] That court found testimony admissible if it "bore sufficient indicia of reliability and afforded the trier of fact a satisfactory basis for evaluating the truth of the prior statement * * *" Such reliability can be established if the statement was of a firmly rooted hearsay exception. Further, where the preliminary hearing testimony has been tested by questioning that was equivalent to cross-examination and where the witness was unavailable, the testimony was admissible.

Ohio v. Roberts has been reversed by *Crawford v. Washington*. [80] Under *Crawford*, the statement is inadmissible if it is testimonial in nature unless the accused has an opportunity to cross-examine the maker of the statement. It should be noted that Crawford applies to all statements, not only preliminary hearing statements.

---

[77] *State v. Smith*, 58 Ohio St. 2d 344, 390 N.E. 2d 778 (1979).

[78] *State v. Roberts*, 55 Ohio St.2d 191, 378 N.E.2d 492 (1978).

[79] *Roberts v. Ohio* 448 U.S. 56, 65 L. Ed. 2d 597, 100 S Ct. 2531 (1980).

[80] *Crawford v. Washington* ,124 S.Ct. 1354 (2004).

CHAPTER 5

1. Interrogations.

2. Garrity Statements.

1. Interrogations

The United States Supreme Court held in *Edwards v. Arizona*, once an accused invokes his right to counsel all police interrogation must cease and may not be resumed without counsel present, unless there is a subsequent waiver, or if the accused renews the conversation. [81]

Interrogation "refers not only to express questioning, but also to any words or action on the part of the police (other than those normally attendant to arrest and custody) that the police should know are reasonably likely to elicit an incriminating response from the subject." *Rhode Island v. Innis.* [82]

---

[81] *Edwards v. Arizona*, 451 U.S. 477, 101 S. Ct. 1880 (1981).

[82] *Rhode Island v. Innis*. 446 U.S. 291, 100 S. Ct. 1682 (1980).

[82] *State v. Williams*, 6 Ohio St. 3d 281, 452 N.E. 2d 1323 (1983).

[82] *Harrington v. California* 395 U.S. 250, 89 S. Ct. 1726 (1969).

In *State v. Williams*, an interrogation was found to be illegal where the police did not honor the accused's request for counsel and then initiated the conversation. They prompted the defendant into speaking by telling him that they knew his accomplice's side of the story, but not his side. This technique by the police "* * * can certainly be expected to engender incriminating statements, particularly, when appellant is aware that his accomplices have already implicated him. It is hardly surprising then that, under such circumstance, an accused, feeling himself evidentially outnumbered, will admit to some degree of complicity in the criminal offense." [83]

Even though the conversation was ruled inadmissible, the conviction was upheld, such violation having been found harmless beyond a reasonable doubt. See also, *Harrington v. California* [84]

In *State v. Knuckles*, the accused invoked his right to counsel, but instead of stopping the conversation the police told him that they did not want to talk to him about his arrest for bad checks, but about "Bobby Bennett" [a murder victim]. The defendant agreed to talk, signed a *Miranda* waiver, and made incriminating statements. The questioning of the accused concerning the matter not related to his arrest was, nevertheless, a "further interrogation" prohibited by *Edwards*, *supra*.[85]

---

[85] *State v. Knuckles*, 65 Ohio St. 3d 494, 605 N.E. 2d 54 (1992).

In *Knuckes, supra., the* court further held that any statement that is reasonably likely to elicit an incriminating response is an interrogation, citing *Rhode Island v. Innis* (1980), 446 U.S. 291, 301 S.Ct. 1682, 64 L. Ed. 2d 297.

The court reiterated its holding in *Williams, supra*, that all interrogation must cease once the accused invokes his right to counsel.

Where the accused invokes his right to counsel, two inquires must be made:

1. It must be determined if the right to counsel was invoked.

2. If the right to counsel was invoked, before the responses can be admitted into evidence, it must be shown that:

(a) The accused initiated the subsequent questioning with his interrogators, and

(b) He knowingly and intelligently waived his previously invoked right to counsel. See *Smith v. Illinois* [86]

2. Garrity Statements.

A Garrity[87] statement is an administrative statement made by an employee in the course of an investigation. The nature of this statement is of a compelled statement. The terms of which are that the statement will not be used against the person and that if it is not given truthfully the person can be discharged from

---

[86] *Smith v. Illinois* 469 U.S. 91, 105 S.Ct. 490 (1984).

[87] *Garrity v, New Jersey*, 385 U.S. 493, 87 S. Ct. 616.

employment. The prohibition against the use of the statement against the defendant includes its direct or derivative use.

Hence If the statement is given to a prosecutor or if there is an investigating officer present who later participates in the prosecution of the defendant, the defendant's constitutional rights have been violated.

The burden is on the prosecution to show that the statement was not used in the prosecution of the defendant including its use to obtain an indictment.

There is a two-prong test:

1. The state must deny any use of the statement in the criminal proceedings. 2. The state must show that the evidence used at trial was from other sources totally separate from the Garrity statement.[88] [89]

---

[88] *State v, Conrad* (1990), 50 Ohio St. 3d 1, 552 N.E. 2d 214.

[89] *State v. Jackson*, 125 Ohio St. 3d 218, 2010-Ohio-621.

CHAPTER 6

Grand Jury

1. **Revealing Grand Jury Matters.**
2. **Particularized Need.**
3. **Substantial Discrepancies Required for Disclosure.**
4. **Control of the Court of Common Pleas.**
5. **Number of Grand Jurors.**
6. **Recording of Grand Jury Testimony.**
7. **Municipal Court.**
8. **Testimony Used to Refresh Recollection.**
9. **Impeachment of Own Witness Prohibited.**

For the most part, the issues that have come before the court concerning the Grand Jury have concerned access to the testimony of witnesses who have appeared before the Grand Jury.

To view grand jury testimony, the defendant must show a *particularized need* to review the transcripts. "Grand jury proceedings are secret, and an accused is not entitled to inspect grand jury transcripts either before or during trial unless the ends of justice require it and there is a showing by the defense that a particularized need for disclosure outweighs the need for secrecy." [90]

Notwithstanding the requirement of a particularized need to gain access to grand jury testimony, Crim. R. 16(B)(1)(a)(iii)

---

[90] *State v. Patterson*, 28 Ohio St.2d 181, 277 N.E.2d 201 (1971).

permits a defendant to review his or her own grand jury testimony, and also the recorded grand jury testimony of any co-defendant.

1. Revealing Grand Jury Matters.

Crim. R. 6 (E) provides that grand jury matters may be revealed "only when so directed by the court preliminary to or in connection with a judicial proceeding, or when permitted by the court at the request of the defendant upon a showing that grounds may exist for a motion to dismiss the indictment because of matters occurring before the grand jury."

Thus, in *State v. Greer*, in addition to requiring the trial court to consider the particularized need alleged by the defendant, the court held that the trial court may inspect *in camera* the grand jury minutes with the assistance of counsel.

This inspection is allowed under the theory that if a particularized need is established " * * * the necessity of preserving grand jury secrecy is lessened, largely because the witness, in testifying at trial, has given up any anonymity he might have had and has made public the events which are the subject of the grand jury testimony being sought." [91]

Exactly what established the particularized need in this case was not discussed in the opinion. The court was concerned only whether the trial court was satisfied that a particularized need had been established.

The court further held that when grand jury transcripts are to be used, the trial court should delete irrelevant and extraneous matters and issue protective orders if required.

[91] *State v. Greer*, 66 Ohio St. 2d 139, 420 N.E. 2d 982 (1981).

2. Particularized Need.

Particularized need to inspect grand jury transcripts was established in *State v. Sellers.*[92] In *Sellers*, the defendant was charged with several counts of rape and importuning, the indictment and the bill of particulars used broad non-specific dates of the occurrences. For instance, "* * * on or about a date certain between April 1, 1982, and May 31, 1982." It was revealed during the testimony that some of the victims were aware of more specific dates of the alleged crimes than were contained in the indictment.

The court held: "* * * this court finds that the accused demonstrated a particularized need to inspect the grand jury testimony and that the trial court thus erred in refusing to allow an in-camera inspection of the relevant portions of grand jury testimony."

These relevant portions pointed toward the possibility that the victims could have testified to more specific dates, or suddenly remembered at trial specific dates. In addition, if the grand jury testimony contained more specific dates, this could have been relevant as to whether the prosecutor was aware of the dates, and chose to withhold this information, thus creating grounds for a mistrial.

---

[92] *State v. Sellers,* 17 Ohio St. 3d 169, 478 N.E. 2d 781 (1985).

3. Substantial Discrepancies Required for Disclosure.

In *State v. Grewell,*[93] particularized need for grand jury testimony of the rape victim was not established where the discrepancies in her testimony were not *substantial.* The time periods testified to at trial were similar to those listed in the indictment. Further, other specific dates testified to were from sources other than the victim. That being the case, there was no established inference that the victim's testimony was inconsistent.

To conclude, a defendant under Crim. R. 16 (B)(1)(a)(iii) has a right to his own grand jury testimony, or that of a codefendant. In regard to the grand testimony of any other person, Crim. R. 6 (E) controls, and the disclosure of the testimony is left to the sound discretion of the trial court.

---

[93]*State v. Grewell,* 45 Ohio St. 3d 4, 543 N.E. 2d 93 (1989).

4. Control of the Court of Common Pleas.

Grand Jury proceedings are under the control of the court of common pleas, not the prosecutor. "The grand jury is essentially an arm of the court. R.C. 2939.10, the court then gives the prosecuting attorney or assistant prosecuting attorney access to the grand jury * * *." [94]

5. Number of Grand Jurors.

A proper indictment requires that the grand jury that hears the testimony be composed of at least nine jurors, Crim. R. 6. This is so even though R. C. 2939.02 requires fifteen jurors, and R.C. 2939.20 requires that twelve of the fifteen agree.

When there is a conflict between a statute and a rule, the rule prevails if the right involved is procedural. Since the court has held that the manner in which a person is charged is procedural, the rule prevails. [95]

---

[94] *State ex rel. Shoop v. Mitrovich*,4 Ohio St 3d 220, 448 N.E.2d 800 (1983).

[95] *State v. Brown*, 38 Ohio St. 3d 305, 528 N.E. 2d 523 (1988).

6. Recording of Grand Jury Testimony.

Although recording of grand jury testimony is not required under the United States Constitution. In Ohio, Grand Jury testimony must be recorded pursuant to Crim. R. 22, "in all serious offenses." Pursuant to Crim.R. 2, a felony is a "serious offense."

Grand Jury proceedings are included in the term "all proceedings shall be recorded" under Crim. R. 22. Although Crim. 6(D) states that a stenographer or operator may, be present, this language only: * * * "relieves the state of the obligation to record grand jury testimony without using a county reporter," but it does not eliminate the obligation to record the proceedings." [96]

7. Municipal Court.

Supervisory authority is solely in the hands of the court of common pleas, *State ex rel Shoop v. Mitrovich, supra*. The "court" referred to in Crim.R. 6 is the court of common pleas.[97]

Notwithstanding this rule, it is permissible for the court of common pleas to corroborate with the municipal court in order to determine if there exists a particularized need for disclosure. See *Petition for Disclosure of Evidence*, "* * *[t]he supervising court is in the best position to access the need to preserve secrecy * * * it may not be in the best position to decide the extent of need * * *." Since the transcripts are sought by a different court, a cooperative

---

[96] *State v. Grewell*, 45 Ohio St. 3d 4, 543 N.E. 2d 93 (1989).

[97] *State ex rel. Collins v. O'Farrell*, 61 Ohio St. 3d 142, 573 N.E. 2d 113 (1991).

effort may be necessary. [98] See also *Douglas Oil Co. of California v. Petrol Stops Northwest.* [99]

A municipal court may not order the prosecuting attorney to disclose testimony before the grand jury of witnesses in a case that is pending in the municipal court. This is so because the municipal court has no supervising authority over the grand jury.

8. Testimony Used to Refresh Recollection.

A witness who testifies inconsistently with his grand jury testimony may be read his grand jury testimony to refresh his recollection, and to assist him in explaining the inconsistencies between his trial testimony and his grand jury testimony.

9. Impeachment Of Own Witness Prohibited.

Where a witness, at trial, insists that the grand jury transcript is not authentic, it is improper for the prosecutor to call the court reporter from the grand jury to read the same transcript at trial. Since "using another witness, like the reporter to read [the witnesses] grand jury testimony violates the principal of not impeaching one's own witness, as established in State v. Dick (1971), 27 Ohio St. 2d 162." See also, *State v. Diehl.*[100]

---

[98] *Petition for Disclosure of Evidence*, 63 Ohio St. 2d 212, 407 N.E. 2d 513 (1980).

[99] *Douglas Oil Co. of California v. Petrol Stops Northwest,* L. Ed. 2d 156, 99 S.Ct. 1667 (1979).

[100] *State v. Diehl,* 67 Ohio St. 2d 389, 423 N.E. 2d 1112 (1981).

Ordinarily, an indictment cannot be amended where it changes the name or identity of the crime, Crim. R. 7(D). And although it was error for the trial court to amend the indictment so that it changed the name and identity of the crime, it was not plain error since:

1. The amendment was bargained for.
2. The defendant was being represented by an attorney, and The defendant was not prejudiced. [101]

[101] *State v. Rohrbaugh*, 126 Ohio St. 3d 421, 2010-Ohio-3286.

CHAPTER 7

Discovery

1. No Duty to Disclose the Significance of Evidence.
2. Disclosure of Rebuttal Witnesses.
3. Subjecting the Witness to Harm or Coercion.
4. Withholding of Evidence by the Prosecutor.
5. Motion to Compel not a Prerequisite to Sanctions.
6. Continuing Duty to Disclose.
7. Discovery of Police Reports.
8. In Camera Inspection.
9. Appeal of Discovery Orders.
10. Inadvertent Failure to Disclose.
11. Inspection of In Camera Statement by Defense Counsel.
12. Misdemeanor Convictions.
13. Comment on the Failure to Call an Alibi Witness.
14. Defense Recordings of Witness Statements.
15. Failure to Disclose Where Defense Counsel Has Knowledge of Significance of the Material.
16. Grand Jury Testimony of Employees of a Corporation.
17. Where the Failure to Provide Timely Discovery is not Willful.
18. Depositions.

19. Where Denial of Deposition is proper.
20. Information Contained on a Hard Drive.
21. Public Records Requests.

"The purpose of the discovery rule is to prevent surprise and the secreting of evidence favorable to one party." [102]

1. No Duty to Disclose the Significance of Evidence

"Crim. R. 16(B) does not require the prosecution to disclose the significance of evidence sought to be discovered by the defendant. The rule only requires the prosecution to disclose, and permit the defendant to obtain the information sought." [103]

In *Parker*, the prosecutor did not reveal to defense counsel that the tape recording provided through discovery was used to identify the defendant. Defense counsel did not object to the content of the tape, but objected to the fact that the state did not disclose that it was used to identify the defendant.

[102] *Lakewood v. Papadelis*, 32 Ohio St. 3d 1, 511 N.E. 2d 1138 (1987).

[103] *State v. Parker*, 53 Ohio St. 3d 82, 558 N.E. 2d 1164 (1990).

This case is illustrative of the general rule that the prosecutor is not required to disclose *how* the evidence is to be used.

2. Disclosure of Rebuttal Witnesses.

The duty to disclose the names of witnesses also applies to rebuttal witnesses. If the name of the rebuttal witness is not provided to opposing counsel, the court may impose the sanctions of Crim. R. 16(E) (3). "Thus, if the prosecution does not provide the name of a rebuttal witness * * * the court may impose sanctions on the prosecution." [104]

> The sanctions available to the court pursuant to Crim. R. 16 (E)(3) are:
>
> (1) permit the discovery or inspection, (2) grant a continuance, (3) prohibit the introduction of the evidence, (4) or any order the court determines is proper.

In *State v. Howard*, the court held that if the prosecutor *reasonably anticipates* it is likely to call a witness in its case in chief, or in rebuttal, the name should be provided to defense counsel. Where the state fails to provide the name of a rebuttal witness pursuant to Crim. R. 16(B)(1)(e), the proper procedure is to use the "failure to comply" options of Crim. R. 16(E)(3). [105]

---

[104] *State v. Finnerty*, 45 Ohio St. 3d 104, 543 N.E. 2d 1233 (1989).

[105] *State v. Howard* 56 Ohio St. 2d 328, 383 N.E. 2d 912 (1978).

In *Howard*, the state did not provide the name of a rebuttal witness, as a result, the court offered to grant defense counsel a continuance. However, after a voir dire of the witness, defense counsel did not request a continuance. Because of the failure to request the continuance, the trial court was not required to exclude the rebuttal testimony.

In *Finnerty*, the court held: "[h]owever, because no request for a continuance was made by the defendant and because the trial court explicitly instructed the jurors to limit the rebuttal witness' testimony to the issue of the defendant's credibility, the trial court had not committed prejudicial error.

Where it is established that the prosecution could not reasonably anticipate the need to call a rebuttal witness, the sanctions of Crim. R. 16(E)(3) will not apply:

"Faced with an insanity defense, we cannot say that the prosecution should have 'reasonably anticipate[d]' that it would be able to use this witness to rebut testimony as to appellee's character. The prosecutor could use the testimony of the rebuttal witness only if appellee first put his character into evidence." *Finnerty*, at 108.

3. Subjecting the Witness to Harm or Coercion.

Pursuant to Crim. R. 16(B)(1)(e), the prosecutor is not required to disclose the names of witnesses if it is certified to the court that to do so would subject the witness to physical or substantial economic harm or coercion.

This rule contains two alternatives: (1) Relief from the obligation of providing the names of witnesses, or (2) The perpetuation of the witness' testimony in a hearing before the court where both parties can participate.

Regardless of which alternative is sought, the trial judge cannot be the judge who hears the motion. "* * * when the state seeks to obtain relief from discovery or to perpetuate testimony under Crim. R. 16(B)(1)(e), the judge who disposes of the motion may not be the same judge who will conduct the trial." [106] However, a violation of this rule is subject to a harmless error analysis: *Gillard, at 229*.

The court established this requirement in order to eliminate possible prejudice on the part of the trial court who will later preside over the trial of the case.

> In *Gillard*, the prosecution's motion included allegations of witness intimidation and references to other crimes of the defendant, which could have proved to be detrimental to a fair trial.

A violation of this rule is not per se prejudicial; any error may be found to be harmless, as was the case in *Gillard* where, despite this procedural violation, the state produced overwhelming evidence of guilt.

---

[106] *State v.Gillard*, 40 Ohio St. 3d 226, 533 N.E. 2d 272 (1988). See also State v. Dean, 127 Ohio St.3d 140, 2010-Ohio-5070.

4. Withholding of Evidence by the Prosecutor

"Pursuant to Crim. R. 16(B)(1)(a)(i), a defendant is entitled to relevant written or recorded statements made by him, and it is not within the province of the state to determine, and then to provide, only that which the state believes to be relevant to the defense * * *" [107]

For example, the conviction was reversed in *Moore*, because the prosecution withheld a tape recording from discovery that was later used at trial to impeach the defendant.

The conviction was reversed because the withholding of the tape recording affected the defendant's right to plan an adequate trial strategy. Had the defendant known of the undercover tape recording, he would not have denied under cross-examination that he had a conversation with the undercover informant on the date of the recording.

A trial court abuses it discretion by dismissing a case with prejudice without giving the parties an opportunity to brief the issues.

Where an aggravated murder conviction was sent back to the trial court for either a dismissal or new trial and where the trial court then reversed the conviction because the prosecution failed to provided possible exculpatory evidence through discovery, the trial court abused its discretion by dismissing the case by assuming that the defendant can no longer receive a fair trial because of the passage of time and the unavailability of witnesses.

---

[107] *State v. Moore*, 40 Ohio St.3d 63, 531 N.E.2d 691 (1988).

Although dismissal may have been warranted, the parties should have been given an opportunity to brief the issues before such determination .[108]

5. Motion to Compel not a Prerequisite to Sanctions

A motion to compel discovery is not a prerequisite that must be met in order for the trial court to impose sanctions of Crim. R. 16(E)(3), for failure to provide discovery. Even though the rule requires a two-step process, that is: (1) a demand for discovery and if not complied with, (2) a request for an order for failing to comply to the demand, the duty of the parties to respond is not lessened because the court is not involved. "The rule does not grant discretion to a party to ignore a request of an opposing party until a court orders compliance. * * * the fact that the court is not involved does not diminish the duty of the parties to comply with the rules at that point in the discovery process. [109]

6. Continuing Duty to Disclose.

Crim. R. 16(D) provides for a continuing duty to disclose. Where additional information that is subject to discovery is found, the original order for discovery covers such information.

[108] State v. Keenan, 143 Ohio St. 3d 397, 2015-Ohio-2484.

[109] *City of Lakewood v. Papadelis*, 32 Ohio St. 3d 1, 511 N.E. 2d 1138 (1987).

Where defense counsel was given a laboratory report that concluded that the amount of residue on the hands of the defendant was too small to conclude that he had fired a weapon, the prosecutor failed to follow-up that report since he was told later by his expert witness that due to the particular ammunition used, the defendant could have fired the weapon.

The court, in reversing the conviction, held: "It is certainly reasonable to conclude that the trial strategy employed by the defense and its pre-trial preparations would have been materially altered by prior knowledge of the * * * testimony." [110]

7. Discovery of Police Reports.

Notwithstanding the general prohibition of Crim. R.16(B)(2), a police report is not exempt from discovery if it is a witness statement by an observing police officer.

"Those portions of a testifying officer's signed report concerning his observation and recollection of the events are statements within the meaning of Crim.R. 16(B)(2) and therefore excepted from the general prohibition of Crim.R. 16(B)(2)."[111] Although all portions of a police report may not be discoverable and may indeed be privileged under Crim. R. 16(B)(2), "* * * [I]t becomes apparent that those portions of a testifying police officer's

[110] *State v. Wilson*, 30 Ohio St. 3d 99, 507 N. E.2d 1109 (1987).

[111] *State v. Jenkins*, 15 Ohio St. 3d 164, 473 N.E.2d 264 (1984).

signed report concerning his observations and recollections of the events are 'statements' within the meaning of Crim. R. 16(B)(1)(g) * * *" Attorneys for all parties must be given the opportunity to inspect the statement personally."

8. In Camera Inspection.

The police report must be requested in the same manner as any other statement for an in-camera inspection: "It is clear that under Crim. R. 16(B)(1)(g) a defendant must move for an in-camera inspection of witness statements on apparent inconsistencies between the prior statement and the witness' testimony on direct examination. This motion can be made any time after completion of the witness' direct examination, but prior to the completion of the witness' cross-examination.[112] A court may also *sua sponte* inspect these statements.

---

[112] *State v. Schipper*, 22 Ohio St.3d 158, 489 N.E.2d 820 (1986).

9. Appeal of Discovery Orders.

A party may seek leave to appeal any pretrial discovery order pursuant to R.C. 2945. [113]

10. Inadvertent Failure to Disclose.

Where the prosecutor fails to provide discovery due to an inadvertent error, the admission of the evidence is not necessarily barred where:

(1) The failure to disclose was not willful.
(2) Foreknowledge would not have benefited the defendant.
(3) No prejudice was shown.[114]

In Parsons, in responding to a discovery request the prosecutor stated the defendant did not make an oral statement. At trial, a police officer testified as to an oral statement of the defendant, the court found the trial court did not abuse its discretion in allowing the testimony after analyzing the three factors above.

---

[113] *State ex rel. Corrigan v. Griffin*, 14 Ohio St.3d 26, 470 N.E.2d 894 (1984).

[114] *State v. Parsons*, 6 Ohio St. 3d 442, 453 N.E.2d 689 (1983). See also *State v. Cooper*, 52 Ohio St. 2d 163, 370 N.E.2d 725 (1977), for prejudicial effect discussion.

The sanctions required by the rule apply equally to the state as to a defendant. Where the state unintentionally violates the rules of discovery by failing to disclose the existence of evidence [here it was contraband] the available sanctions always require the consideration of the least severe sanction.

A trial court abuses its discretion by dismissing the case with prejudice for an unintentional discovery violation without considering the least severe sanction.

Here the abuse of discretion is more compelling since the trial court failed to inquire as to whether the omitted evidence was exculpatory.[115]

11. Inspection of In Camera Statement by Defense Counsel.

Where a party moves pursuant to Crim. R. 16(B)(1) (g) for an in camera inspection of the witness' statement, the trial court, after reviewing the report must make it available to defense counsel before finding that it did not contain any material inconsistencies. "We construe Crim.R. 16(B)(1)(g) to mean that, once the trial court independently determines that a producible out-of-court witness statement exists, attorneys for all parties must be given the opportunity to inspect the statement personally. * * * An advocate is frequently in better position than the court in evaluating whether there are inconsistencies between the testimony of such witness and the prior statement." [116]

[115] *State v. Darmond*, 135 Ohio St.3d 343, 2013-Ohio-966

The failure of the trial court to "afford defense counsel the opportunity to inspect the witness' statement personally and call to the court's attention any perceived inconsistencies constitutes reversible error per se."

A finding of material inconsistencies allows the attorney to impeach the witness with the document.

12. Misdemeanor Convictions.

Although felony conviction records of all prosecution witnesses must be provided to defense counsel through discovery, the defendant has no right to the misdemeanor convictions of the prosecution witnesses under Crim. R. 16(B)(1)(b).[117] Whether misdemeanor records are to be furnished is within the sound discretion of the trial court.[118]

13. Comment on the Failure to Call an Alibi Witness.

It is reversible error and a violation of Crim. R. 16(B)(4) for the prosecutor to comment on the failure of defense counsel to call an alibi witness.[119]

---

[116] *State v. Daniels*,1 Ohio St. 3d 69, 437 N.E. 2d 1186 (1982).

[117] *State v. Spikes*, 67 Ohio St 2d 405, 423 N.E.2d 1122 (1981).

[118] *State v. Edwards*, 49 Ohio St. 2d 31, 358 N.E.2d 1051 (1976).

[119] *State v. Hanna*, 54 Ohio St.2d 84, 374 N.E.2d 1359 (1978); *State v. Jackson*, 50 Ohio St. 2d 253, 364 N.E.2d 236 (1977).

14. Defense Recordings of Witness Statements

A tape recording of a witness statement made by defense counsel is not discoverable under Crim. R. 16(C)(1)(a) as a tangible object. It was error for the trial court to prevent defense counsel from impeaching the state's witness with the recording. This is so because Crim. R. 16(C)(2) does not authorize the discovery of "statements made by prospective witnesses to the defense attorney or his agents." [120]

15. Failure to Disclose Where Defense Counsel Has Knowledge of Significance of the Material.

Although the state should have provided the defendant a copy of his waiver of rights form because it is a statement under Crim. R. 16(B)(1)(a). The trial court did not abuse its discretion in admitting the statement because defense counsel had already secured two other waiver forms and was on notice that the police officer was capable of testifying as to the circumstances of the waiver. [121]

---

[120] *State v. Lockett*, 49 Ohio St. 2d 71, 358 N.E.2d 1077 (1976).

[121] *State v. Hall*, 48 Ohio St. 2d 325, 358 N.E.2d 590 (1976) [vacated in part by *Ohio v. Hall* 438 U.S. 910.

16. Grand Jury Testimony of Employees of a Corporation.

The grand jury testimony of an employee of a corporation may be discovered pursuant to Crim. R. 16(B)(1)(a) as a statement of a defendant during grand jury proceedings if "the statement concerns an alleged criminal act or omission performed on behalf of the corporation and within the scope of employment.[122]

17. Where the Failure to Provide Timely Discovery is not Willful.

Where the prosecutor fails to provide the name of a prosecution witness until the day before she testified, such failure does not necessarily prohibit that witness from testifying. "Crim. R. 16(E)(3) provides for the admissibility of the testimony of the witness if it can be shown that the failure to provide discovery was not willful, foreknowledge of the statement would not have benefited the defendant in the preparation of the defense, and the defendant was not prejudiced by the admission of the evidence." *State v. Heinish.*[123]

---

[122] *State v. CECOS Intern., Inc.*, 38 Ohio St.3d 120, 526 N.E.2d 807 (1988).

[123] *State v. Heinish,* 50 Ohio St. 3d 23, 553 N.E.2d 1026 (1990).

In Heinish, the prosecutor stated that he did not learn the significance of the testimony until the day before the witness was due to testify. The prosecutor was willing to give defense counsel the opportunity to cross-examine the witness, take measurements, and recall the witness to cross-examine her with no objection.

This testimony was permitted because foreknowledge of the testimony would not have benefited the defense. "There is no question that the state had a duty to disclose the name of this witness. However, there is no evidence that foreknowledge of this testimony would have benefited appellant or that he was prejudiced by the admission of this testimony."

Where the witness list provided by the state was supplemented the second day before trial, and where the court did not grant a continuance, no error occurred since the witness' testimony would not have had great impact and the new witnesses did not alter defense strategy.[124]

The trial court did not err in admitting the testimony of a police officer whose name was not provided to defense counsel because:

1. There was no reason to believe the defense was surprised.
2. The police officer's partner's name was on the witness list.
3. The partner had a heart attack the night before.

---

[124] *State v. Kehn,* 50 Ohio St.2d 11, 361 N.E.2d 1330 (1977).

4. Much of the witness' testimony was identical to that of the coroner.

5. Defense counsel did not move for a continuance.

The trial court has latitude in supervising pretrial discovery; hence it was not an abuse of discretion where the court allowed the testimony of a police officer whose name did not appear on the list of prospective witnesses furnished by the state. The court permitted the testimony because it appeared that the prosecutor had inadvertently omitted the witness' name and that defense counsel was not surprised by the testimony, much of which was identical to that given by the coroner's investigator.[125]

18. Depositions

Crim. R. 15 allows the prosecuting attorney or defense counsel to file a motion for the taking of a deposition of a material, prospective witness who will be unable to attend the trial or will be prevented from attending the trial.

The notice of deposition must be timely to afford the other party time to prepare and to travel. For instance, where defense counsel did not receive timely notice of the deposition and consequently did not attend the deposition, a video deposition of a seriously ill undercover agent showing his identification of a photo array of the defendant, which was used at trial, was improperly admitted.

Notice was given the day before the deposition was to be taken. Defense counsel would have had to travel 90 miles to the deposi~~tion. The court stated, "Any~~ testimony was defective

[125] *State v. Edwards*, 49 Ohio St. 2d 31, 358 N.E. 2d 351 (1976).

because they [defense counsel] were not afforded the opportunity for cross-examination and confrontation." [126]

The introduction into evidence of the deposition was not harmless error because the defense was alibi, and the agent was the only witness whose direct testimony identified the defendant.

19. Where Denial of Deposition is Proper.

The trial court did not abuse its discretion in overruling a motion to take a deposition, pursuant to R.C. 2945.50, where the witnesses would be available to testify at trial a week later, and where it was possible that the request for the depositions was a fishing expedition. Further, there was no showing that the outcome of the trial would have been different had the deposition been permitted. [127]

20. Information Contained on a Hard Drive.

Where the state has furnished discovery that is a summary of information contained on a computer hard drive in the possession of the police department, the defendant does not have

---

[126] *State v. Wilkerson*, 64 Ohio St. 2d 308, 415 N.E. 2d 261(1980). See Crim. R. 15, and Rule of Superintendence, C.P. R. 15(B).

[127] *State v. Hill*, 12 Ohio St. 2d 88, 232 N.E. 2d 394 (1987)

a right to acquire a mirror image of the hard drive under the theory that the state is withholding evidence. There must be some prima facie showing that the state's response to the discovery request is incomplete.[128]

21. Public records requests.

Where a defendant makes a public records request from the state the reciprocal duty to provide discovery to the state is invoked even though no formal Rule 16 demand has been made:

"When an accused directly or indirectly makes a public records request for information that could have been obtained from the state though discovery, that public records request is the equivalent of a demand for discovery, and a reciprocal duty of disclosure arises in accordance with Crim.R. 16."[129]

---

[128] *State v. Revas*, 121 Ohio St. 3d 469, 2009-Ohio-1354.

[129] *State v. Athon*, 136 Ohio St.3d 43, 2013-Ohio-1956

CHAPTER 8

1. **Pleadings and Motions Made Before Trial.**
2. **Pretrial Motions and Speedy Trial Rights.**

1.Pleadings and Motions Made Before Trial.

Crim. R. 12 governs both pleadings and motions that *may* be made before trial, and also those that are *required* to be made before trial. Under Crim. R. 12(B) any defense, objection, or request that can be determined before trial may be before trial by motion. However, the following defenses, objections, or motions *must* be made before trial.

1. Defenses and objections based on defects in the institution of the prosecution.
2. Defenses and objections based on defects in the indictment, information, or complaint.
3. Motions to suppress evidence including * * * statements and identification testimony * * * illegally obtained.
4. Requests for discovery.
5. Requests for severance of charges of defendants.

Under Crim. R. 12 (G), failure by the defendant to raise the defenses or objections constitutes a waiver thereof.

Crim. R. 12 (H) allows a defendant who pleads no contest to appeal an error by the trial court in ruling on a pretrial motion.

Crim. R. 12 (J) allows the state to appeal a granting of a motion to suppress and a granting of a motion to return property.

2. Pretrial Motions and Speedy Trial Rights.

The period of delay caused by a defendant's motions toll the time in which a prosecution may be brought. This also applies to a later prosecution arising out of the same facts of the initial case in which the motions were filed.

There is a difference between a waiver of speedy trial and a tolling of the time in which a trial may go forward. A waiver of a speedy trial does not toll the time in which a subsequent charge may be brought arising out to the same facts. This is so because a waiver of a speedy trial involves relinquishing the fundamental right to a speedy trial and if there is a subsequent charge the defendant would have had no way of knowing of the new charge and could not have knowingly waived his speedy trial rights as to it.

R.C. 2945.72 tolls the time in which a prosecution may be brought, including motions for discovery and to obtain counsel. [130]

---

[130] *State v. Blackburn*, 118 Ohio St. 3d 163, 887 N.E. 2d 319. (2008).

A pretrial motion to suppress by a co-defendant does not toll the time the defendant is to be brought to trial. R.C. 2945.72 contains the circumstances in which a speedy trial can be waived. The list contained in this section is exhaustive of the circumstances that may be considered. The only other way to approve a speedy trial delay is if it can be determined that the delay is reasonable pursuant to R.C. 2945 (H) second subsection.[131]

Where a defendant in custody in another state attempts to take advantage of the Interstate Agreement on Detainers (IAD). (The Interstate Agreement on Detainers is a compact that allows a jurisdiction to procure temporary custody of a prisoner in another jurisdiction for the purpose of trial. The defendant does not have to be in prison, per se, incarceration can include a county jail as well as a state prison. As a result of the prosecutor's mistaken belief that the defendant had not begun his incarceration in the other state because the defendant was in a county jail and not in a prison, a defendant's speedy trial rights were violated because the prosecution did not go forward within the speedy trial requirements. [132]

---

[131] *State v. Ramey*, 132 Ohio St.3d 309, 2012-Ohio-2904

[132] State v. Black, 142 Ohio State 3d 332, 2015-Ohio-513.

By The Defendant:

Motions to Suppress/Dismiss

1. Where Defense Counsel Had Prior Opportunity to Become Aware of Suppression Issue.
2. Burden to Establish Probable Cause.
3. Waiver of Motion to Suppress by filing a Stipulation of Facts.
4. Appeal Where Denial of Motion Destroys Defense.
5. Where a Motion in Limine is Treated as a Motion to Suppress.
6. Motion to Dismiss Based on Inability to Obtain Expert Testimony.
7. Notice Requirements.

1. Where Defense Counsel Had Prior Opportunity to Become Aware of Suppression Issue.

Where defense counsel has had an adequate opportunity at an unrelated suppression hearing to become aware of a possible Miranda issue, the trial court properly denied the defendant's motion at trial to suppress statements made to police supposedly in violation of his Miranda Rights. [133]

[133] *State v. Moody*, 55 Ohio St. 2d 64, 377 N.E. 2d 1008 (1978).

Even though appellant in *Moody* argued that the Miranda issue was not discovered until trial, the court found at the hearing that defense counsel had an opportunity to cross-examine three police officers who were involved in the identification process. As a result, defense counsel become aware that the defendant was not permitted to make a telephone call for about three hours after his arrest. Defense counsel at trial made a motion to strike the testimony of the police officers. However, since defense counsel failed to file a *timely* motion to suppress, the motion was waived. Crim. R. 12(G).

"The failure to move within the time specified by Crim. R. 12 (C) for the suppression of evidence on the basis of its illegal obtainment constitutes a waiver of the error."[134]

2. Burden to Establish Probable Cause.

In a motion to suppress the admission of evidence acquired as a result of a warrantless search or seizure; or if the defendant properly raises a lack of probable cause to conduct the search, the burden of going forward to show probable cause to search, falls on the prosecution.[135]

---

[134] *State v. Wade*, 53 Ohio St. 2d 182, 373 N.E. 2d 1244 (1978).

[135] *Xenia v. Wallace* , 37 Ohio St. 3d 216, 524 N.E. 2d 889 (1988).

3. Waiver of Motion to Suppress by filing a Stipulation of Facts.

A motion to suppress was not timely filed where the defendant first filed a stipulation of facts and then later a motion to suppress. The stipulation of facts is "tantamount to the commencement of trial on the merits." Because the stipulation was filed before the motion to suppress, any issue regarding the admissibility of the evidence was waived.[136]

4. Appeal Where Denial of Motion Destroys Defense.

Crim. R. 12 (C) provides that any defense, objection, or request that is capable of determination without trial may be raised by motion before trial.

Where a motion to suppress is denied and the remaining issue is not in dispute and points toward guilt, an immediate appeal is proper.

For example, in a prosecution for driving under the influence of alcohol, if the motion to suppress were overruled, the only remaining issue would be whether the defendant was operating the vehicle in Ohio. The defense would thereby be destroyed because of the ruling. "If the defendant pleads no contest after such a ruling, judicial economy will be served by appeal of the

[136] *State v. F.O.E. Aerie,Port Clinton*, 38 Ohio St. 3d 53, 526 N.E. 2d 66 (1988).

pivotal issue rather than forcing the defendant through a futile trial * * * A plea of no contest does not waive a defendant's appeal from an adverse ruling on the motion." *City of Defiance v. Kretz,* 60 Ohio St. 3d 1, 573 N.E. 2d 32. (1991).

5. Where a Motion in Limine is Treated as a Motion to Suppress.

The court in *State v. ULis,*[137] affirmed the principal of judicial economy referred to in *Kretz*, *supra*, by approving the decision of the court of the appeals in State v. Hall.[138] In *Hall* it was held that where a motion in limine is treated as a motion to suppress, that is, where a hearing is held and a fully presented cross-examination occurs, any error of the trial court in ruling on the motion is preserved as long as the court informs the defendant that he has a right to appeal the ruling after he pleads no contest.

6 Motion to Dismiss Based Inability to Obtain Expert Testimony.

In a motion to dismiss an indictment a trial court may consider evidence not on the face of the indictment pursuant to Crim. R. 12(F)

Where a motion to dismiss was based on defendant's allegation that an expert could not properly prepare for trial

[137] *State v. ULis,*[137] 65 Ohio St. 3d 83, 600 N.E. 2d 1040 (1992)

[138] *State v. Hall*, 57 Ohio App. 3d 144, 567 N.E. 2d 305 (1989).

because of the restrictions in obtaining evidence because of the child pornography law, this court reversed the court of appeals dismissal of the indictment. The court noted that the expert was free to examine the evidence in the office of the prosecutor. [139]

*7. **Notice Requirements***

The minimum standards for a court to consider a motion to suppress pursuant to Crim. R. 47 can be met when the motion states with "particularity to place the prosecutor and the court on notice of the issues to be decided."[140] "A highly detailed pleading of the facts and law is not required to satisfy the notice requirements of Shindler to trigger the right to a hearing on a motion to suppress."[141]

---

[139] *State v.Brady*, 119 Ohio St. 3d 375, 894 N.E. 2d 671 (2008).

[140] State v. Shindler, 70 Ohio St 3d 54, 636 N.E. 2d 319 (1994).

[141] State v. Codeluppi, 139 Ohio St. 3d 165, 2014-Ohio-1574.,

BY THE STATE

Crim R. 12(J) authorizes a prosecutor to appeal the trial court's granting of a defense motion to suppress evidence or to return property. The prosecutor must certify to the court that the appeal is not taken for delay, and that the granting of the motion weakened its case such that any reasonable possibility of effective prosecution has been eliminated. The state must comply with the time limits of the rule, and an appeal not timely filed will be denied.[142]

7. Appeal by the State during Trial.

Crim. R. 12(J) allows for appeals by the prosecution of adverse evidentiary rulings during trial, such appeal does not impermissibly interfere with the defendant's interest in having an uninterrupted trial.

---

[142] *State v. Buckingham,* 62 Ohio St. 2d 14, 402 N.E. 2d 536 (1980).

Where the trial court improperly ordered the state to continue the trial, despite the state's attempt to appeal the ruling, the state had no choice but to tell the court it could not go forward. The trial court subsequently dismissed the case for failure to prosecute.

This court in ordering a retrial held:

"* * * [W]e hold that the Double Jeopardy Clause does not bar re-prosecution where a criminal prosecution has erroneously required the state to proceed with trial despite the states properly filed Crim. R. 12 (J) appeal." [143] The state must satisfy the certification requirements of 12(J) that the appeal is not done for purposes of delay and that the ruling has destroyed the state's case.

8. Appeal by State to Prevent a Miscarriage of Justice.

The state is permitted to appeal to prevent a miscarriage of justice. For example, where the trial court grants the defendant's motion for a polygraph examination, for purposes of the rule, the hearing was a 'special proceeding' [144] and the granting of the motion was a *final order*, *State ex rel Leis v. Kraft* [145]

---

[143] *State v. Malinovsky*, 60 Ohio St. 3d 20, 573 N.E. 2d 22 (1991).

[144] A "special proceeding" includes a pretrial motion to suppress. *State v. Collins*, 24 Ohio St. 2d 261, 265 N.E. 2d 107 (1970).

In *Leis,* the trial court granted the defendant a polygraph examination at state's expense. Because the prosecutor did not agree to the admission of the test as is required by *State v. Souel,*[146] the results could not be admitted into evidence.

The state has an absolute right to appeal pursuant to R.C. 2945.67 under four situations.[147] The granting of the motion in this case does not fall under one of the four situations, as a result, any appeal must be by *leave of court*. Noting that the court of appeals can only entertain appeals of judgments or final orders, the court found this to be a final order since a final order is one that affects a substantial right made in a special proceeding. The substantial right being of the state to proceed with the prosecution and its lack of ability of appeal a final verdict.

9. State's Appeal of Motion to Suppress after Acquittal.

Crim. R. 12(J) gives the state a right to appeal a trial court's ruling granting the defendant's motion to suppress

---

[145] *State ex rel Leis v. Kraft* 10 Ohio St. 3d 34, 460 N.E. 2d 1372 (1984).

[146] *State v. Souel*, 53 Ohio St. 2d 123, 372 N.E. 2d 1318 (1978).

[147] The prosecutor may appeal: (1) motion to suppress; (2) a motion to dismiss; (3) a motion to return property; (4) a grant of post-conviction relief. See also State v. Ross, Slip Opinion No. 2010-Ohio-6282.

evidence. This right to appeal is in effect whether the motion to suppress was granted before or during trial. The state may appeal even where a judgment of acquittal was granted, although the acquittal cannot be appealed.

> "Where such a motion to suppress is granted, it is not for the trial court to determine the sufficiency of the state's evidence, proceed with the prosecution and hence enter a judgment of acquittal. Rather the state must be permitted to determine whether it will seek a stay of proceedings in order to exercise its right of appeal pursuant to Crim. R. 12(J), or alternatively to proceed to a final verdict or judgment. The choice is that of the prosecutor.[148]

Under R.C. 2945.67, a court of appeals has jurisdiction to grant the state leave to appeal a trial court's ruling on the admissibility of evidence, even though the defendant has been acquitted.[149]

In Arnette, the state objected to the testimony of a psychologist and a psychiatrist regarding the state of mind of the defendant at the time of the crime.

The court in *State v. Keeton*, 18 Ohio St. 3d 379, 481 N.E. 2d 629 (1985) held: "The state in seeking 'appeal by leave of court to which the appeal is taken under R. C. 2945.67(A) must follow

[148] *State v. Fraternal Order of Eagles Aerie 0337*, 58 Ohio St. 3d 166, 569 N.E. 2d 478 (1991).

[149] *State v. Arnette*, 22 Ohio St. 3d 186, 489 N.E. 2d 284 (1986).

the procedure outlined in *State v. Wallace*, 43 Ohio St. 3d 1, 330 N.E. 2d 697 (1975). This includes compliance with App. R. 5(A). Under the procedural guidelines, the court of appeals in this case must decide, upon remand, whether in its sound discretion the state should be granted leave to appeal the above-mentioned decision of the trial court."

10. State's Appeal of Improper Sentence

The state may appeal the trial court's failure to sentence the defendant to the statutory minimum sentence.[150]

In *Beasley*, the court failed to sentence the defendant to a two to fifteen-year sentence, as required by the statute for felonious assault.

Such an appeal does not suggest a double jeopardy issue because, "any attempt by a court to disregard statutory requirements when imposing a sentence renders the attempted sentence a nullity or void. * * * We therefore hold that the trial court's correction of a statutorily incorrect sentence did not violate appellant's right to be free from double jeopardy."[151]

---

[150] *State v. Beasley*, 14 Ohio St. 3d 74, 471 N.E. 2d 774 (1984).

[151] *Beasley, supra*.

11. State's Right to Appeal Dismissal.

A state has the right to appeal when the trial court dismisses any part of an indictment.[152]

In Haynes, the court of appeals held that the trial court's ruling that the term "in loco parentis" was unconstitutionally vague did not constitute a final appealable order. This court, in finding the state has a right to appeal, held that the trial court's ruling as to vagueness of the term "in loco parentis" had the effect of dismissing part of the indictment, since the state could not have proceeded on the remaining count of the indictment.

It should be keep in mind that there is no abuse of discretion in failing to grant leave of court to appeal where the state has failed to comply with the appellate rules.[153]

---

[152] *State v. Haynes*, 25 Ohio St. 3d 173, 495 N. E. 2d 578 (1986).

[153] *State v. Fisher*, 35 Ohio St. 3d 22, 517 N.E. 2d 911 (1988).

12. Denial of Leave to Appeal.

The denial of leave to appeal is properly appealable to the Supreme Court. Pursuant to R.C. 2953.14, the state may appeal where a court superior to the trial court makes a finding adverse to the state.[154]

A substantive ruling of law may be reviewed by a court of appeals even though there has been a verdict of acquittal, as long as the *judgment* is not appealed. Since R.C. 2945.67 allows leave to appeal for "any other decision" except the final verdict it permits the court of appeals to exercise its discretion in granting an appeal.[155]

---

[154] *State ex rel Corrigan v. Lawther,* 39 Ohio St. 3d 157, 529 N.E. 2d 1377 (1988).

State v. Bistricky, 51 Ohio St. 3d 157, 555 N.E. 644 (1990) (See also) *State v. Arnette*, 22 Ohio St.3d 186, 489 N.E. 2d 284 (1986).

13. Motions to Suppress in Municipal Court.

A municipal court conducting a preliminary hearing does not have authority to entertain a motion to suppress illegally obtained evidence. The motion must be made in the court of common pleas after arraignment and before trial

Crim. 12(J) contemplates a proceeding by the trial court where the charge is a pending felony. A municipal court engaged in a preliminary hearing can exclude evidence under the Rules of Evidence, but evidence that may have been acquired unconstitutionally may not be suppressed. One reason for this tenet is the suppression of the evidence may involve the return of the evidence to the defendant, which could destroy the prosecution's case. Further, because Crim. R. 12(J) does not authorize an appeal by a prosecutor from a ruling at a preliminary hearing, there would be no means to appeal the suppression of the evidence.[156]

14. Trial Court Must State Findings on the Record.

Where a trial court entertains a motion under Crim. R. 12 (E), that court must state on the record its findings whenever factual issues are involved. A failure to do so will result in reversal and remand.[157]

---

[156] *State v. Mitchell*, 42 Ohio St. 2d 447, 329 N.E. 2d 682 (1975).

[157] *City of Bryan v. Knapp*, 21 Ohio St.3d 64, 488 N. E. 2d 142 (1986).

15. Mandamus.

Where the state otherwise has *an adequate remedy at law* to appeal an error in sentencing, mandamus will not lie. [158]

A prosecuting attorney * * * may appeal by leave of court to which the appeal is taken any other decision, except the final verdict, of the trial court in a criminal case * * *" R.C. 2945.67(A).

Where the trial court fails to follow the law by finding the defendant guilty of a lesser-included offense, for instance, the verdict cannot be challenged through mandamus because mandamus is not available to control the discretion of the trial court.Because mandamus cannot control judicial discretion, a grant of a writ in this circumstance would unconstitutionally subject the defendant to double jeopardy.[159] An appeal is the appropriate vehicle.

---

[158] *State ex rel. Zoller v. Talbert* , 62 Ohio St. 2d 329, 405 N.E. 2d 724 (1980).

[159] *State ex rel Sawyer v. O' Conner*, 54 Ohio St. 3d 380, 377 N.E. 2d 494 (1978).

CHAPTER 9

Broadcasting in Courtroom

The broadcasting of a trial is authorized by C.P. Sup. R. 11 and Canon 3(A)(7) of the code of judicial conduct. The trial court must make a finding that the presence of the broadcasting media does not "distract the participants, impair the dignity of the proceedings, or materially interfere with the achievement of a fair trial or hearing."[160]

In *Grinnell*, the court held that the trial court must permit the broadcasting of the trial unless a fair trial will be impaired pursuant to Canon 3 A(7)(c)(ii). The court has given credence to the presumption of regularity by the Canon as stated in the Canon and the Rule of Superintendence (C.P. Sup. R.11).

Accordingly, the trial court may not "call the validity of this presumption into question, but it is its responsibility to scrutinize the case before it to determine if any of the factors which rebut this presumption is present. A failure to make a specific determination of the existence of a disqualifying factor falling within the purview of Canon 3A (7)(c)(ii) or (iii) dictates that media coverage be permitted." Here a limited writ of mandamus was issued directing the trial court to permit broadcast coverage absent a determination of a factor under Canon 3A (7)(c)(ii) or (iii).[161]

---

[160] *State ex rel. Grinnell Communications Corp v. Love,* 62 Ohio St. 2d 399, 406 N.E. 2d 809 (1980)

[161] See also, *State v. Rogers*, 17 Ohio St. 3d 174, 478 N.E. 2d 984 (1985).

CHAPTER 10

Bail

1. **Factors to Consider in Deciding to Grant Bail.**

2. **Where Denial of Bond is an Abuse of Discretion.**

1. Factors to Consider in Deciding Whether to Grant Bail.

Factors that should be considered by a court prior to granting or denying bail are, in addition to the nature and circumstances of the offense, the "petitioner's family ties, employment, financial resources, character and possible access to a foreign refuse." [162]

---

[162] *Burch v. Perini*, 66 Ohio St. 2d 174, 420 N.E. 2d 1001 (1981).

2. Where Denial of Bond is an Abuse of Discretion.

The Court of Appeals abused its discretion in denying bail where the risk factors, including appellant's age, length of residency in the community, home ownership, activity in community affairs, responsible employment, lack of a prior criminal record, and the minimum potential sentence was only six months, would ordinarily support a decision for release on bond.

The court of appeals further erred by denying the defendant's motion for bail without stating why the motion was denied. Although a court's failure to state why bail is denied does not necessarily indicate there were no grounds to deny bail, however, in examining what information was available to the court, an independent review of the facts and background by the court found both were sufficient to comply with the requirements of Crim. R. 46(E)(1) that bail should be granted since there was no evidence that would support a belief in risk of flight or danger.[163]

---

[163] *Liberatore v. McKeen*, 63 Ohio St. 2d 175 , 407 N.E. 2d 23 (1980). Overruled on unrelated matter. *Dapice v. Stickrath*, 40 Ohio St.3d 298, 533 N.E.2d 339 (1988).

CHAPTER 11

Sureties

1. Where the Defendant Flees the Jurisdiction.
2. Notice Requirements.

1. Where the defendant Flees the Jurisdiction.

Where a defendant flees the jurisdiction, the surety who posted bond forfeits the bond even though the defendant is later located and extradited to the original jurisdiction.

In *State v. Hughes*, the surety found the defendant and caused the authorities to initiate extradition proceedings, however the defendant did not waive extradition, and was given bond in the new jurisdiction. Even though he was subsequently returned to the original jurisdiction, since the surety did not meet its obligation pursuant to Crim. R. 46 (A) to insure the defendant's appearance at all stages of the criminal proceedings, a forfeiture was appropriate. [164]

The court so held notwithstanding R.C. 2937.36, which allows for relief for a showing of good cause by the production of the body or otherwise. Even though the surety went to great expense in locating the defendant, he

---

[164] *State v. Hughes,* 27 Ohio St. 3d 19, 501 N.E. 2d 622 (1986).

did nothing after alerting the authorities in Cuyahoga County.

"Yet having already gone to great time and expense in locating [the defendant] appellants might have met their obligation by appearing before the Cook County court to argue against the allowance of the extradition bond which freed him."

The release by Cook County did not exonerate appellant (although the Local Rule 34(P) provides for some relief so that a portion of the bond can be returned.

2. Notice Requirements.

The notice requirements of Crim. R. 46 (J) were satisfied by the court's journal, which stated the defendant was to remain on bond. "* * * a surety is charged with knowledge of when its defendant is to appear in court on the date set for trial. The surety by posting bail bond, guarantees that it will produce the defendant in court when called." (citations omitted) Here the date the defendant pled guilty was the trial date and the surety, had it followed the case, would have known that the defendant pled guilty, and his bond had been continued. Further, the surety had constructive notice because of the existence of the court's journal entry. *State v. Stevens.*[165]

A surety is relieved of responsibility under Crim. R. 46(m) even though the defendant enters a county in violation of the condition of bond, where the defendant was apprehended due to the efforts of the surety, and both appeared in court the date of the hearing

[165] *State v. Stevens*, 30 Ohio St. 3d 25, 505 N.E. 2d 972 (1987).

The appearance of the defendant in court due to the efforts of the surety can establish good cause in accordance with R.C.2937.36(C) "* * * simply because a condition of release may be imposed upon a defendant does not mean that the breach of a condition of release requires a forfeiture of a bail bond. The procedure for the forfeiture of bail is not governed by the breach of a condition of release but is governed by the procedures set forth in R.C.2937.36. *State v. Homes.*[166]

---

[166] *State v. Homes,* 57 Ohio St. 3d 11, 564 N.E. 2d 1066 (1991).

PART TWO: TRIAL ISSUES

It should be noted that the defendant has a 6th Amendment right of self-representation. Whenever the defendant invokes this right it must be determined that he or she "voluntarily, and knowingly and intelligently elects to do so."[167] Denial of this right is reversible error.[168] This request must be granted unless it is determined that it was made for the purpose of delay or as part of a scheme counter to the integrity of the trial proceedings.[169]

State v. Gibson (1976), 45 Ohio St.2d 366, 74 O.O.2d 525, 345 N.E.2d 399.

[168] *State v. Reed* (1996), 74 Ohio St.3d 534, 535, 660 N.E.2d 456.

[169] *State v. Dean*, 127 Ohio St.3d 140, 2010-Ohio-5070.

CHAPTER 12

Burden and Degree of Proof.

Under R.C. 2901.05, the burden of proving all elements of a crime is on the prosecution. The burden of going forward with an affirmative defense is on the accused by a preponderance of the evidence. An affirmative defense is one that is either designated as affirmative, or which involves excuse or justification that is, "peculiarly within the knowledge of the accused, on which he can fairly be required to adduce supporting evidence."

R. C. 2901.05(B) (1), (2).

1. Affirmative Defenses: Burden of Proof and Persuasion.

For a time, the burden to disprove an affirmative defense was on the state. This was based on the court's interpretation of R.C. 2901.05(A) in State *v. Robinson*,[170] "The approach is to require the state to bear the burden of persuasion beyond a reasonable doubt upon every issue necessary to convict and to impose upon the defendant the burden of coming forward with evidence sufficient to raise any affirmative defense. The state need not disprove an affirmative defense unless the defendant comes forward with evidence sufficient to raise that defense, and the defendant is not required to prove the mitigating circumstances of his affirmative defense by a preponderance of the evidence, 'but

---

[170] *State v. Robinson*, 47 Ohio St. 2d 103, 351 N. E. 2d 88 (1976).

need only introduce evidence of such circumstance to raise a reasonable doubt of his guilt. *People v. Cornett* (1948), 33 Cal. 2d 33'."

The court so held and the legislature enacted the statute, so that the burden of proof always remained upon the state under the theory that the defendant should never have to be in a position to prove his or her innocence, which would be the case if he or she were assigned any specific burden in proving the defense. All that was required was that the defendant produce evidence sufficient that a jury instruction would be warranted so that the jury could consider the defense without imposing on the defendant a high degree of proof.

However, as a response to the *Robinson* ruling, the legislature amended R.C. 2901.05(A) wherein the burden of proving an affirmative defense by a preponderance of the evidence was shifted back to the defendant, as can be seen by the court's opinion in *Klein v. Leis.* [171]

---

[171] *Klein v. Leis*, 99 Ohio St. 3d 537, 795 N.E. 2d 663 (2003).

CHAPTER 13

Joinder of Offenses.

If it appears that the defendant or the state is prejudiced by a joinder of offenses * * * in an indictment * * * the court shall order an election or separate trial of counts * * * or provide such other relief as justice requires. Crim. R. 14.

The court *in State v. Torres*[172] discussed three criteria to be used to determine an improper joinder of offenses:

(1) Whether the defendant's rights were prejudiced,

(2) Whether at the time of the motion to sever the counts of the indictment the defendant provided the judge with sufficient information with which to weigh the joinder against the right to a fair trial,

(3) Whether the trial court abused its discretion by failing to sever the charges.

In *State v. Benner*, the defendant was indicted, inter alia, with two counts of aggravated murder and two counts of attempted murder. All of the counts were unrelated, although the means employed were similar. Appellant argued that the joinder cumulated the evidence and convicted him of an offense of which he would not have been convicted had the counts not been joined. [173]

[172] *State v. Torres*, 66, Ohio St. 2d. 340, 421 N.E. 2d 1288 (1981).

Under Evid. R. 404 evidence of other crimes is admissible to prove *identity*. The facts of each case were similar (four rapes were attempted or committed, and two of the victims were strangled by their brassieres) if the trials had been separated into four different trials, the evidence would have been admissible in each trial.

This rationale was previously stated in *State v. Hamblin*: "Where evidence of each of the joined offenses would be admissible at separate trials, severance is not required because prejudice due to the cumulation of evidence or the inference of a criminal disposition is largely absent." [174]

This ability of the jury to separate the charges has been discussed *in State v. Brooks*, "The jury demonstrated its ability to segregate the proof on each charge. The jury acquitted the defendant of the drug and gun charges and specifications relating to the events * * *." [175] The *Hamblin* court also held: "Joinder of offenses is favored because it conserves resources by avoiding duplication inherent in multiple trials and minimizes the possibility of incongruous results that can occur in successive trials before different juries."

In *Hamblin*, the counts of attempted murder, having a weapon under disability, aggravated murder, and aggravated robbery, were properly joined as being part of a course of criminal

---

[173] *State v. Benner, 4*0 Ohio St. 3d 301, 533 N.E. 2d 701 (1988).

[174] *State v. Hamblin*, 37 Ohio St. 3d 153, 524 N.E. 2d 476 (1988).

[175] *State v. Brooks*, 44 Ohio St. 3d 185, 542 N.E. 2d 636 (1989).

conduct. The two criminal acts of which the crimes were composed occurred about one eighth of a mile apart and within twenty minutes of each other.

The evidence as to both crimes was also related. The burden is on the defendant to show prejudicial joinder. To prevail, on appeal, the defendant must show that the trial court abused its discretion in not separating the charges for trial.

In *State v. Schaim*, although the crimes were properly joined in the indictment because they were similar, although not the same, the trial court abused its discretion by failing to sever the counts at trial. Crim. R. 14 allows for severance if the defendant or the state would otherwise be *prejudiced.* [176]

In regard to the principal that, if the evidence of other crimes would be admissible at separate trials, any prejudice of hearing the evidence in a joint trial would be no different if there were separate trials, the trial court mistakenly found that the evidence was admissible because it showed a pattern of the defendant molesting women.

For the most part the evidence did not show a "pattern or any fact relevant to the other crimes." Identity was not an issue. "Instead of separate trials that carefully limited the admissibility of other acts evidence, the defendant was subjected to one trial where the jury was permitted to simultaneously consider the evidence of three different offenses." The evidence was also not simple and distinct as mentioned in *Roberts*, supra.

In regard to whether the court was furnished sufficient information so it could weigh the considerations favoring joinder against the defendant's right to a fair trial, there were several pretrial motions "that required a discussion of the evidence that the state expected to introduce at trial * * *." The court was aware of

---

[176] *State v. Schaim* ,63 Ohio St.3d 1452, 590 N.E.2d 281 (1992).

the evidence the state planned to introduce and the defendant pointed out the danger of using the other acts evidence.

The court abused its discretion in refusing to sever, "particularly when its reasons for doing so were based on the fact that committing one of these crimes shows a propensity to commit another - an inference that a jury is forbidden to draw"

In *State v. Watson*, the court upheld the joinder of the separate crimes of murder and theft where it was necessary for the state to prove possession of the murder weapon by presenting evidence that the defendant stole it. Here as stated above, if during a single trial the evidence of the other crimes is admissible, they may be joined in a single trial. If the murder were tried by itself, the evidence of the possession of the other weapon would have been admissible. [177]

A defendant is not entitled to separate trials when faced with multiple individual charges unless it can be established that the defendant is prejudiced by a joinder. Criminal Rules R. 8 and 14 should be consulted. It is not improper to join crimes that were the result of a common scheme or plan, similar character or course of criminal conduct. This court held in State v. Lott, 51 Ohio St. 3d 160, regarding Crim. R. 8 that the law favors joining multiple charges.

Further, if other acts evidence can be introduced pursuant to Evid. R. 404(B) there is no prejudice per se also such evidence may be introduced if the evidence is “direct and simple” and without confusion.

Here, the defendant wanted to testify about some of the charges but not others, This court in quoting State v. Roberts, 62 Ohio St. 3d 170, held: “Defendant must produce sufficient information regarding the nature of the testimony he wishes to give in the one case and his reasons for not wishing to testify in the other, so as to satisfy the court that his claim of prejudice is genuine.” [178]

---

[177] *State v. Watson,* 28 Ohio St. 2d 15, 275 N.E. 2d 153 (1971).

[178] State v. Dean, 2015 Ohio St. 3d 4347.

CHAPTER 14

Principals and Aiders and Abettors

It is no defense to a charge of aiding and abetting that the principal was not convicted of the crime. Under R.C. 2923.03 (B) the aider and abettor is to be punished as though he or she were the principal offender.[179]

"Each crime is equal in status and punishment, yet separate and distinct in identity. This allows, and even requires, the characterization of the aider and abettor as a principal offender. It is illogical to propose that the prosecution must show that the principal, who is not on trial, violated the statue beyond a reasonable doubt."[180]

It is not necessary to know the identity of the principal. It is only necessary that the state prove the principal committed the offense. The identity of the principal is not an element of complicity.[181]

Although presence alone at the scene of a crime does not prove a person was an aider and abettor, presence plus

---

[179] *State v. Bell*, 48 Ohio St. 2d 270, 358 N.E. 2d 556 (1976).

[180] *State v. Graven*, 52 Ohio St. 2d 112, 69 N.E. 2d 1205 (1977).

[181] *State v. Perryman* (1976), 49 Ohio St. 2d 14, 358 N.E. 2d 1040 (rev. other grounds).

some action taken on the part of the defendant can be sufficient evidence to characterize the defendant as an aider and abettor. This can be true even if that action is not directed specifically towards the crime.

As an example, the defendant was charged with attempted murder because he was the driver of a car in which his brother, the passenger, attempted to shoot a police officer. The actions of the defendant included his failure to turn off the car motor and to produce identification when requested to by the police officer. He then drove the car away. "The driver failed to terminate the flight. Instead with full knowledge that a firearm was discharged by the passenger, continued to drive away. These intentional evasive actions by the appellee clearly aided the passenger in the attempted murder of the [victim]." [182]

---

[182] *State V. Widner,* 69 Ohio St. 2d 267, 431 N.E. 2d 1025 (1982).

CHAPTER 15

Bar of Subsequent Prosecution (Double Jeopardy).

1. **State and City Sovereignty.**
2. **Where a Civil Penalty is Punitive.**
3. **Retrial as a result of Court Error.**

The Double Jeopardy Clause prohibits "(1) a second prosecution for the same offense after acquittal, (2) a second prosecution for the same offense after conviction, and (3) multiple punishments for the same crime." [183]

Where a single act violates two statutes, a conviction or acquittal under either statute does not necessarily bar a subsequent prosecution. Concerning multiple punishments for the same crime, the Supreme Court of Ohio has looked for guidance to the United States Supreme Court's decision in *Blockburger v. United States.*[184]

[183] *State v. Uskert*, 85 Ohio St. 3d 593, 709 N.E. 2d 1200 (1999).

[184] *Blockburger v. United States* 284 U.S. 299, 76 L. Ed. 306, 52 S.Ct. 180. (1932)

The Blockburger court adopted the language of the Supreme Court of Massachusetts in *Morey v. Com.* 108 Mass. 433: "A single act may be an offense against two statutes; and if each statute requires proof of an additional fact which the other does not, an acquittal or conviction under either statute does not exempt the defendant from prosecution and punishment under the other."

In Blockburger, the court held that the defendant was properly convicted of two drug violations from a single transaction. One violation was for selling drugs not pursuant to a written prescription, the other was for selling drugs not in the original package.

The Blockburger court further stated, "Each of the offenses created requires proof of a different element. The applicable rule is that where the same act or transaction constitutes a violation of two distinct statutory provisions, the test to be applied is to determine whether each provision requires proof of an additional fact which the other does not."

If offenses have identical elements, or if one of the offenses is a lesser-included one of the other, any subsequent prosecution is barred.

One act may separately violate two statutes because the elements are different, nevertheless a subsequent prosecution may be barred where that prosecution requires a relitigation of facts already determined in the first. *State v. Thomas.*[185]

[185] *State v. Thomas.* 61 Ohio St. 2d 254, 400 N.E. 2d 897 (1980) (overruled to extent of holding that denial of motion to dismiss for double

In *Thomas*, the defendant pled guilty to robbery. Subsequent to the defendant's plea, the victim of the robbery died, and the defendant was indicted for involuntary manslaughter. The state was not barred from proceeding with the involuntary manslaughter prosecution. Citing *Harris v. Oklahoma*, *437 U.S. 682* (1977), the *Thomas* court held, " The import of Harris is that a person may not be subjected to multiple prosecutions when proof of the one offense is necessary, as a practical matter, to prove the other, and both completed offenses arose out of the same criminal conduct."

The court found that robbery and involuntary manslaughter are offenses that can be distinguished under *Blockburger* because involuntary manslaughter requires death, while robbery requires a commission or an attempt to commit a theft offense. The court held that if the victim had died before the first trial, the defendant could have been prosecuted and sentenced for both crimes in one trial.

A subsequent prosecution will be barred if it requires a relitigation of facts already determined. However, where the facts "necessary to sustain the conviction have not occurred or have not been discovered, the state may proceed when it is impossible for the state to join all substantive offenses at one trial, the inconvenience to the defendant is clearly outweighed by the

---

jeopardy grounds is a final appealable order) See *State v. Crago*, 53 Ohio St.3d 243, 559 N.E.2d 1353 (2000).

[186] *State v. Thomas*, 61 Ohio St.2d 254, 400 N.E.2d 897 (1980).

public's interest in assuring that the defendant does not fortuitously escape responsibility for his crimes."[186]

If one act violates two statutes because the elements are different, a subsequent prosecution may be barred where that prosecution requires a relitigation of facts already determined in the first prosecution. Further, if the facts have not occurred or have not been discovered at the time of the first trial, an exception to the rule of *Ashe v. Swanson*, may be in effect. (Ashe prohibited the relitigation of facts already determined in a prior proceeding). [187]

In *State v. Tolbert*, the defendant pled no contest to misdemeanor assault before it was determined that the extent of the injuries was more serious than believed. The defendant was later charged with felonious assault. In this instance, although the facts of the injuries had occurred at the time of the indictment, the seriousness of the injuries was not discovered until a few hours after the defendant was found guilty because the victim had not yet been examined by her doctor. In allowing the prosecution for felonious assault to go forward, the court held, "* * * even though the facts necessary to sustain the charge of felonious assault occurred prior to Tolbert's plea, these facts were not discoverable despite the exercise of due diligence." [188]

A motion to dismiss alleging double jeopardy is a final appealable order[189]

---

[187]*Ashe v. Swanson* 397 U.S. 436, 25 L. Ed. 2d 469, 90 S. Ct. 1189 (1970).

[188] *State v. Tolbert,* 60 Ohio St 3d 89, 573 N.E. 2d 617 (1991).

[189] State v. Anderson, 138 Ohio St 3d 264, 2014-Ohio-542

1. State and City Sovereignty.

Because the state and a city are part of the same sovereignty, "double jeopardy stands as a bar to a prosecution by one, after an accused has been in jeopardy for the same offense in a prosecution by the other this principal Includes lesser included offenses." [190]

2. Where a Civil Penalty is Punitive.

A fine imposed in addition to criminal sanctions is not punishment for the same crime where the fine is not punitive. A court is required to "examine the purpose of the legislation and its effects in determining whether it is punitive such as to constitute a double jeopardy violation" *State v. Uskert.*[191] The focus must be on the penalty's effect.

In *Uskert*, the defendant was convicted of Driving Under the Influence (DUI) and received an Administrative License Suspension (ALS) suspension. After paying his criminal fine and serving his sentence, he was required to pay a reinstatement fee that, he argued, was additional punishment for his DUI conviction. In finding the reinstatement fee not punitive the court utilized the following seven factors: (1) "[w]hether the sanction involves an

---

[190] *State v. Best*, 42 Ohio St. 2d 530, 330 N.E. 2d 421 (1975).

[191] *State v. Uskert* ,85 Ohio St. 3d 593, 709 N.E. 2d 1200 (1999)

affirmative disability or restraint," (2) "whether it has historically been regarded as punishment," (3) "whether it comes into play only on a finding of scienter," (4) "whether its operation will promote the traditional aims of punishment-retribution and deterrence," (5) "whether the behavior to which it applies is already a crime," (6) "whether an alternative purpose to which it may rationally be connected is assignable for it," and (7) "whether it appears excessive in relation to the alternative purpose assigned." Further, "only the clearest proof' will suffice to override legislative intent and transform what has been denominated a civil remedy into a criminal penalty."

3. *Retrial as a Result of Court Error.*

The prohibition against double jeopardy does not prevent a retrial where a court error results in a reversal of conviction. Accordingly, where the defendant was convicted and some of the evidence presented at trial was erroneously admitted, a retrial is proper and an appellate court may consider all of the evidence presented, including the erroneously admitted evidence.[192]

The key to understanding this ruling is that where evidence was admitted by the court that proved to be improper it is possible that the prosecution could have but did not produce additional evidence. The prosecution should not be penalized by being denied a retrial where it could have produced additional evidence but did not under the belief that it has met its burden as the result of evidence that the trial court admitted

This scenario should be contrasted with that in which the appellate court finds that the evidence admitted is insufficient to sustain a conviction. Such an instance is similar to a judgment of acquittal that is not appealable.[193] [194]

---

[192] *Lockhart v. Nelson*, 488 U.S. 33 109 S.Ct. 285 102 L.Ed.2d 265

[193] See *State v. Lovejoy*, 79 Ohio St. 3d 440, 683 N.E. 3d 1112.

[194] *State v. Brewer* 121 Ohio St. 3d 202, 2009-Ohio-593.

CHECKLIST.

The Double Jeopardy Clause prohibits:

☐ A second prosecution for the same offense after acquittal.

☐ A second prosecution for the same offense after conviction.

☐ Multiple punishments for the same crime.

<u>In analyzing double jeopardy issues</u>:

☐ Does the offense require proof of an addition fact that the other does not?

☐If so, an acquittal or conviction does not bar further prosecution for the other offense.

☐ Are the elements identical?

☐ If so, prosecution is barred.

☐ Is the offense a lesser included one of the previously prosecuted one?

☐ If so, prosecution is barred.

☐ Although the elements are different, does the prosecution require relitigation of facts already determined?

☐ If, so prosecution is barred.

☐ Were the facts necessary for conviction not discovered or had they not occurred at the time of the previous trial?

☐ If so, prosecution may proceed.

☐ Is the offense the same in the state statute and the city ordinance?

- ☐ If so, prosecution is barred.

☐ Is the civil fine punitive in nature?

- ☐ If so, prosecution is barred.
  - ☐ Look to the “seven factors.”

CHAPTER 16

Corpus Delicti of a Crime.

The *Corpus Delicti* of a crime is the body of the crime and usually consists of two elements (1) The act, and (2) The criminal agency of the act."[195]

In a murder prosecution, corpus delicti was defined in *State v. Manago.*[196] "The Corpus Delicti, meaning the body of the crime charged, in a homicide prosecution involves two elements, i.e. (1) the fact of death and (2) the existence of the criminal agency of another as the cause of death."

"* * * [I]t is important to understand that *corpus delicti* does not mean a dead body and that proof of the corpus delicti of murder does not require production of a dead body.[197]

In *Nicely*, there was only circumstantial evidence of the crime and no body, the conviction was affirmed under the principal that circumstantial evidence may support a conviction, and the reviewing court may not substitute its

---

[195] *State v. Edwards*, 49 Ohio St 2d 31, 358 N.E. 2d 1051 (1976).

[196] *State v. Manago,* 38 Ohio St. 2d 223, 33 N.E. 2d 10 (1974).

[197] *State v. Nicely*, 39 Ohio St. 3d 147, 529 N.E. 2d 1236 (1988).

judgment for that of the jury where substantial credible evidence is presented concerning the guilt of the defendant. The *corpus delicti* of the crime was complete where the circumstantial evidence and the *corpus delicti* of the crime were present.

The issue of the corpus delicti of a crime can be present where there is an issue as to whether the crime has occurred within the applicable statute of limitations. In the case of fraud the corpus delicti of the crime is not complete until the fraud is discovered even though the statute of limitations has expired.[198]

---

[198] *State v. Cook*, Slip Opinion No. 2010-Ohio-6305.

CHAPTER 17

Requirements for Criminal Liability Where a Specific Degree of Culpability is not Specified.

Where a criminal statute does not specify a degree of culpability, and does not impose strict liability, pursuant to R.C. 2901.21(B) recklessness is the degree of culpability necessary to commit the offense. *State v. Young* [199]

1. Recklessness.

In *State v. Adams*, the court of appeals reversed the conviction because the trial court failed to instruct the jury on the degree of mental culpability of recklessness: "a defendant is entitled to have the jury instructed on all elements that must be charged, and where specific intent or culpability is an essential element of the offense, a trial court's failure to instruct on that mental element constitutes error." [200]

An appellate court must review the entire record to determine whether the omission of a charge on the degree of

---

[199] *State v. Young,* 37 Ohio St. 3d 249, 525 N.E. 2d 1363 (1988).

[200] *State v. Adams,* 62 Ohio St. 2d 151, 404 N.E. 2d 144 (1980).

culpability has constituted substantial prejudice. This court found no prejudice because the defense was that the defendant was not the person who caused the injuries to the child and, accordingly, recklessness was never an issue.

Where a defendant has been charged with having a weapon while under disability in violation of R.C. 2923.13(A)(3). And further, where the defendant did not know he was under indictment for a drug related crime, in order to convict, it must be shown that the defendant acted "recklessly with regard to being aware that he was under indictment * * *" [201]

Further, in a weapons under disability prosecution, the state is not required to prove a mental state in regard to the prior offenses that subjected the defendant to the charge or any mental state showing that he was presently prohibited from possessing weapons.[202]

Where the indictment does not contain a mens rea it must be determined whether recklessness or strict liability is the proper mens rea. Under R.C. 2901.21(B) if an offense "plainly indicates a purpose to impose strict liability * * * culpability is not required. Where there is no culpability specified and no strict liability is present, recklessness is "sufficient culpability to commit the offense."[203]

---

[201] *State v. Clay*, 120 Ohio St. 3d 528, 900 N.E. 2d 1000 (2008).

[202] *State v. Johnson*, Slip Opinion No. 2010-Ohio-6301

[203] *State v. Lester*, 122 Ohio St. 3d 396, 2009-Ohio-4225.

One way to determine whether strict liability is the standard is to compare the liability for mere *possession* of an instrument of crime with the *use* of the instrument. For example, the use of a deadly weapon element of R.C. 2911.02(A)(c) does not require recklessness since mere location on the defendant's person is sufficient. This can be contrasted with the actual use of the weapon, which requires a specific intent. Accordingly, if a specific intent is required, the indictment must contain the mens rea, if not, the proper jury instruction must contain it.

It is not necessary for the indictment to indicate a mens rea where the statue describing the crime does not contain a mens rea. It is sufficient that the indictment track the language of the statute. Previously the court had held that an indictment could be defective even though it tracked the exact language of the indictment where no mens rea was indicated.[204]

Further, where one section of statute specifies a mean rea if one or more of the remaining sections does not specify a mens rea, a determination must be made whether strict liability or recklessness is to be the standard.[205]

---

[204] *Colon II*, 119 Ohio St.3d 204, 2008-Ohio-3749, 893 N.E.2d 169.

[205] *State v. Horner*, 126 Ohio St.3d 466, 2010-Ohio-3830.

CHAPTER 18

Proof of Physical Harm.

In a prosecution where one of the elements to be proven is "physical harm" or "serious physical harm," it is not necessary that an examining physician, or the custodian or preparer of the hospital or medical treatment records testify. In *State v. Spikes*, footnote 10 the court stated:

"Based on [the victims] testimony, the jury could have found, beyond a reasonable doubt, that he experienced 'acute pain of such duration as to result in substantial suffering.' Therefore, any error which might have resulted from admitting the medical records would be harmless. See State v. Moritz (1980), 63 Ohio St. 2d 150, 157."

The import of this holding is that the elements of serious physical harm can be proven beyond a reasonable doubt solely by the testimony of the victim.

Where medical records are admitted with no testimony as to the authenticity of the medical records; R.C. 2317.422 merely requires the following:

1. A verified certification of either the person who made them, the custodian or the person under whose supervision they were made.

2. A certification showing the mode and the time they were prepared.

3. A statement that they were made in the usual course of business.

4. That the records were provided to the attorney of record for each adverse party not less than five days before trial.

Of course, this statute does not take away the right of any party to call the preparer or the custodian to testify as to the authenticity.

CHAPTER 19

Constitutionality of Prior Convictions.

The criminal statutes are replete with provisions for the enhancement of penalties due to prior convictions. Although it is rare, in some instances the issue of the constitutionality of the plea in the prior conviction arises.

Although an uncounseled prior conviction cannot be used to enhance a sentence based on a subsequent conviction, *Baldasar v. Illinois*, where a defendant stipulates to a prior conviction, the stipulation acts as a stipulation also to the constitutionality of the prior conviction. [206]

The defendant must object to the conviction at any time before or during trial, but he may not do so on appeal. If a constitutional question of a prior conviction is raised, the defendant "must present sufficient evidence to establish a prima facie showing of a constitutional infirmity."[207]

Where defense counsel raises an objection to the use of a prior conviction for enhancement purposes, he must present some evidence supporting this claim. Sufficient evidence to raise the issue can be presented by asking the defendant while on the stand

---

[206] *Baldasar v. Illinois,* 446 U.S. 222, 64 L.Ed. 2d 169, 100 S.Ct. 1585. (1980).

[207] *State v. Adams*, 37 Ohio St. 3d 295, 525 N.E. 2d 1361 (1988).

whether he was counseled during the prior conviction. “This one question and answer would have placed on the state the burden of proving that appellee’s prior convictions were counseled.” *State v. Brandon* [208]

[208] *State v. Brandon,* 45 Ohio St. 3d 85, 543 N.E. 2d 501 (1989).

CHAPTER 20

Aiders and Abettors.

An inference of purpose to kill can be established where the facts show that "The participants in a felony entered into a *common design* and either the aider or abettor knew that an inherently dangerous instrumentality was to be employed to accomplish the felony or, the felony and the manner of its accomplishment would be reasonably likely to produce death." *State v. Scott.*[209] In *Scott*, the inherently dangerous instrumentality was a handgun.

If a jury is instructed that a purpose to kill may be inferred because the defendant participated in a common design to commit the crime by force or violence, the jury must be instructed that this is a *nonconclusive inference,* R.C. 2903.01. However, it is not necessary that the jury instruction state the exact words the "inference is nonconclusive." A jury instruction is sufficient if it includes the requirement of specific intent, and it states that mere association with the perpetrators does not make that person a participant.[210]

---

[209] *State v. Scott* ,61 Ohio St. 2d 155, 400 N.E. 2d 375. (1980).

[210] *State v. Coleman*, 37 Ohio St. 3d 286, 525 N.E. 2d 792 (1988).

It makes no difference if an aider and abettor did not know his accomplice was going to kill the victim if it can be shown that the means to rob the victim employed inherently dangerous devices. "* * * the defendant participated in the planning and commission of the robbery, and also acquiesced in the employment of a deadly weapon to accomplish this crime. Under these circumstances appellant must have realized that the victim's life would be endangered by the manner and means of performing the act conspired, and accordingly, appellant is bound by consequences naturally resulting from the furtherance of the conspiracy to commit the aggravated robbery." [211]

---

[211] *State v. Clark,* 55 Ohio St.2d 257, 379 N.E.2d 597 (1978) (reversed on other grounds)

CHAPTER 21

Inconsistent Verdicts

Where different verdicts are returned on multiple count indictments, it has been argued that these inconsistencies require reversal of the convictions. However, inconsistent verdicts are not reversible. "The several counts of an indictment containing more than one count are not interdependent. A verdict responding to a designated count will be construed in the light of the count designated, and no other. Inconsistency in a verdict does not arise out of inconsistent responses to different counts, but only arises out of inconsistent responses to the same count." *State v. Adams*,[212] quoting *Browning v. State.* [213]

In *Adams*, the defendant was charged with aggravated robbery and aggravated murder premised on the count of aggravated robbery, he was found not guilty of aggravated robbery, but guilty of aggravated murder. This verdict does not violate the general rule against inconsistent verdicts.

---

[212] *State v. Adams,* 53 Ohio St. 2d 223, 373 N.E. 2d 137 (1978), vacated, in part, for unrelated issue *Adams v. Ohio*, 439 U.S. 811, 99 S.Ct. 69, 58 L.Ed.2d 103 (1978)

[213] *Browning v. State,* 120 Ohio St. 62, 165 N.E. 566 paragraph 4, of the syllabus (1929).

In *State v. Brown*,[214] a more blatant, less than consistent verdict was returned. The defendant in Brown was convicted of one of three counts of rape in addition to other counts. He was found not guilty of two of the rape counts by reason of insanity, but sane as to the other rape, and the other remaining counts.

The court found the verdicts not inconsistent; relying on *Adams*, *supra*., the court concluded that the verdict was consistent with the testimony of the defense expert witness, who testified that appellant could fade in and out of sanity. The court held, "the jury could have found that appellant was insane from the time he first accosted Daily until the time he and Daily went into the kitchen for coffee." Since the inconsistency was to different counts, the verdict will not be set aside as it would be if there were inconsistencies to the same count.

---

[214] *State v. Brown,* 12 Ohio St.3d 147, 465 N.E. 2d 889 (1984).

CHAPTER 22

Jurors

1. **Exclusion of Jurors by Religion.**
2. **Hearing Impaired Defendant or Juror.**
3. **Alternate Jurors Present during Deliberations**
4. **Juror Misconduct.**

1. Exclusion of Jurors by Religion.

Where the defendant challenges the array of the grand jury and /or the petit jury because members of a particular religion have been excluded from jury duty, it must be established that the procedure used to choose grand jurors caused substantial under representation of an identifiable group.

The defendant lacked standing since he was not a member of the Old Older Amish religious faith. However, the practice of not putting the names of the Amish on the jury list was violative of R.C. 2313.08, but this violation does not per se cause a reversal of a valid conviction unless it can be shown that the grand jurors were not qualified.

Without a showing of prejudice, "* * * no indictment shall be quashed or verdict set aside for any such irregularities or

---

[215] *State v. Fulton*, 57 Ohio St. 3d 120, 566 N.E. 2d 1195 (1991). See also, *State v. Puente*, 69 Ohio St. 2d 136, 431 N.E. 2d 987 (1982); and R.C. 2313.41

misnomers if the jurors who formed the same possessed the requisite qualifications to act as jurors."[215]

In regard to the challenged petit jury, appellant failed to establish there was a systematic exclusion of the religious sect.

2. Hearing Impaired Defendant or Juror.

Evidentiary Hearing Required

The Sixth Amendment requires an evidentiary hearing when expert testimony is proffered that the defendant is hearing impaired and cannot hear all of the testimony at trial. "A trial court should carefully balance the state's interests and the defendant's rights, and take reasonable steps to compensate for the disability. The judge can consider the cost of alternative measures, the extent to which a particular method will disrupt trial, the degree of the defendant's impairment, and any other relevant factors."[216]

In order to seat a hearing impaired juror, the court must determine whether an accommodation established by the court is sufficient for the juror to serve competently and whether there is any possibility of the defendant being deprived of a fair trial. If as a part of the state's case the jurors are asked to evaluate factors that are beyond the impaired juror's capacity such as patterns of speech, demeanor, and voice inflections, the defendant will be denied a fair trial if such a juror is seated.[217]

---

[216] *State v. Schaim*, 65 Ohio St. 3d 51, 600 N.E. 2d 661 (1992).

[217] *State v, Speer*, 124 Ohio St. 3d 564, 2010-Ohio-649.

3. Alternate Jurors Present during Deliberations.

It is violation of Crim. R. 24(G)(1) and R.C. 2313.37(C) to allow an alternate juror to be present during jury deliberations. See *State v. Murphy* (2001), 91 Ohio St.3d 516, 531, 747 N.E.2d 765. Whenever an alternate juror is allowed to be present with or without objection there is error. With objection, the burden shifts to the state to show there was no prejudice. The failure of the state to show a lack of prejudice requires a new trial.[218]

4. Juror Misconduct.

Where there is an allegation of jury misconduct and where the trial court does not thoroughly inquire as to whether the juror can be rehabilitated before declaring a mistrial, this lack of diligence can arise to the level of being unreasonable causing double jeopardy to attach making it necessary to discharge the defendant. [219]

---

[218] *State v. Downour,* 126 Ohio St.3d 508, 2010-Ohio-4503.

[219] *State v. Gunnell*, 132 Ohio St.3d 442, 2012-Ohio-3236

CHAPTER 23

Corporate Liability

Concerning the criminal liability of a corporation, an employee of the corporation whose criminal conduct can be attributed to the corporation "constitutes the corporate defendant. The court held in State v.CECOS Internl, Inc: a corporation may be found guilty only if the criminal act or omission was "approved, recommended, or implemented by high managerial personnel with actual or implied authority to approve, recommend or implement same. High managerial personnel are those who make basic corporate policy." See R.C. 2901.23.[220]

---

[220] *State v. CECOS Internl.* Inc., 38 Ohio St. 3d 20, 526 N.E. 807 (1988).

CHAPTER 24

Lesser-Included and Allied Offenses

1. Lessor Included offenses.
2. Offenses of an Inferior Degree Distinguished.
3. Allied Offenses.

R.C. 2945.74 provides in pertinent part: "* * * When the indictment or information charges an offense, including different degrees, or if other offenses are included within the offense charged, the jury may find the defendant not guilty of the degree charged but guilty of an inferior degree thereof or lesser included offense."

1. Lessor Included Offenses.

The court held in *State v. Deem*, "an offense may be a lesser included of another if (i) the offense carries a lesser penalty than the other; (ii) the greater offense cannot, as statutorily defined, ever be committed without the lesser offense, as statutorily defined, also being committed; and (iii) some element of the greater offense is not required to prove the commission of the lesser offense." [221]

Part (ii) of Deem has been modified by the court. The "ever" language has been deleted:

---

[221] *State v. Deem* ,40 Ohio St 3d 205, 533 N.E. 2d 294 (1988).

"This clarification does not modify the *Deem* test, but rather eliminates the implausible scenarios advanced by parties to suggest the remote possibility that one offense could conceivably be committed without the other also being committed. *Deem* requires a comparison of the elements of the respective offenses in the abstract to determine whether one element is the functional equivalent of the other. If so, and if the other parts of the test are met, one offense is a lesser included offense of the other."[222]

Even though an offense may be found to be a lesser-included offense, the key to whether a charge for a lesser-included offense is to be given is whether the evidence presented at trial so warrants.

In order to assist the trial court in determining whether a lesser included offense should be charged, the court has held: "Even though so defined, a charge on the lesser included offense is not required unless the trier of fact could reasonably find against the state and for the accused upon one or more of the elements of the crime and against the accused on the remaining elements which by themselves would sustain a conviction upon a lesser included offense." [223]

An offense can fail to be a lesser-included offense of another, but may be an offense of an *inferior degree*. If an offense is found to be of an inferior degree and the evidence so warrants, the court must give a jury instruction on that offense as it would a lesser-included offense.

---

[222] *State v. Evans*, 122 Ohio St.3d 381, 2009-Ohio-2974

[223] *State v. Kidder*, 32 Ohio St 3d 279, 513 N.E. 2d 311 (1987).

2. *Offenses of an Inferior Degree Distinguished.*

Offenses of an inferior degree were discussed in, *State v. Deem, supra.*: "an offense is an 'inferior degree' of the indicted offense where its elements are identical to or contained within the indicted offense, except for one or more additional mitigating elements which will generally be presented in the defendant's case."

The *Deem* court gave as an example the offense of kidnapping under R.C. 2905.01 (A) (B). Kidnapping is a felony of the first degree unless the offender releases the victim in a safe place unharmed, which would be a felony of the second degree. "An 'offense, including different degrees' is an offense which, upon proof of a mitigating or aggravating element, is assigned a different degree of punishment."

In *Deem*, the court found that aggravated assault is of an inferior degree to felonious assault, but not a lesser-included offense, since one can commit felonious assault without serious provocation. It is an offense of inferior degree because the elements are identical, except for the mitigating element of serious provocation. In *Deem*, because the evidence was insufficient for a lesser charge, the court's refusal to charge aggravated assault was affirmed.

Concerning jury deliberation, when a jury or finder of fact has been charged with considering a lesser-included offense, the jury does not have to first find unanimously that the defendant is not guilty of the principal charge before it can begin

---

[224] *State v. Thomas*, 40 Ohio St. 3d 213, 533 N.E. 2d 286 (1988).

to consider whether the defendant is guilty of the lesser-included offense.[224]

The court in *Thomas,* adopted the reasoning of the court of appeals in *State v. Muscatello*, paragraph three of the syllabus:

"3. A jury must unanimously agree that the defendant is guilty of a particular criminal offense before returning a verdict of guilty on that offense. If a jury is unable to agree unanimously that a defendant is guilty of a particular offense, they may proceed to consider a lesser-included offense upon which evidence has been presented. The jury is not required to determine unanimously that the defendant is not guilty of the crime charged before they may consider a lesser included offense."[225]

In the same vein, not only should the jury be charged to consider a lesser included offense for purposes of benefiting the defendant, that is, where the evidence is sufficient for a finding of guilt on the lesser charge and not guilty of the indicted offense, it is also possible that giving a lesser included charge to the jury can harm the defendant.

" * * * If evidence tending to prove a lesser included offense is present and a jury is inhibited by the charge from finding the defendant guilty thereof, the collective conscience of that body may too easily be disposed to fabricate the elements of the crime charged rather than risk, by a verdict of acquittal, turning the malefactor loose upon a society grievously harmed by his act. If a defendant is not guilty of murder, his liberty should not be dickered away by a compromised verdict upon another crime, which is supported by the evidence."[226]

[225]*State v. Muscatello* 57 Ohio App.2d 231, 387 N.E. 2d 627 (1977).

[226] *State v. Loudermill*, 2 Ohio St. 2d 79, 206 N.E. 2d 198 (1965).

Directing the fact finder to consider a lesser-included charge could create an "unreasonable conclusion." [227]

In *Nolton*, the court held: "if the evidence adduced on behalf of the defense is such that if accepted by the trier it would constitute a complete defense to all substantive elements of the crime charged, the trier will not be permitted to consider a lesser included offense for the reason that an unreasonable compromise would be invited on the "state's evidence."

Therefore, for instance, if the evidence adduced by the defendant tended to establish an alibi for a murder charge, it would be unreasonable to cause a jury to consider a lesser-included offense, because if the defense is believed, the defendant would be acquitted, because this would be a complete defense of all substantive elements of the crime charged. In addition, concerning affirmative defenses, it would also be unreasonable to charge a lesser-included offense where the essential elements of the indicted offense are admitted, such as in the case of an automobile manslaughter where the defendant admits the death was caused by operation of the vehicle and the defendant requested a charge of assault and battery.[228]

Where two statutes do not have identical elements, in order to successfully argue that the second prosecution is barred by double jeopardy it must be established that one is a lesser included offense of the other.

---

[227] *State v. Nolton* 19 Ohio St. 2d 133, 249 N.E. 2d 797 (1969).

[228] *State v. Champion*, 109 Ohio St. 281, 142 N. E. 2d 141 (1924).

For instance, reckless operation of a motor vehicle under R.C. 4511.20 is not a lesser included offense of the felony of failure to comply with a signal or order of a police officer pursuant to R.C. 2921.331(C)(5)(a)(ii) . Accordingly, where one is first convicted of reckless operation, and later indicted for failure to comply with a signal or order of a police officer the subsequent prosecution is not barred by double jeopardy.

The two statutes do not have identical elements. Moreover, they are not lesser-included offenses. It should be noted that the court of appeals in finding reckless operation a lesser included offense of failure to comply determined that recklessness was the culpable mental state contained in the charge of failure to comply, and since recklessness is the culpable mental state in reckless operation reckless operation is a lesser included offense of failure to comply.

This court found that the state of mind of recklessness is not required in order to commit the offense of failure to comply, and further since the statute does not have a specified mental state, the only inquiry should be whether a substantial risk of physical harm to persons or property was present. [229]

Where the defendant was charged with robbery and was convicted of theft, a fifth-degree felony as a lesser included offense of robbery, the trial court properly determined that theft is a lesser included offense of robbery. This court applied the two-step test of State v. Deem and modified the Deem holding to include cases where there are alternative elements the commission of either of which can constitute guilt of the offense. In robbery, a person can be convicted either by committing or attempting to commit a theft offense. In the case of theft one of the alternatives of the robbery statue is theft which is a lesser included offense of robbery.

[229] *State v. Fairbanks,* 117 Ohio St. 3d 543, 885 N.E. 2d 888 (2008).

Because these alternatives exist, each of the alternatives must be examined to determine whether the offense is a lesser include offense of one of the alternatives.[230]

3. Allied Offenses

When considering allied offenses of similar import pursuant to the dictates of R.C. 2941.25, the conduct of the defendant must be examined to determine whether a merger should take place or whether more than one offense has been committed thereby resulting in two or more separate offenses of which the defendant can be found guilty and sentenced on each.

State v. Rance (1999) 85 Ohio St. 3d is now overruled. Rance required the court to compare the elements of the crimes in the case of multiple offenses in the abstract without regard to the conduct of the defendant. And even though Rance had been modified by State v. Cabales, 118 Ohio St. 3d 54, 2008-Ohio-1645, 886 N.E. 2d 181, to establish that the elements do not have to strictly coincide, such a rule nevertheless left the courts in a quandary in interpreting and applying R.C.2941.25.

As a result of State v. Johnson, when a court is faced with possible allied offenses, the court must:

1.Determine if the offenses were committed by the same conduct.

2.Determine if it is possible to "commit one offense and commit the other with the same conduct."

If the commission of one offense also is the commission of the other they are allied offenses of similar import and the offenses will be merged.[231]

---

[230] *State v. Smith*, 117 Ohio St. 3d 447, 884 N.E. 2d 595. (2008).

In an aggravated assault prosecution where the defendant was convicted of two separate parts of R.C 2903.12(A)(1) where one part imposes criminal liability where one causes or attempts to cause physical harm to another; and where the other part imposes criminal liability where one causes or attempts to cause physical harm by means of a deadly weapon, if there is but one animus, the defendant can only be convicted of one of the counts of aggravated assault. It should be noted that the defendant can be tried on both counts but only convicted of one count.

Technically, a comparison of the elements under the two-tier test shows that the commission of one will not necessarily result in the commission of the other. Accordingly, the legislative intent must also be considered in determining allied offenses. Here, the court noted that the intent of each part of the statute is to prevent harm. Accordingly, these offenses are allied offenses of similar import. [232]

Murder and felonious assault are allied offenses. Felonious assault under R.C. 2903.11(A)(1) is an allied offense of attempted murder under R.C. 2903.02(B). Further felonious assault under R.C. 2903.11(A)(2) is an allied offense of attempted murder under R.C. 2903.02(A) and 2903.02. [233]

---

[231] *State v. Johnson*, Slip Opinion No. 2010-Ohio-6314.

[232] State v. Brown, 119 Ohio St. 3d 447, 895 N.E. 2d 149 (2008).

[233] *State v. Williams*, 124 Ohio St.3d 381, 2010-Ohio-147

Where a defendant is incorrectly sentenced for two or more offenses that are allied offenses of similar import the court of appeals can properly reverse the sentence so that the prosecutor can choose which offense to which the defendant will be sentenced. The convictions are not to be merged. The prohibition against double jeopardy only prevents multiple sentences for the same crime not multiple convictions of allied offenses. [234]

Where a defendant is convicted of allied offenses, he can only be sentenced for one of the crimes. The prosecutor, at sentencing, must choose which offense the defendant is to be sentenced to. It is error to sentence the defendant on both charges and run the sentences concurrently. Although practically, such a sentence may have the same effect in regard to sentence length assuming the prosecutor will choose the offense that has the longest potential sentence. Nevertheless, such multiple convictions are prohibited. [235]

Aggravated robbery under R.C. 2911.01(A)(1) which requires possession of a deadly weapon used, shown, or brandished and robbery under R.C. 2911.02(A) (2) which prohibits a threat to inflict physical harm are allied offenses of similar import. Accordingly, "a defendant cannot be convicted of both offenses when both are committed with the same animus against the same victim." Felonious assault under R.C. 2903.11(A) (1) and under R.C. 2903.11(A)(2) are allied offenses of similar import if committed with the same animus.[236]

---

[234] State v, Whitfield, 124 Ohio St. 3d 319, 2010-Ohio-2

[235] State v. Damron, 129 Ohio St. 3d 86, 2011-Ohio-2268. See also State v. Johnson, 128 Ohio St. 3d 153, 2010-Ohio-6314,and R.C. 2929.41.25 which prohibits multiple sentences.

A conviction under the RICO statute does not cause the underling crime to be an allied offense because under RICO the defendant is convicted of a "pattern" of offenses, this pattern is the crime under RICO which is separate from the underlying crime which is not an allied offense.[237]

In regard to the minimum monetary amount required to trigger the statute, where two individuals' actions fall short of the requirement 500-dollar amount but in the aggregate, does meet the amount the individual amounts are to be used. This is because the statute is ambiguous and ambiguity must be decided in favor of the defendant.[238]

---

[236] State v. Harris, 122 Ohio St.3d 373, 2009-Ohio-3323.

[237] State v. Miranda, 138 Ohio St. 3d 184, 2014-Ohio-451,

[238] State .Stevens 138 Ohio St. 3d 247, 2014-Ohio-1932.

Aggravated Burglary and rape and not allied offenses of similar import. When deeming whether crimes are allied offenses the conduct, the animus and the import must be separately considered.

Here the court further articulated the consequence of State v. Johnson, 128 Ohio St 3d. 153, 2010-Ohio-6314. The court held that offenses that result in separate and identifiable harm are of dissimilar import. The court then analyzed what "import "means.

The court held: "When a defendant's conduct victimizes more than one person, the harm for each person is separate and distinct, and therefore, the defendant can be convicted of multiple counts. Also, a defendant's conduct that constitutes two or more offenses against a single victim can support multiple convictions if the harm that results from each offense is separate and identifiable from the harm of the other offense."[239]

[239] State v. Ruff, 143 Ohio St, 3d 114, 2015-Ohio-995.

CHAPTER 25

Motion for Judgment of Acquittal

1. Standard of Proof.
2. Appeal of Judgment of Acquittal.

Pursuant to Crim. R. 29, a defendant, or the court on its own motion shall order an entry of a judgment of acquittal for one or more offenses under the following circumstances:

1. The motion was made after the evidence on either side was closed.
2. The evidence was insufficient to sustain a conviction of one or more offenses.

1. Standard of Proof

The standard in determining whether to grant a motion for a judgment of acquittal is whether "reasonable minds can reach different conclusions as to whether each material element of a crime has been proved beyond a reasonable doubt."[240]

In order to preserve as error the trial court's failure to grant a directed verdict of acquittal, the defendant, in a jury trial, as oppos~~ed to a trial to the court, mus~~t renew the motion for a

[240] State v. Swinger, 5 Ohio St. 2d 151, 214 N.E. 2d 417 (1966). See also State v. Bridgeman, 55 Ohio St. 2d 261, 381 N.E. 2d 184 (1978).

directed verdict of acquittal at the close of all evidence. If the case is tried to the court, "* * *the defendant's plea of not guilty serves as a motion for judgment of acquittal, and obviates the necessity of renewing a Crim. R. 29 motion at the close of all evidence." [241] The purpose of a Crim. R. 29 motion is to take the case from the jury, and where there is no jury, the subsequent motion is not necessary.

The *Bridgeman* court also discussed the factors that constitute evidence sufficient to overcome a rule 29 motion, such as eyewitness testimony and corroboration.

Crim. R. 29(C) includes a 14-day time limit in which to file the motion. A motion for reconsideration filed after the 14-day time limit is not valid and will be denied.[242]

2. Appeal of Judgment of Acquittal

Where a trial court grants a judgment of acquittal pursuant to Crim. R. 29(C) this judgment is a final verdict and is not appealable by the state with, or without leave of court.[243]

Pursuant to R.C. 2945.67(A) a judgment of acquittal for improper venue is a final verdict and is not appealable.[244]

---

[241] Dayton v. Rogers, 60 Ohio St. 2d 162, 398 N.E. 2d 781 (1976) (overruled on other grounds).

[242] *State v. Ross*, Slip Opinion No. 2010-Ohio-6282.

[243] State v. ex rel Yates v. Court of Appeals for Montgomery Cty., 32 Ohio St. 3d 30, 512 N.E. 2d 343 (1987).

[244] State v. Hampton, 134 Ohio St.3d 447, 2012-Ohio-5688

CHAPTER 26

Use of a Firearm.

1. Operability.
2. Use of Circumstantial Evidence.
3. Discharging a Firearm into a Habitation

R.C. 2929.14 (formally R.C. 2929.71) requires the offender who is convicted of, or pleads guilty to a specification charging him with having a firearm on or about his person, to serve an additional three years of actual incarceration, before and consecutive to the indefinite term of imprisonment or life sentence.

1.Operability.

The establishment of a firearm specification requires proof that the firearm is operable.

The operability of the firearm can be proven beyond a reasonable doubt with direct or scientific evidence. Operability of a firearm must be proven in order to impose a term of actual incarceration. The court in *State v. Gaines*[245] held that proof the

[245] *State v. Gaines* 46 Ohio St. 3d 65, 545 N.E. 2d 68 (1989).

defendant possessed a "deadly weapon" pursuant to R.C.2911.01 is not sufficient to prove the defendant possessed a "firearm" pursuant to R.C. 2929.71(A), it is necessary to show operability even if with circumstantial evidence.

The court suggested proof of operability could be established by way of testimony of gunshots, smell of gunpowder, bullets or bullet holes, etc.

The court subsequently modified *Gaines* concerning the evidence necessary to prove the firearm specification, holding that the state may rely on all of the "surrounding facts and circumstances in establishing whether a firearm was used in the commission of a felony." *State v. Murphy*. [246]

In *Murphy,* the defendant, while robbing a convenience store, pointed a gun at a customer, and announced if not given money that he would kill the clerk.

The court found these facts sufficient to establish beyond a reasonable doubt that the defendant possessed a firearm pursuant to R.C. 2923.11(B). The operability of the firearm can be proven "* * * by the testimony of lay witnesses who were in a position to observe the instrument and the circumstances surrounding the crime." The state is not required to introduce the firearm at trial.

In *State v. Thompkins*, the court included implicit threats as sufficient to show operability of a handgun. In *Thompkins*, the defendant pointed the gun and told the clerk to "be quick." The court held: "However, the fact that Thompkins did not explicitly threaten Brinkman does not take away from the fact that Brinkman thought her life was in danger. Even absent any explicit verbal threats on the part of Thompkins, the trier of fact in this case could

[246] *State v. Murphy*,, 49 Ohio St. 3 206, 551 N.E. 2d 932 (1990).

have reasonably concluded, based on the totality of the circumstances, that Thompkins was in possession of a firearm at the time of the offense, that is a deadly weapon capable of expelling projectiles by an explosive or combustible propellant." [247]

2. Use of Circumstantial Evidence.

R.C. 2923.11(B)(2) allows the establishment of the operability of a firearm by the use of circumstantial evidence. When determining whether a firearm is capable of expelling or propelling [projectiles] * * * the trier of fact may rely on circumstantial evidence* * *"

Where the defendant is indicted for felonious assault, a felony of the second degree with a firearm specification, and was later convicted of the lesser-included offense of aggravated assault a felony of the fourth degree, the requirements of R.C. 2929.11(G), R.C. 2929.71(C) , R.C. 2929.141(A) and R.C. 2941.143 requiring the indictment to contain a deadly weapon specification, does not mean that the lesser included third or fourth degree felony must be in a separate count of the indictment with a firearm specification for R.C. 2929.11(B)(7) to apply. "* * * if this * * * indictment, count in the indictment, or information charg[is] him with* * * the offense * * * ' (emphasis added) of a greater degree than a third or fourth degree felony the indictment or count necessarily and simultaneously charges the defendant with lesser included offenses as well."[248]

---

[247] *State v. Thompkins* 78 Ohio St. 3d 380, 678 N.E. 2d 541 (1997). (superseded by statute for other grounds).

[248] *State v. Lytle*,49 Ohio St. 3d 154, 551 N.E. 2d 950 (1990).

Where a burglar enters a dwelling unarmed, and acquires a firearm from the burglarized home, this act of acquiring the firearm is sufficient evidence to find the defendant guilty of having a firearm in possession during the commission of a felony.[249]

3. Discharging a Firearm into a Habitation.

The offense of discharging a firearm into a habitation (R.C. 2923.161) coupled with a firearm specification (R.C. 2941.145) is proper because they do not constitute allied offenses of similar import. The discharging of a firearm into a habitation is a statutory crime. The firearm specification is not a criminal offense but is a penalty enhancement and cannot be joined with a criminal offense to constitute an allied offense of similar import.[250]

---

[249] *State v. Powell*, 59 Ohio St. 3d 62, 571 N.E. 2d 125 (1991).

[250] *State v. Ford,* 128 Ohio St. 3d 398, 2011-Ohio-765.

CHAPTER 27

Pleas

1. Defendant Must be Informed of Rights.
2. Notification of Probation Eligibility.
3. Notification of Right to Confront Accusers.
4. No Contest Pleas May Result in a Conviction of a Lesser Offense.
5. Jeopardy.
6. Participation by Court in Plea Negotiations.
7. Guilty Pleas after Trial.
8. Notification of Post Release Requirements.
9. Statements to a Polygraph Examiner.

1. Defendant Must be Informed of Rights

Until the court's holding in State v. Veney, the trial court was required, pursuant to Crim. R. 11(C), to inform the defendant the following rights before accepting a guilty plea:

(1) The defendant is waiving his privilege against self-incrimination.

(2) The defendant has a right to a jury trial.

(3) The defendant has a right to confront his accusers.

(4) The defendant has a right to compulsory process.[251]

[251] *State v. Ballard*, 66 Ohio St. 2d 473, 423 N.E. 2d 115 (1981).

There is no ground for vacating a plea if the trial court fails to use the exact language when explaining these rights to the defendant. "* * * we hold that a rote recitation of Crim. R. 11(C) is not required, and failure to use the exact language of the rule is not fatal to the plea. Rather, the focus, upon review, is whether the record shows that the trial court explained or referred to the right in a manner reasonably intelligible to that defendant.[252]

In *Ballard*, the court linked two separate statements of the trial court to conclude that the defendant was reasonably informed of his right to a trial by jury.

The trial court told the defendant: (1) neither the judge nor the jury could draw any inference if he failed to testify. (2) He was entitled to a fair and impartial trial under the law. The above was a reasonable substitute for the "right to jury trial" language of Crim. R. 11(C).

(5) The fifth right is to have the state prove guilt beyond a reasonable doubt. It should be kept in mind that this right is included in Crim. R. 11(C)(2)(c), but the court never required it to be strictly complied with. Now failure to inform the defendant of this right will invalidate the plea. [253]

If at the time of accepting a defendant's plea the trial court fails to explain the defendant's constitutional rights, the plea is invalid. If certain non-constitutional rights are not explained literally in compliance with Crim. R. 11, the plea may be upheld if it has not been prejudicial to the defendant. [254]

---

[252] *Ibid.*

[253] *State v. Veney*, 120 Ohio St. 3d 176, 897 N.E. 2d 621 (2008).

[254] *State v. Clark*, 119 Ohio St. 3d 239, 893 N.E. 2d 462 (2008).

When the trial court in informs the defendant of the rights contained in Crim. R. 11 it is not necessary to precisely track the wording of Crim. R. 11 (C) (2) (c) which state: "to have compulsory process for obtaining witnesses in the defendant's favor." It is sufficient to state: "you have the right to call witnesses on your behalf." Although the preferred method is for the trial court to track the language of the above rule, "the court's failure to literally comply with Crim. R. 11(C) does not invalidate a plea agreement if the record demonstrates that the trial court explained the constitutional right 'in a manner reasonably intelligible to the defendant'" Further, any other portion of the record can be examined to verify compliance with the rule, including the written plea agreement.[255]

[255] *State v, Barker*, 129 Ohio St. 3d 472, 2011-Ohio-4130.

2. Notification of Probation Eligibility.

If the trial court fails to inform the defendant prior to accepting his plea that he is ineligible for probation in violation of Crim. R. 11 (C) the defendant cannot attack his conviction by post-conviction relief under R.C. 2953.21. The doctrine of res judicata bars this action: "* * * a final judgment of conviction bars a convicted defendant who was represented by counsel from raising and litigating in any proceeding except an appeal from that judgment, any defense or any claim of lack of due process that was raised or could have been raised by the defendant at trial. * * * Under the doctrine of res judicata the Crim. R. 11(C) question is merged with the judgment of conviction and defendant cannot now relegate the issue." [256]

Although Crim. R. 11(C)(2)(a) requires the trial court to inform the defendant prior to accepting a plea whether he is eligible for probation, there is no error where there was substantial compliance with the rule. Substantial compliance means that under the totality of the circumstances the defendant understands the rights he is waiving and the implications of his plea.

For example, in *State v. Nero,*[257] the court concluded the defendant knew he was ineligible for probation from the circumstances surrounding his plea. Defense counsel told the court defendant knows that he will be incarcerated. In addition, the defendant stated to the judge that he would just like some time to straighten out his affairs.

"We hold, therefore, that where the totality of the circumstances indicated that the defendant knew he was ineligible

---

[256] *State v. Ishmail*, 67 Ohio St. 2d 16, 423 N. E. 2d 1068 (1981).

[257] *State v. Nero* ,56 Ohio St. 3d 106, 564 N.E. 2d 474 (1990).

for probation and was not prejudiced by the trial court's failure to comply with Crim. R. 11(C)(2)(a), the trial court's acceptance of the defendant's guilty plea to the nonprobational crime of rape without personally advising the defendant that he was not eligible for probation constitutes substantial compliance with Crim. R. 11." *Nero, supra.*

3. Notification of Right to Confront Accusers.

Failure of the trial court to inform defendant he has a right to confront his accusers prior to accepting his guilty plea requires the plea to be vacated.[258]

4. No Contest Plea may result in Conviction of Lesser Offense.

A trial court may find a defendant guilty of a lesser-included offense upon a plea of no contest.[259]

5. Jeopardy

Jeopardy attaches at the time a plea of no contest is entered because the defendant is "put to trial before a trier of facts * * *" [260]

---

[258] *State v. Sturm*, 66 Ohio St. 2d 483, 422 N.E. 2d 853 (1981).

[259] *Sawyer v. O'Connor*, 54 Ohio St. 2d 380, 377 N.E. 2d 494 (1975).

[260] *Surface v. United States,* 420 U.S. 377 (1975); *State ex rel. Leis v. Gusweiler*, 65 Ohio St. 2d 60, 418 N.E. 2d 397 (1981).

6. Participation by Court in Plea Negotiations.

"A judge's participation in plea negotiations does not cause the plea to be involuntary per se but, because of the possibility that the plea may have been coerced requires that the circumstances of the plea be carefully scrutinized to determine if the judge's participation affected the voluntariness of the plea."[261]

In State v. Byrd, the court found that the judge's participation in the plea process made the plea involuntary for the following reasons:

> (1) The judge spoke privately with the defendant's mother and sister urging them to have the defendant plead guilty.
> (2) The judge remarked about the possible sentence.
> (3) It appeared that the judge had joined forces with the prosecutor in deciding the defendant was guilty.
> (4) The judge talked about the problems in having a jury trial.

7. Guilty Pleas after Trial.

Where a defendant is found guilty and subsequently enters into a plea before sentencing, he has waived all errors that may have occurred at trial unless those errors can be shown to have prejudiced the defendant in voluntarily entering the plea.[262]

---

[261] *State v. Byrd*, 63 Ohio St. 2d 288, 407 N.E. 2d 1384 (1980).

[262] *State v. Kelly*, 57 Ohio St. 3d 127, 566 N.E.2d 658 (1991).

8. Notification of Post Release requirements.

In determining whether a plea is knowing, intelligent, and voluntary, the trial court must include in its colloquy any post-release requirements and any possible additional sentence that must be served if the post-release requirements are not met. A failure to inform the defendant is a violation of Crim. R. 11 requiring a vacation of the plea. [263]

[263] *State v. Sarkozy*, 117 Ohio St. 3d. 86, 881 N.E. 2d 1224 (2008).

9. Statements to a Polygraph Examiner.

Evid. R. 410(A)(5), Which provides that statements made during plea negotiations are not admissible does not prevent the admission of statements made to a polygraph examiner prior to indictment. The court reiterated the fact that the statement must be made during active plea negotiations for it to be covered under this rule. [264]

---

[264] *State v. Jeffries*, 119 Ohio St. 3d 265, 893 N.E. 2d 487 (2008).

CHAPTER 28

Attempt/Tampering with Evidence

1. Purpose.
2. Substantial Step.
3. Overt Action.
4. Tampering with Evidence

The elements of attempt are the "mens rea of purpose or knowledge, and conduct directed toward the commission of an offense." [265]

Where one purposely and knowingly, but unsuccessfully, engages in conduct that would result in an offense, that person is guilty of attempt under R.C. 2923.02.

There are several exceptions under this statute. A person cannot be convicted of attempt to commit a minor misdemeanor, or an attempt to engage in a conspiracy. In addition, anyone convicted of an offense cannot be convicted of an attempt to commit the same offense, nor can a person be convicted of complicity to commit the same offense. R.C. 2923.02(C).

If a person abandons his effort to commit the crime or prevents the commission of the crime so that there is a

---

[265] *State v. Woods*, 48 Ohio St. 2d 127, 357 N.E. 2d 1059 (1976), overruled on other grounds.

State v. Downs, 51 Ohio St.2d 47, 364 N.E.2d 1140 (1977).

"complete and voluntary renunciation of his criminal purpose," this act of abandoning or prevention may be asserted as an affirmative defense to a charge of attempt to commit the crime. 2923.03(D).

A defendant cannot defend a charge of attempt on the theory that the offense could not have been committed either factually or legally. It is sufficient that the "offense could have been committed had the attendant circumstances been as the actor believed them to be." 2923.02(B).

The penalty for an attempt to commit of an offense is usually that of the next lesser degree than the attempted offense. R.C. 2923.02(E) specifies the penalties for attempted offenses.

1. Purpose.

In an attempted theft prosecution, *purpose* to deprive the owner of property must be clearly shown. For example, merely looking into a store window is insufficient to constitute an attempted theft. "* * * the act of peering through the window could constitute conduct directed to the commission of a theft offense, but without a showing of purpose to deprive the store owner of property, an attempt was not shown." [266]

3. *Substantial Step*

In *Woods, supra.*, the co-defendant climbed the roof of a store in order to rob the store manager; he left the roof after hearing a fire engine siren. Because the statute does not say how

---

[266] *State v. Reed* , 65 Ohio St. 2d 117, 418 N.E. 2d 1359 (1981).

far one must proceed toward the commission of the offense in order to have attempted to commit the offense, the court cited with approval the Model Penal Code: "* * * the standard adopted in the latter code appears to us workable, reasonable, and consistent with the language of R.C. 2923.02(A). Under section 5.01 of the Model Penal Code, an attempt is when one 'purposely does or omits to do anything which is * * * an act or omission constituting a substantial step in a course of conduct planned to culminate in his commission of the crime.'

The court further held: "to constitute a *'substantial step'* the conduct must me 'strongly corroborative of the actor's purpose.' * * * [B]ut this standard does properly direct attention to overt acts of the defendant which convincingly demonstrate a firm purpose to commit a crime, while allowing police intervention, based upon observation of such incriminating conduct, in order to prevent the crime when the criminal intent becomes apparent."

In *State v. Group*, the court further expounded the elements of attempt. The issue in *Group* was how far one must solicit another for the act of soliciting to constitute a substantial step sufficient to constitute an attempt.

Group arranged for a co-inmate to firebomb a house. He provided the address of the victim's house, showed the person how to make the bomb, promised him $150,000.00, and encouraged him to carry out the act.

These actions are *overt acts* which constitute *substantial steps* in carrying out the crime and are sufficient to constitute attempt.[267]

---

[267] *State v. Group,* 98 Ohio St. 3d 248, 781 N.E. 2d 980 (2002).

In *State v. Powell*, the defendant attempted rape where he ordered a seven- year- old girl to take her clothes off. "But a step need not be necessary to the commission of the crime to constitute an attempt it need only be 'substantial' as *Woods* defines that term." [268]

It should be kept in mind that the facts of Powell included an admission by the defendant that he intended to have sex with the victim, which buttressed the court's analysis in finding attempted rape since his admission showed his purpose. This finding can be contrasted with that of *State v. Heinish,* where attempted rape was not found although the evidence showed that the victim's pants were partially pulled down.[269]

---

[268] *State v. Powell* ,49 Ohio St.3d 255, 552 N.E.2d 191 (1990).

[269] *State v. Heinish,* 50 Ohio St.3d 231, 553 N.E.2d 1026 (1990).

3. Overt Action.

Where the issue is whether the defendant attempted to have sexual intercourse with the victim, the "action is not criminally punishable as an attempt to commit a particular crime unless the accused had the intent to commit the crime. To convict appellee of attempted statutory rape the prosecution was required to prove that appellee undertook some overt action * * * with the intent of having sexual intercourse with her." [270] $

4. Tampering with Evidence

In order to be convicted of this crime that it must be proven beyond a reasonable doubt that the defendant knew of an investigation of that crime or that an investigation was likely.[271] R.C. 2921.12(A)(1) defines tampering with evidence as when a person either knows that an official preceding or investigation is in progress or is likely to be instituted. This court has discussed this issue in State v. Straley, 139 Ohio St. 3d 339, 2014-Ohio-2139. Which held the mere concealing of crime does not necessarily point to a tampering with evidence crime.

Here the defendant concealed heroin in her vagina several days prior to the auto in which she was riding in was stopped by a law enforcement officer. She admitted she had concealed the drugs in her body.

The state argued that an" unmistakable crime "was committed thereby giving the defendant constructive knowledge

---

[270] *State v. Curry*, 43 Ohio St. 2d 66, 330 N.E. 2d 720 (1975).

[271] State v. Barry, Slip Opinion No. 2015-Ohio5449

that an investigation was likely. The unmistakable crime doctrine has never been approved by this court.

The court finally concluded: “It is not proper to impute knowledge of a pending or likely investigation merely because one commits a crime.”

CHAPTER 29

JURY INSTRUCTIONS/Closing Argument

1. The Epperson Rule.
2. Eyewitness Identification.
3. Failure to Object to Jury Instructions.
4. Special Jury Instructions, Writing Required.
5. Where an Objection is Required.
6. Where Failure to Object is not a Waiver of Review.
7. Preliminary Instructions.
8. Defective Verdict Form.
9. Waiver of Closing Argument.

1. The Epperson Rule.

If requested jury instructions are correct, pertinent, and timely presented, they should be included, in substance at least, in the general instruction. This principal is known as the *Epperson Rule.* [272]

---

[272] *City of Cincinnati v. Epperson* , 20 Ohio St. 2d 59, 253 N.E. 2d 785 (1969).

However, where the substance of the special instruction is not fully contained in the general instruction, this omission does not necessarily constitute error because the requested instructions may not be necessary. If the jury is not clearly assisted by the instruction, there is no abuse of discretion for refusing to give the instruction.

Epperson also required the trial court to respond to any question from the jury regarding the instructions. This requirement has been overruled. It is now the law that an abuse of discretion in responding to the jury's questions must be shown to reverse a conviction.[273]

2. Eyewitness Identification.

A trial court does not err where it refuses to give a supplementary jury instruction on eyewitness identification where the evidence does not support the instruction.

Where the facts show that the defendant was viewed for a considerable period by a trained police officer; the physical circumstances were idea for observation (a brightly lighted hallway); the intervals of observation were sufficient for accurate memory and recall; the original description of the defendant was given the same night of the shooting, and was generally consistent with the physical characteristics of the defendant; and the identification at the lineup was immediate and without equivocation, the court did not abuse its discretion in not giving a special instruction on eyewitness identification.

"In short, it is evident to us that the exercise of discretion by the trial court in deciding that the factual issues present in the

---

[273] *State v. Carter*, 72 Ohio St.3d 545, 651 N.E.2d 965 (1995).

case did not require, and would not have assisted by, the requested instructions, and that the issue of determining identity beyond a reasonable doubt was adequately covered by other instructions." *State v. Guster*.[274]

The court concluded that the requested instruction would not have clearly assisted the jury under these facts. Whether or not to give such an instruction is always fact determinative.

3. Failure to Object to Jury Instruction.

Failure to object to an erroneous jury instruction precludes review pursuant to Crim. R. 30. The rule requires an objection before the jury retires, counsel must state specifically the grounds of the objection, unless plain error can be shown.[275]

In *State v. Durkin*, defense counsel failed to object to an erroneous jury instruction regarding the burden of proof. The conviction could have only been reversed upon a showing of plain error pursuant to Crim. R. 52(B).[276]

The philosophy behind the *Durkin* holding and Crim. R. 30 can be seen in *State v. Williams*: "This court has consistently held that an appellate court need not consider an error which a party complaining of could have called, but did not call to the trial courts attention at a time when such error could have been avoided or corrected by the trial court."[277]

---

[274] *State v. Guster* , 66 Ohio St. 2d 266, 421 N.E. 2d 157 (1981).

[275] See *State v. Roberts*, 48 Ohio St. 2d 221, 358 N.E. 2d 530 (1976).

[276] *State v. Durkin* ,66 Ohio State 2d 158, 420 N.E. 2d 124 (1981).

A defendant cannot assign as error the failure of the trial court to give a requested instruction where he subsequently objects to the giving of any lesser-included instructions after his original request was denied. [278]

Crim. R. 30 requires that the party who assigns as error the instruction given by the court, to make the objection. The defendant cannot use the fact that the error in the instruction was brought the court's attention by the prosecutor. *State v. Roberts, supra*.

4. Request for a Special Jury Instruction, Writing Required.

A special jury instruction pursuant to Crim. R. 30 must be in writing, "Such a request must be in writing and made at the close of the evidence or at such earlier time as the court reasonably directs in order to be proper, appellant's request was improper." [279] The defendant would have prevailed had he followed the correct procedure for the submission of special instructions. The trial court has a "mandatory constitutional duty" to instruct the jury that it may not consider the defendant's failure to testify, a failure to give the instruction *upon proper request* is reversible error. See *Carter v. Kentucky,* 450 U.S. 288, (1981).

---

[277] *State v. Williams* 51 Ohio St 2d 112, 364 N.E. 2d 1364 (1977).

[278] *State v. Parra*, 61 Ohio St. 2d 236, 400 N. E. 2d 885 (1980).

[279] *State v. Fanning*, 1 Ohio St. 3d 19, 437 N.E. 2d 583 (1982).

5. Objection Required.

There was no plain error where the trial court improperly charged the jury that the state must prove "extreme emotional stress as an element of voluntary manslaughter where defense counsel did not object to the charge. In *State v. Muscatello*,[280] the court affirmed the reversal of the conviction for this erroneous instruction. However, plain error was never addressed.

Since November 1978, the defendant has been required to prove extreme emotional stress by a preponderance of the evidence. No plain error was found here since there was very little evidence of extreme emotional stress, and there was overwhelming evidence of the elements of the charge. "The facts in this case fall far short of meeting the criteria for plain error."[281]

6. Where Failure to Object is not a Waiver of Review.

Where defense counsel fails to object to a jury charge, the objection is not waived where the record shows the trial court is aware of the correct law of the disputed issue and where the defendant was unable to cause the court to correctly charge the jury.

---

[280] *State v. Muscatello,* 55 Ohio St. 2d 201, 378 N.E. 2d 738 (1978).

[281] *State v. Underwood*, 3 Ohio St. 3d 12, 444 N.E. 2d 1332 (1983).

In *State v. Wolons*, defense counsel and the court discussed the cases that supported defendant's contention concerning the intoxication defense. "Defendant attempted to persuade the court that the evidence and case supported his position and made it clear that the trial court understood his objection to the court's refusal to so instruct." [282]

As a result, there was no waiver of objection by failure to object on the record after defense counsel's discussion with the trial court.

Where the trial court is required to give an instruction such as a correct or complete instruction on the elements of a crime and the defenses, the error is preserved where defense counsel objects pursuant to Crim. R. 30(A), even though there is a failure to proffer written instructions as is required by the rule.[283]

7. Preliminary Instructions.

Where the trial court gave preliminary instructions of law pursuant to Crim. R. 30(B), that are vital to the defendant's rights, the fact that they were given preliminarily does not excuse the court from repeating the instructions after arguments of counsel. However, there was no error where the trial court refused to repeat all of the preliminary instructions, such as the instructions on credibility and weighing of the evidence, where prejudice has not been shown. [284]

---

[282] *State v. Wolons,* 44 Ohio St. 3d 64, 541 N.E. 2d 443 (1989)

[283] *State v. Williford,* 49 Ohio St. 3d 247, 551 N.E. 2d 1279 (1990).

8. Defective Verdict Form.

Under R.C. 2945.75(A), the jury verdict form, if there is the presence of an element of the crime that can make the charged crime an offense of a more serious degree, the jury form must state either the degree of the offense or the underlying facts that make it a crime of a higher degree. Accordingly, In the case of a tampering with records conviction where the crime was found to be of a higher degree because there were government records involved, and where this fact was not on the verdict form, the verdict was reversed since the defendant can only be convicted of the least degree of the offense.[285]

Where the jury verdict form does not specify the drug of which the defendant is charged with possessing, but where the indictment, jury instructions, and the evidence presented at trial correctly specify the drug, the defendant is properly convicted of the crime.[286]

---

[284] *State v. Comen*, 50 Ohio St. 3d 206, 553 N.E. 2d 640 (1990).

[285] *State v. Pelfrey*, 112 Ohio St. 3d 422, 860 N.E. 2d 735 (2007).See also State v. McDonald, slip opinion 2013-Ohio-5042.

[286] *State v. Efford*, 132 Ohio St.3d 159, 2012-Ohio-2224

9. Waiver of Closing Argument.

The right to counsel in closing argument can be waived. This includes waiver by silence. Where, after hearing testimony, the trial court immediately determines guilt or innocence there is a waiver of closing argument where counsel "neither requests a closing argument nor objects to its omission. See also State v. Pasqualone 121 Ohio St. 3d 186, which delineates what rights can be waived by counsel and what rights must be personally waived.[287]

[287] *State v. McCaulsland*, 124 Ohio St. 23d 8, 2009-Ohio-5933.

PART THREE: CRIMES

CHAPTER 30

Aggravated Murder

1. **Prior Calculation and Design.**
2. **Instantaneous Deliberation and Prior Calculation.**
3. **Purpose or Intent to kill.**
4. **Aiders and Abettors.**
5. **Sentences.**

R. C. 2903.01 establishes two forms of aggravated murder. The first under R.C. 2903.01(A) is murder committed *purposely* and with *prior calculation and design*, or the *unlawful termination of another's pregnancy*.

The second form is felony-murder under R.C. 2903.01(B) where the act of homicide is connected with a specific felony. Under this section it must be established that the killing was done *purposely* while committing or attempting to commit or while fleeing immediately after committing or attempting to commit kidnapping, rape, aggravated arson or arson, aggravated robbery or robbery, aggravated burglary or burglary, terrorism, or escape. This section also includes other acts which subject the defendant to the death penalty, including the killing of a person under thirteen years of age, or a law enforcement officer (under certain circumstances). This section as in (A) above includes the unlawful termination of another's pregnancy while committing any of the above offenses.

A conviction under this section can subject the defendant to the death penalty if the indictment contains one or more aggravating circumstances.[288] A defendant who is not the principal offender may nevertheless be subjected to the death penalty if he or she was an aider and abettor of the principal and the murder was committed with the aider and abettor's prior calculation and design.

1. Prior Calculation and Design.

Under prior Ohio law, aggravated murder was differentiated from murder as being "premeditated murder," which by definition included a spur of the moment killing. The present aggravated murder statute's operative term is "prior calculation and design."

The Legislative Service Commission's comments indicate that it was the legislature's intention that the use of the term "prior calculation and design" was "to indicate studied care in planning or analyzing the means of the crime, as well as a scheme compassing the death of the victim. Neither the degree of care nor the length of time the offender takes to ponder the crime beforehand are critical factors in themselves, but they must amount to more that momentary deliberation."

---

[288] Aggravating circumstances are discussed below.

2. Instantaneous Deliberation and Prior Calculation and Design.

To illustrate the difference between instantaneous deliberation and prior calculation and design, an analysis of the following cases is helpful.

In *State v. Reed,*[289] the suspicious occupants of a vehicle were stopped by the police. The police vehicle contained two police officers. One of the officers approached with his gun drawn. The defendant exited the vehicle, immediately shot, and killed one of the police officers. There was evidence produced at trial that the defendant had stated to co-workers, "If a cop got in his way [during a robbery] he would blow him away."

This scenario established instantaneous deliberation, and *not* prior calculation and design: "* * * the evidence at most indicated the presence of <u>instantaneous deliberation."</u>

Concerning the defendant's prior statements about blowing the cop away, the court held: "[they] do not show that appellant designed a scheme in order to implement a calculated decision to kill. Not only were the remarks significantly removed from the killing in terms of a time frame but they were very general in nature and thus were not relevant to the killing * * * "

However, words followed more closely to the acts can be relevant in establishing prior calculation and design.

In *State v. Toth,*[290] the defendant's actions combined with his words established prior calculation and design. The defendant stated if he found the person who damaged his car, he would "waste~~" that person. After he found~~ the woman (who was with two

[289] *State v. Reed* ,65 Ohio St. 2d 117, 418 N.E. 2d 1359 (1981).

[290] *State v. Toth,* ,52 Ohio St. 2d 206, 371 N.E. 2d 831 (1977).

friends), he grabbed one of the women by the hair, shot her in the jaw, and then shot the two other women.

The court held: "The appellant's method of shooting the three girls as well as his apparent determination to follow through on a specific cause of action, sufficiently supported the finding that appellant had adopted a plan to kill."

The *plan to kill* constituted prior calculation and design. See also *State v. Robbins.* In *Robins,* prior calculation and design was found where the offender, after knocking the victim down, left the room and returned with a "sword" he obtained from under his mattress and stabbed the victim to death. [291]

A case with similar facts is *State v. Cotton.*[292] In *Cotton,* the court restated the general principal that instantaneous deliberation is not sufficient to constitute prior calculation and design. After attempting to pass a stolen check, the defendant, was pursued by two police officers. He struggled with one officer, took his gun, assumed a shooting position and shot the officer to death.

The court held: "The evidence reveals the presence of sufficient time and opportunity between the appearance of the police officers on the scene and the fatal shot into officer Hutchison for the planning of the killing and for the planning to constitute prior calculation. The circumstances surrounding the firing of the non-fatal shots and the circumstances surrounding the firing of the last shot justify a finding of design."

Prior calculation and design was also found in *State v. Moreland.* [293] The defendant, after arguing with his girlfriend, left

---

[291] *State v. Robbins,* 58 Ohio St. 2d 74, 388 N.E. 2d 755 (1979).

[292] *State v. Cotton* 56 Ohio St 2d 8, 381 N.E. 2d 190 (1978).

the house returned with a rifle, stood in front of her, and shot her to death. He then reloaded the rifle and either killed or attempted to kill several other people in the house. The court held that these facts indicated that the offender had "sufficient time and opportunity for the planning of appellant's acts." Further, the killing, and attempted killing, of the others present "showed a scheme to implement the calculated decision to kill * * *"

In *State v. Claytor*, [294]under facts similar to those of *Cotton, supra*. The offender, after being stopped for trespassing, first shot and killed one of two security officers. He then chased the other officer around a parking lot where he caught him and fatally shot him. The court found the first killing did not constitute prior calculation and design, because it appeared to be a spur of the moment killing. Concerning the second shooting, the court held: "* * * [it] could be viewed as going beyond the impulse of the moment to constitute prior calculation and design." See also *State v. Wickline*. [295]

3. Purpose or Intent to Kill.

"Purposely" is defined in R.C. 2901.22(A) "A person acts purposely when it is his specific intention to cause a certain result, or when the gist of the offense is a prohibition against conduct of

---

[293] *State v. Moreland* 50 Ohio St. 3d 58, 552 N.E. 2d 894 (1990).

[294] *State v. Claytor,* 61 Ohio St. 3d 234, 574 N.E. 2d 472 (1991).

[295] *State v. Wickline,* 50 Ohio St. 3d 114, 552 N.E. 2d 913 (1990).

a certain nature, regardless of what the offender intends to accomplish thereby, it is his specific intention to engage in conduct of that nature." In regard to "purposely" as it applies to aggravated murder, the following cases are illustrative.

In *State v. Johnson,* the defendant while robbing his landlord, hit him with the barrel of a sawed-off shotgun, causing his death. The court held, "It is a fundamental principal that a person is presumed to intend the natural, reasonable and probable consequence of his voluntary act * * * The mere fact that the shotgun was not fired at [the victim] but was used as a club does not negate the presumption of an intent [and hence purpose] to kill since such a weapon is capable of causing death by either method." [296]

Purpose to kill can also be established from coroner's photographs that show a victim's wounds. The court has upheld the admission of coroner's photographs because they can show: "* * * intent behind infliction of the wounds." [297]

4. Aiders and Abettors.

An inference of purpose to kill can be established where the facts show "[T]he participants in a felony entered into a common design and *either,* the aider or abettor knew that an inherently dangerous instrumentality was to be employed to accomplish the felony or the felony and the manner of its

---

[296] *State v. Johnson,* 56 Ohio St. 2d 35, 381 N.E. 2d 637 (1978).

[297] *State v. Franklin*, 62 Ohio St. 3d 118, 580 N.E. 2d 1 (1991).

accomplishment would be reasonably likely to produce death." The inherently dangerous instrumentality was a handgun. [298]

If a jury is instructed that a purpose to kill may be inferred because the defendant participated in a common design to commit the crime by force or violence, the jury must be further instructed that this is a nonconclusive inference. However, it is not necessary that the jury instruction state the exact words the "inference is nonconclusive." A jury instruction is sufficient if it includes the requirement of specific intent, and states that mere association with the perpetrators does not make that person a participant.[299]

"It makes no difference if an aider and abettor did not know his accomplice was going to kill the victim. If it can be shown that the means to rob the victim employed inherently dangerous devices. That the defendant participated in the planning and commission of the robbery, and also acquiesced in the employment of a deadly weapon to accomplish this crime. Under these circumstances appellant must have realized that the victim's life would be endangered by the manner and means of performing the act conspired, and accordingly, appellant is bound by consequences naturally resulting from the furtherance of the conspiracy to commit the aggravated robbery." *Coleman, supra.*

---

[298] *State v. Scott*, 61 Ohio St. 2d 155, 400 N.E. 2d 375 (1980).

[299] *State v. Coleman*, 37 Ohio St. 3d 286, 525 N.E. 2d 792 (1980).

5. Sentences.

If the indictment or count of the indictment does not contain any specifications of aggravating circumstances, the defendant is not subject to the death penalty. The maximum sentence can be life imprisonment without parole. See R.C. 2929.03 for the other possible sentences.

CHAPTER 31

Death Penalty

21. The Insanity Standard Compared with the Mitigation Standard.
22. Harmless Error.
23. Prohibiting the Introduction of Mitigation Evidence.
24. Prosecutorial Comment on Unsworn Statement.
25. Victim Impact Statements.
26. Presentence Report.
27. Residual Doubt.
28. Sentencing Issues: Expert Witness Appointment.
29. Imposition of Sentence.
30. Resentencing upon Demand.
31. Trial Court's Failure to Articulate Its Reasoning in Its Weighing Duties.

Introduction.

The Supreme Court of Ohio declared the most recent death penalty statute, R.C. 2929.03 *et seq.*, constitutional in *State v. Jenkins* [300]

Ohio's previous death penalty statute was declared unconstitutional by the United States Supreme Court in *Lockett v. Ohio.*[301] *Lockett* was one of a string of cases in which the Supreme Court invalidated death penalty statutes nationwide beginning with the landmark decision of *Furman v. Georgia,*[302]

---

[300] *State v. Jenkins* 15 Ohio St. 3d 164, 473 N.E. 2d 264 (1984).

[301] *Lockett v. Ohio* , 438 U.S. 586 (1978).

[302] *Furman v. Georgia*, 408 U.S. 238 (1972).

holding that the death penalty was being applied arbitrarily and capriciously, and was therefore unconstitutional.

Later in *Gregg v. Georgia*,[303] the Supreme Court held if safeguards could be implemented to lessen the arbitrary and capricious nature of the application of the death penalty, a sentence of death would not be per se unconstitutional.

The same day *Gregg* was decided, the court decided *Woodson v. North Carolina* which invalidated North Carolina's mandatory death sentence statute that required that all persons convicted of first-degree murder be sentenced to death. [304]

The court in *Woodson*, held that mandatory death statutes are unconstitutional because such statutes treat "all persons convicted of a designated crime not as uniquely individual human beings, but as members of a faceless, undifferentiated mass to be subjected to the blind infliction of the penalty of death." [305]

As a result of the above United States Supreme Court decisions, Ohio law now provides that the class of persons eligible to be sentenced to death be limited to those whose crimes consist of one or more aggravating circumstances.

---

[303] *Gregg v. Georgia,* 428 U.S. 153 (1976).

[304] *Woodson v. North Carolina*, 428 U.S. 280 (1976).

[305] Ibid, at 304 (plurality opinion of Stewart, J., Powell, J., and Stevens, J.)

The aggravated murder trial where the death penalty is sought is bifurcated. It consists of a guilt phase and a penalty phase. In order to be subjected to the death penalty, the defendant must have been found guilty of the principal charge of aggravated murder, as well as one or more "aggravating circumstances."

The aggravating circumstances established must then be weighed by the fact finder, in the penalty phase, against any mitigating factors the defendant was able to establish during the penalty phase. The burden is on the defendant to establish any mitigating factors. The state is then required to prove that the aggravating circumstances outweigh the mitigating factors beyond a reasonable doubt.

1. Possible Sentences.

If the trial is by jury, the jury recommends the appropriate sentence after a finding of guilt. The possible sentences are death, life imprisonment without parole, life imprisonment with no possibility of parole until having served thirty years, life imprisonment with no possibility of parole until having served twenty-five years. The trial judge is not bound by the jury's decision to sentence the defendant to death. The trial court is free to reject a sentence of death and impose one of the above lesser sentences. However, the judge cannot sentence the defendant to death without a recommendation of death from the jury. See 2929.03 for several other provisions concerning death eligibility and parole eligibility.

2. Appellant Review.

3. Aggravating Circumstances.

In order to be subjected to the death penalty it is necessary that the defendant be convicted of the primary charge of aggravated murder, in addition to one or more statutory aggravating circumstances.

Ohio Revised Code § 2929.04 delineates the requisite aggravating circumstances that must be proven beyond a reasonable doubt as a condition for the imposition of the death penalty.

4. Principal Offender and Prior Calculation and Design.

It should be noted, that a finding that the murder was committed with prior calculation and design cannot by itself, subject a defendant, who is a principal offender, to the death penalty. A finding of prior calculation and design is only significant if the defendant was not the principal offender, but was an accomplice who possessed the kind of culpability required for the act.[306]

In other words, the principal offender can be sentenced to death without a finding of prior calculation and design (indeed cannot be sentenced to death with only a finding of prior calculation and design), and an accomplice cannot be subjected to the death penalty unless he or she commits the murder with prior calculation and design.

---

[306] *State v. Coleman*, 37 Ohio St. 3d 286, 525 N.E. 2d 792 (1988).

"Prior calculation and design is an aggravating circumstance only in the case of an offender who did not personally kill the victim." [307]

5. Non-Statutory Aggravating Circumstances.

Because R.C. 2929.04 defines with particularity the only aggravating circumstances that must be proven in order to subject the defendant to the death penalty, any failure by the trial court to follow the law in this regard can invalidate the proceeding.

One area where this failure to follow the law has been where the jury or three-judge-panel has considered, or where the indictment has contained, non-statutory aggravating circumstances. Because the fact-finder is required to weigh any aggravating circumstances against any mitigating factors, before it can impose the death penalty, the consideration of non-statutory aggravating factors deprives the defendant of a fair trial.

The consideration of non-statutory aggravating circumstances, affects the crucial weighing process. That process may become unconstitutionally tilted toward the imposition of the death penalty. Such a tilt would defeat the legislatively dictated narrowing function, which defines those acts which when committed can subject the offender to the death penalty. The guidance needed by a capital jury, "so as to avoid the arbitrary and selective imposition of the death penalty," would be lost.[308]

---

[307] *State v. Penix*, 32 Ohio St.3d 369, 513 N.E.2d 744 (1987).

[308] *State v. Johnson*, 24 Ohio St. 3d 87, 494 N.E. 2d 1061 (1986).

6. Non-statutory Aggravating Circumstances Contained in the Indictment.

In *Johnson, supra*, the indictment improperly designated a firearm specification as an aggravating circumstance, instead of merely as a firearm specification. The court held, "presenting the jury with specifications not permitted by statute impermissibly tips the scales in favor of death, and essentially undermines the required reliability in the jury's determination."

7. Non-statutory Aggravating Circumstances Not in the Indictment but Considered by the Court.

In *State v. Davis*, the court reversed a death sentence because the trial court's opinion listed the following as aggravating circumstances:

"1) The manner by which the defendant purchased the gun, used to kill the victim in this case.

"2) The manner by which the defendant purchased the ammunition for the gun.

"3) The shooting of the victim, the firing at close range and finally placing the gun almost against her skull and discharging the weapon.

"4) The prior purposeful killing of his wife in 1970 by multiple stab wounds.

"5) Committing the present offense while on parole for the murder of his wife." [309]

In addition, the court in *Davis* improperly considered prior calculation and design as an aggravating circumstance, since the

---

[309] *State v. Davis*, 38 Ohio St. 3d 361, 528 N.E. 2d 925 (1988).

defendant was a principal offender. Here, the only proper aggravating circumstance was number 4.

8. The Court's Consideration of the Nature and Circumstances of the Crime Improperly Attacked as Non-Statutory Aggravating Circumstances.

Other than in the most blatant cases as in *Johnson, supra.* where the opinion of the court or three judge panel specifically lists improper aggravating circumstances, or where the indictment contained non-statutory aggravating circumstances, the Ohio Supreme Court has consistently held that it is very difficult, if not impossible, to successfully show that the fact finder considered non-statutory aggravating circumstances.

In many cases, the trial court, in its opinion, cites the nature and circumstances of the crime in its analysis of the case; such an opinion has been unsuccessfully attacked under the theory that the court converted the nature and circumstances of the crime into non-statutory aggravating circumstances.

The citing of the nature and circumstances of the crime does not, standing by itself, constitute a consideration of non-statutory aggravating circumstances. Indeed R.C. 2929.03 (F) requires the court to compare the nature and circumstances of the crime to any mitigation factors found, and to any aggravating circumstances established.

Thus, in *State v. Stumpf*, the court held, "[U]nder R.C. 2929.03 (F) a trial court or three judge panel may rely upon and cite the nature and circumstances of the offense as reasons

---

[310] *State v. Stumpf* ,32 Ohio St. 3d 95, 512 N.E. 2d 598 (1987).

supporting its finding that the aggravating circumstances of the offense outweigh the mitigating factors." [310]

The Supreme Court of Ohio has read 2929.03 (F) in para materia with 2929.04 (B), concluding that it would be illogical to allow a three judge panel to consider the nature and circumstances of the offense in determining whether the aggravating circumstances outweigh the mitigating factors, "yet to forbid that panel from relying upon and citing such nature and circumstances as reasons for its decision." [311]

9. History, Character, and Background.

Similarly, in *State v. Spirko*, the trial court's consideration of the defendant's history, character, and background was found not to be a non-statutory aggravating circumstance. [312]

10. Future Trends in Light of Cleamons v. Mississippi.

Since the U.S. Supreme Court decision in *Clemons v. Mississippi,* it is unlikely whether a trial court's consideration of nonstatutory aggravating circumstances will be grounds for reversing a death sentence. [313] The court in *Clemons* upheld a

---

[311] *State v. Stumpf, supra.*

[312] *State v. Spirko*, 59 Ohio St. 3d 1, 570 N.E. 2d 229 (1991).

[313] *Clemons v. Mississippi* ,494 U.S. 738, 108 L Ed. 2d 725, 110 S.Ct. 1441 (1990).

death sentence based in part on an invalid aggravating circumstance (an "especially heinous, atrocious or cruel killing)" the use of such words had been declared unconstitutional in *Maynard v. Cartwright*. [314]

The court concluded that where the reviewing court can reweigh the legitimate aggravating circumstance or where the consideration of the invalid aggravating circumstance is harmless error, a reversal is not warranted.

A more blatant departure from the *Johnson-Davis* holdings is *State v. Lott.* The trial court in *Lott,* for all practical purposes listed and considered non-statutory aggravating circumstances. The trial court in its opinion held: "[setting the victim] on fire and the leaving him unattended with the probability of death was a factor in aggravation." In upholding the conviction and death sentence, the court independently weighed the aggravating circumstances against the mitigating factors and concluded that the aggravating circumstances outweighed the mitigating factors, citing *Clemons, supra.* [315]

Although *Johnson* and *Davis* are still law, the court has consistently used its independent review powers to reweigh the aggravating circumstance against the mitigating factors and has affirmed the convictions.[316]

---

[314] *Maynard v. Cartwright*, 486 U.S. 356 (1988).

[315] *State v. Lott.* 51 Ohio St. 3d 160, 555 N.E. 2d 293 (1990).

[316] *State v. Johnson*, 112 Ohio St. 3d 210, 858 N.E. 2d 1144 (2006).

11. Duplicative Aggravating Circumstances.

Where duplicative aggravating circumstances are present, the balancing function of the fact finder is flawed because the mitigating factors are improperly measured against one or more improper aggravating circumstances. The result is not unlike that where non-statutory aggravating circumstances have been considered, except that the aggravating circumstances are legitimate and statutory, although duplicative.

12. Merger of Duplicative Aggravating Circumstances.

The court has dealt with the problem of duplicative aggravating circumstances, in most instances, by merging or excluding the duplicative aggravating circumstances and affirming the conviction, if it finds that the remaining aggravating circumstances outweigh the mitigating factors. This act of merging is based on the court's duty as stated in R.C. 2929.05(A) to independently weigh the aggravating circumstances against the mitigating factors. Thus, in *State v. Jenkins* [317] the court stated the following rule:" * * * [I]n the penalty phase of a capital prosecution, where two or more aggravating circumstances arise from the same act or indivisible course of conduct and are thus duplicative, the duplicative aggravating circumstances will be merged for purposes of sentencing. Should this merging of aggravating circumstances take place upon appellate review of a death sentence, re-sentencing is not automatically required where the reviewing court independently determines that the remaining aggravating circumstances outweigh the mitigating factors beyond a

[317] *State v. Jenkins* 15 Ohio St 3d 164, 473 N.E. 2d 294 (1984).

reasonable doubt and that the jury's determination of duplicative aggravating circumstances in the penalty phase did not affect the verdict."

In *State v. Landrum*,[318] the court considered the duplicative aggravating circumstances of aggravated burglary, and murder to escape detection. The court then merged the duplicative aggravating circumstances into one count of aggravated burglary, and independently reweighed the remaining aggravating circumstance and sustained the conviction citing *Clemons v. Mississippi, supra.*[319]

13. Where the Consideration of Duplicative Aggravating Circumstances does not Affect the Verdict.

In *State v. Spizak*, the court sustained the death sentence where the indictment contained duplicative aggravating circumstances. The court held: "although the court of appeals did not apply the merger doctrine below, we have determined that the jury's consideration of the duplicative aggravating circumstances did not affect their verdict." [320] See also *State v. Wiles*. [321]

---

[318] *State v. Landrum,* 53 Ohio St. 3d 107, 559 N.E. 2d 710 (1990).

[319] See also, *State v. Davis*, 76 Ohio St. 3d 107, 666 N.E. 2d 1099 (1996).

[320] *State v. Spizak,* 36 Ohio St. 3d 80, 521 N.E. 2d 800 (1988).

14. Where Consideration of Duplicative Aggravating Circumstance Affected the Verdict.

The court has, however, reversed a death sentence where it was clear that the duplicative aggravating circumstance affected the verdict.

In *State v. Penix,* the indictment contained the aggravating circumstance of prior calculation and design in addition to the aggravating circumstance of felony/murder. The court in reversing the death sentence held that R.C. 2929.04 (A)(7) clearly states that these two particular specifications are to be charged only in the alternative. Prior calculation and design can only be an aggravating circumstance where the defendant is not the principal offender. To charge a defendant with prior calculation and design in addition to felony murder is duplicative.

The problem in *Penix,* was compounded because the trial court charged the jury that the quantity of the aggravating circumstances should be a consideration in weighing the aggravating circumstances against the mitigating factors. The combination of the duplicative aggravating circumstances with the instruction that quantity is an important factor made the death sentence unreliable. [322]

---

[321] State v. Wiles, 59 Ohio St. 3d 71, 571 N.E. 2d 97 (1991).

[322] *State v. Penix,* 32 Ohio St. 3d 369, 513 N.E. 2d 744 (1987).

15. Three Judge Panel Presumption of Correctness.

The option of choosing a three-judge panel is particular to death penalty prosecutions. The Ohio Supreme Court presumes that a three-judge panel correctly interprets the evidence and is not affected by errors that would normally affect a jury in its decision-making function, including the weighing and consideration of aggravating circumstances against the mitigating factors.

In *State v. Brewer*, the court held there is a "usual presumption that in a bench trial in a criminal case the court considered material and competent evidence in arriving at its decision.[323] This presumption was articulated in *State v. Post:* "Based on the foregoing, we find error in the admission of the victim's impact evidence. However, we are not persuaded that such error warrants reversal. The risks of arbitrary and prejudicial sentencing * * *[are] not present * * *[with a] three judge panel rather than a jury." [324]

In *State v. Moreland*, the court presumed the three-judge panel knew the difference between aggravating circumstances and the nature and circumstance of the crime. [325]

It is therefore not fatal to a conviction where there is evidence of duplicative aggravating circumstances in the case of a three-judge panel. The court presumes the panel of three judges correctly weighs the aggravating circumstances. Thus, in *State v.*

[323] *State v. Brewer* 48 Ohio St. 3d 50, 549 N.E. 2d 491 (1990).

[324] *State v. Post* 32 Ohio St. 3d 380, 513 N.E. 2d 754 (1987).

[325] *State v. Moreland* 50 Ohio St. 3d 58, 552 N.E. 2d 894 (1990).

Wickline, the court found that both escaping detection and the purposeful killing of two or more persons, arose from the same act and accordingly, there should have been only one specification, "we assume that the panel did not artificially inflate the aggravating circumstances * * * as such, we find the sentencing decision reliable." [326]

16. Death Qualification of Jury.

Under the principal that the state, as well as the defendant, is entitled to a fair trial, it is permissible to exclude jurors who unequivocally oppose the death penalty, *State v. Esparza* [327]

17. Challenge of Jurors for Cause.

The Supreme Court of Ohio has followed United States Supreme Court decisions concerning the death qualification of jurors. *Witherspoon v. Illinois*, held that veniremen could be excluded for cause if they made [it] unmistakably clear: "(1) that they would automatically vote against the imposition of capital punishment without regard to any evidence that might be developed at the trial of the case before them, or (2) that their

---

[326] *State v. Wickline* 50 Ohio St. 3d 114, 552 N.E. 2d 913 (1990).

[327] *State v. Esparza* 39 Ohio St. 3d 8, 529 N.E. 2d 192 (1988), citing *Lockhart v. McCree* , 476 U.S. 162 (1988).

attitude toward the death penalty would prevent them from making an impartial decision as to the defendant's guilt." [328]

In *State v. Roqers*,[329] while holding that voir dire may constitute reversible error only upon a showing of abuse of discretion by the trial court, the court quoted with approval *Wainwriqht v. Witt* [330] which further refined the *Witherspoon* criteria for excluding jurors for cause.

"The standard is whether the jurors' views would prevent or substantially impair the performance of his duties as a juror in accordance with his instruction and his oath.[331]

In *Rogers, supra*, two jurors where challenged for cause because they believed in the death penalty. In upholding the trial court's refusal to excuse them for cause, after they stated they would nevertheless follow the law, the court held: "* *[the juror's] response to the court's questions indicate that he was not irrevocably committed to a verdict before trial and that his performance of his duties as a juror would not be substantially impaired by his views on the death penalty. He was not therefore, subject to a challenge for cause."

---

[328] *Witherspoon v. Illinois* 391 U.S. 510 (1968).

[329] *State v. Roqers* 17 Ohio St. 3d 174, 478 N.E. 2d 984 (1985). Reversed on other grounds, 32 Ohio St. 3d 70, 512 N.E. 2d 581 (1987).

[330] *Wainwriqht v. Witt* ,469 U.S. 412 (1985).

[331] *Wainwright, supra.*

18. General Questions to the Jury.

A jury may be death qualified with general questions concerning their opinions on capital punishment.

Independent questioning is not required by Ohio's death penalty statutes and the United States Supreme Court has not ruled that it is required by the U.S. Constitution.

The determination of whether a voir dire in a capital case should be conducted in a sequestration is a matter of discretion within the province of a trial judge. Abuse of discretion must be shown. *State v. Mapes* [332]

The court has approved these examples of general questions that may be asked of prospective jurors:

" * * * As you sit here now are there any circumstances that you can foresee that will preclude you from following the court's instructions and fairly considering [sic] the imposition of the death penalty in this case?" *Rogers, supra.*

" * * * Are you stating to me unequivocally that under those circumstances will you follow my instructions as judge and that you cannot and will not consider fairly the imposition of the sentence of death if appropriate, in this case. *Jenkins, supra.*

Concerning peremptory challenges, counsel may challenge jurors who are generally opposed to, or expressed reservations concerning the death penalty. *Esparza, supra.*

Jurors whose opposition to the death penalty is so strong that it would prevent or impair the performance of their duties are not distinctive identifiable groups the challenge of which would be subject to equal protection scrutiny. *Lockhart v. McCree, supra.*

---

[332] *State v. Mapes,* 19 Ohio St. 3d 108, 484 N.E. 2d 140 (1985).

19. Consideration of Mitigating Factors.

R.C. 2929 (C) gives the defendant "great latitude in the presentation of relevant mitigating evidence. Even though the statute permits the defendant to present, "any other factors" that are not delineated in the statute, the jury or three-judge panel does not have to accept any evidence as being mitigating simply because it has been offered. *State v. Moreland* [333] *State v. Steffen* [334] and *Eddinqs v. Oklahoma.* [335]

The fact finder must consider mitigating evidence but it does not have to be *accepted.* It is also not required that the fact finder find the existence of the mitigating factors unanimously before it can be considered.[336]

Even if the fact finder finds that any given mitigating factor has been established, this finding merely allows that factor to be put into the weighing process. The fact finder is nevertheless free to find that the aggravating circumstances outweigh the established mitigating factors beyond a reasonable doubt and thereby sentence the defendant to death.[337]

---

[333] *State v. Moreland,* 50 Ohio St. 3d 58, 552 N.E. 2d 894 (1990).

[334] *State v. Steffen,* 31 Ohio St. 3d 111, 509 N.E. 2d 383 (1987).

[335] *Eddinqs v. Oklahoma,* 455 U.S. 104 (1982).

[336] *McCoy v. North Carolina*, 494 U.S. 433, 108 L. Ed 2d 369 (1990).

[337] *State v. Depew*, 38 Ohio St. 3d 275, 528 N.E. 2d 542 (1988).

20. Counsel's Failure to Present Mitigation Evidence.

There is no ineffective assistance of counsel where defense counsel chooses not to present any mitigating evidence during the penalty phase. As long as there is sufficient evidence showing that counsel was otherwise prepared for the penalty phase. This can best be illustrated by the *Johnson* cases: *Johnson I and Johnson II.*

In *State v. Johnson*, (*Johnson II*): "[defense counsel] was thoroughly familiar with the case, so the decision not to present any other evidence in mitigation may well have been because there was none except for that offered during the guilt phase of trial, or the omission of such evidence may well have been the result of a tactical informed decision by counsel." [338]

In *Johnson I,* the court premised its reversal of the death sentence, in part, on ineffective assistance of counsel where it was clear that defense counsel was not prepared to go forward into the penalty phase. Although there was other evidence of ineffective assistance of counsel in the guilt phase, the gravamen of the reversal was counsel's failure to investigate the background of the defendant for any evidence that could have been used in mitigation. Counsel's only response to the finding of guilt of his client was to request a ten-minute recess in which to explain the mitigation process to the defendant; after which he presented no mitigation evidence. [339, 340]

[338] *State v. Johnson*, (*Johnson II*) 46 Ohio St 3d 96, 545 N.E. 2d 636 (1989).

In summary, although there is no statutory requirement for defense counsel to present mitigation evidence, since the failure to present such evidence could be the result of a reasoned tactical decision. A failure to present mitigation evidence is permissible as long as it appears counsel was otherwise prepared and was truly acting as counsel.[341]

21. Judicial Confusion of the Insanity Standard with the Mitigation Standard of Lack of Substantial Capacity.

The Supreme Court of Ohio has vacated death sentences where it found the aggravating circumstances were insufficient to outweigh the mitigating factors. These cases concerned the defendant's lack of substantial capacity or diminished capacity as defined in R.C. 2929.04(B)(3): "Whether at the time of committing the offense, the offender, because of a mental disease or defect, lacked substantial capacity to appreciate the criminality of his conduct or to conform his conduct to the requirements of the law."

---

[339]See also, *State v. Apanovitch*, 33 Ohio St.3d 19, 514 N.E.2d 394 (1987).

[340] *State v. Johnson*, 24 Ohio St. 3d 87, 494 N.E. 2d 1061 (1986).

[341] *Strickland v. Washington*, 466 U.S. 668 (1984).

In *State v. Claytor*[342] and *State v. Lawrence*,[343] the death sentences were reversed because of a misinterpretation by the trial court and the court of appeals of R.C 2904. (B)(3).

Those courts confused the definition of the mitigating factor with the definition of insanity. The Ohio Supreme Court defined insanity in *State v. Staten*,[344] "In order to establish the defense of insanity, the accused must establish by a preponderance of the evidence that disease or other defect of the mind had so impaired his reason that, at the time of the crime act with which he is charged, either he did not know right from wrong or he did not have the ability to refrain from doing that act."

In *Claytor, supra*, the trial court and the court of appeals applied the stricter insanity standard instead of the proper mitigating factor, which requires a lower threshold of proof.

"The result raises a serious question as to whether the language reflects a flawed analysis that affected the weighing process. Both courts found the mitigating factor to be present, but both appear to have believed that the factor required total inability to refrain and may have been reluctant to accord it the appropriate weight for that reason." *Claytor, supra*.

In *Lawrence, supra*, the prosecutor in his closing argument misstated the law, arguing to the jury that there was no difference between the insanity defense and the mitigating factor defined in 2929.04(B)(3). Defense counsel's objection was sustained but the jury was not instructed to disregard the statement. The court held: "we believe the trial court effectively denied appellant the

---

[342] *State v. Claytor,* 61 Ohio St. 3d 234, 574 N.E. 2d 472 (1991).

[343] *State v. Lawrence,* 44 Ohio St. 3d 24, 541 N.E. 2d 451 (1989).

[344] *State v. Staten*, 18 Ohio State 2d 21, 247 N. E. 2d 293 (1969).

opportunity to have his mental condition considered by the jury in mitigation, for a juror could reasonably have concluded that appellant's mental disorder was to be considered at the sentencing phase exactly as it had been considered at the guilt phase."

Further in *Lawrence* the court held * * * a defendant need not establish the requisites to an insanity defense to have his mental condition considered in mitigation."

The court explained the problem that occurs where an improper test is applied in the mitigation phase. It would be a futile exercise necessary for the defendant to attempt to prove the same factors that have been previously rejected by the trier of fact.

However, see, *State v. Dickerson*, [345] and the application of harmless error analysis. [Next section] The court in *Dickerson* stated, "A clear reading of the foregoing standards indicated recognition of a higher standard for the defense of insanity than the standard established for the mitigating factor of diminished capacity. Insanity requires absolute inability, whereas the mitigating factor of diminished capacity only requires the lack of substantial capacity.[346]

22. Harmless Error.

The holdings of *Claytor* and *Lawrence* are not iron clad, even if the improper test is applied, it is possible that the conviction will be sustained under a finding of harmless error. In *Dickerson,*

---

[345] *State v. Dickerson,* 45 Ohio St. 3d 206, 543 N.E. 2d 1250 (1989).

[346] See generally, *State v. Wilcox*, 70 Ohio St. 2d 182, 436 N.E. 2d 523 (1982).

supra, there was an implication that the trial court used the insanity standard in the mitigation phase because it admitted insanity evidence in that phase. In upholding the death sentence, the court held: "The evidence also contained information relevant to diminished capacity and the finding of that diminished capacity had not been established."

The court found harmless error because:

1. Had the proper test been used, the aggravating circumstances nevertheless outweighed the mitigating factors.
2. The independent review by the court of appeals where it was found that diminished capacity had been established, but that the aggravating circumstances outweighed the mitigating factors.

Even though it may be difficult for jurors to perceive the difference between the two standards, the court is not required to explain that difference, as long as the jury is given a "full and correct statement" of the law. *Rogers, supra.*

23. Prohibiting Defense Counsel from Presenting Mitigating Evidence.

A defendant is permitted to prevent defense counsel from presenting any mitigation evidence.

In *State v. Tyler,* the court held that the trial court was obligated to honor appellant's choice to prevent the introduction of mitigating evidence.[347] See also *Spirko, supra.*

The court in *Tyler* held: "So long as the 'definitional predicates' for the death penalty are proven, we believe that the trial court was obliged to honor appellant's choice." See also,

[347] *State v. Tyler,* 50 Ohio St. 3d 24, 553 N.E. 2d 576 (1990).

Faretta v. California [348] *Illinois v. Allen* [349], and *Adams v. United States, ex rel. McCann.* [350]

24. Prosecutorial Comment on Unsworn Statement.

One of the unique features of a death penalty prosecution is that the defendant is permitted, in the penalty phase, to make an unsworn statement to the jury.

Since an unsworn statement is not subject to cross examination (R.C. 2929.03 (D)(1)), there is potential for abuse by the defendant. It is possible that his unsworn testimony could leave an unfair impression. As a result, the court has held that where a defendant chooses to make an unsworn statement. The state, "may comment that the defendant's statement has not been made under oath or affirmation." This is the extent of the allowable comment. The court further held: "* * * but such statement must be limited to reminding the jury that the defendant's statement was not made under oath in contrast to the testimony of all other witnesses. *Depew, supra*. See also *State v. Durr* [351]

However, if the defendant or another mitigation witness gives false or misleading testimony, the state may

[348] *Faretta v. California,* 422 U.S. 806, 834 (1975).

[349] *Illinois v. Allen,* 397 U.S. 337, 350-351, (1970).

[350] *Adams v. United States, ex rel. McCann,* 317 U.S. 269, 280 (1942).

[351] *State v. Durr,* 58 Ohio St. 3d 86, 568 N.E. 2d 674 (1991).

rebut such evidence in a manner that would normally take place during a trial. *Depew, supra.*

Such rebuttal may be made even if it requires the prosecutor to introduce evidence of the defendant's prior criminal record even though as part of the defense strategy the defendant has chosen not to make a sworn statement for the purpose of keeping out of evidence his prior criminal convictions.

The court held that: "[T]his right is limited, however, to those instances where the defense offers a specific assertion, by a mitigation witness or by the defendant, that misrepresents the defendant's prior criminal history." *Depew, supra.*

In *State v. Jackson,* the prosecutor went a little further, not only did he state that the defendant made an unsworn statement but also stated that by doing so he avoided cross-examination. The comment was improper, but it did not "extend beyond the guidelines for comment on unsworn statements in *State v. DePew* * * *." [352]

25. Victim Impact Statements.

The court held in *State v. Huertas,*[353] that the admission of victim impact statements is prohibited as a result of the decisions in *Booth v. Maryland* [354] and *South Carolina v. Gathers* [355].

---

[352] *State v. Jackson*, 57 Ohio St. 3d 29, 565 N.E. 2d 549 (1991).

[353] *State v. Huertas,*51 Ohio St. 3d 22, 553 N.E. 2d 1058 (1990).

[354] *Booth v. Maryland,* 482 U.S. 496, (1987).

[355] *South Carolina v. Gathers,* 490 U.S. 95, (1989).

The court reversed the death sentence in *Huertas* where the mother of the victim was permitted to testify as to how proud she was of her son and the effect of the murder on the victim's son. "Hate to take him to the graveyard. He always wants to go. He think [s] he [is] going to see his dad." In addition, the father of the victim testified that the defendant should receive the death penalty.

In this regard, the court held: "* * * expressions of opinion by the witness as to the appropriateness of a particular sentence in a capital case violate the defendant's right to have the sentencing decisions made by the jury and judge."

In *Payne v. Tennessee,* [356] the United State Supreme Court overruled portions of *Booth* holding that evidence relating to the victim and the impact of the victim's death on the family is admissible. The issue as to the admissibility of family members' opinions about the crime and the appropriate sentence was not considered by the court.

The *Payne* court focused on the harm caused to the victim as relevant in determining the sentence and the elements of the offense; and compared this with the rule that allows the defendant to proffer relevant mitigating evidence.

The evidence admitted in *Payne* was testimony by relatives as to the effect of the murders of the surviving son. The prosecution also argued to the jury the effect of the murder on the family.

The court held: "It [a victim impact statement] is designed to show instead each victim's 'uniqueness as an individual human

---

[356] *Payne v. Tennesse,* 59 LW 4814.

being' whatever the jury might think the loss to the community resulting from his death might be."

The Ohio Supreme Court cited with approval the *Payne* decision in *State v. Adams.*[357]

26. Presentence Report.

R.C. 2929.03(D)(1) allows a capital defendant to request a presentence investigation and/or a mental examination which may include, in addition to personal history, accurate information on pending charges, *State v. Greer,* [358] and arrests, since they are a part of a defendant's social history, *State v. Hutton.* [359]

Any report made under this section "shall be furnished to the court, to the trial jury, if the offender was tried by a jury, to the prosecutor and to the defendant or his counsel for use under this division."

Due to the broad dissemination and thoroughness of this report, defense counsel often will not request it if the information could be harmful to a favorable sentence. As a result, it is not uncommon for a defendant to waive the preparation of a presentence report and, accordingly, the waiver of a presentence investigation will not be the basis for a finding of ineffective assistance of counsel per *Strickland v. Washington, supra*, as long as the decision is based on sound trial strategy. *State v. Esparaz, supra.*

---

[357] *State v. Adams,* 63 Ohio St. 3d 231, 586 N.E. 2d 1042 (1992).

[358] *State v. Greer,* 39 Ohio St. 3d 236, 530 N.E. 2d 382 (1988).

[359]*State v. Hutton,* 53 Ohio St. 3d 36, 559 N.E. 2d 432 (1990), paragraph one of the syllabus, See also *State v. Cooey, supra.*

27. Residual Doubt No Longer a Valid Mitigation Factor.

At one time, the court held that where there is "residual doubt" of the guilt of a defendant; it might reverse the sentence of death, while upholding the aggravated murder conviction.

In *State v. Watson,* the court reversed the sentence of death where it found such residual doubt.

A combination of factors contributed to this decision.

There was strong circumstantial evidence that another person may have committed the murder; four disinterested witnesses testified that the defendant was not the man whom they saw leaving the scene of the murder; the state's primary witness was the sister of a person who could have committed the murder; the trial court instructed the jury that their sentence was only a recommendation (although this instruction was proper, it may have caused the jury to believe that any residual doubt will be resolved by the court); the defendant did not present any mitigation evidence.[360]

The source of the concept of residual doubt can be found in *Lockhart v. McCree,*[361] where that court held that "residual doubts" of a defendant's guilt are properly considered in mitigation. See also, *State v. Buell,*[362] where the court held that a proclamation of

[360] *State v. Watson,* 61 Ohio St. 3d 1, 572 N.E. 2d 97 (1991).

[361] *Lockhart v. McCree*, 476 U.S. 162.

innocence is a factor that can be considered by the trier of fact.

R.C. 2929.04(B)(7) is a catchall provision permitting the introduction of any other relevant factor in mitigation.

The concept of reversing a sentence of death because of residual doubt is new, and although the reversal is directed toward the penalty phase of the bifurcated trial, it really is directed toward the guilt phase of the trial.

Thus, in *State v. Bonnell*, [363] the court found no error where the trial court refused to give an instruction on residual doubt where there was overwhelming evidence of guilt. See also *State v. Jackson, supra*.

Watson is the first and only case where the court has reversed a conviction because of residual doubt.

The use of residual doubt is no longer valid. As a result of the United States Supreme Court's ruling in *Franklin v. Lynaugh.*[364] The court in State v. Gardner[365] ruled a defendant is not entitled to an instruction on residual doubt, and in State v. McGuire[366] held that residual doubt is not a mitigating factor.

---

[362] *State v. Buell,* 22 Ohio St. 3d 124, 429 N.E. 795 (1986).

[363] *State v. Bonnell,* 61 Ohio St.3d 179, 573 N.E.2d 1082 (1991)

[364] *Franklin v. Lynaugh,* 487 U.S. 164 (1988).

[365] *State v. Gardner*, 74 Ohio St. 3d 49, 656 N.E. 2d 623 (1995).

[366] *State v. McGuire*, 80 Ohio St. 3d 390, 686 N.E. 2d 1112 (1997).

28. Sentencing Issues:

Appointment of Expert Witnesses.

A trial court is not required to appoint a psychiatrist of the indigent defendant's own choosing pursuant to R.C. 2929.024. This statute provides that if the court determines that the services of an expert are "reasonably necessary" the court may appoint an expert; however, the defendant is not entitled to a rebuttal presentence investigation or expert witness psychiatrist.[367]

Similarly, pursuant to R.C. 2929.024, the trial court did not err in refusing to appoint an eyewitness identification expert. The court in approving the decision of the court in *Ake v. Oklahoma,* and *Caldwell v. Mississippi* [368] cited with approval the following quote from *Little v. Armontrout:*

"*Ake* and *Caldwell* taken together hold that a defendant must show more than a mere possibility of assistance from an expert. Rather a defendant must show a reasonable probability that an expert would aid in his defense, and the denial of expert assistance would result in an unfair trial." [369]

This decision follows from *State v. Buell* [370] and adheres to the same principles that it is ordinary not permissible to

---

[367] *State v. Esparza*, 39 Ohio St. 3d 8, 529 N.E. 2d 192 (1988).

[368] *Caldwell v. Mississippi* 472 U.S. 320 (1985).

[369] *Little v. Armontrout,* 835 F. 2d 1240,(C.A. 8, 1987)

[370] *State v. Buell* 22 Ohio St. 3d 124, 489 N.E. 2d 795 (1986)

permit an expert to testify as to a *particular* witness' ability to identify a person, but it is permitted as to the *typical* witness. Here, the defendant failed to show any particularized showing of the necessity of an expert. *State v. Broom.* [371]

29. Imposition of Sentence.

Under R.C. 2929.03(D)(1) where the defendant requests a presentence report, the court is required to order the preparation of the report. The report is required to be submitted to the jury, the prosecutor and the defendant or his attorney.

Because of this distribution, it is error where the report contains statements of witnesses that are irrelevant to mitigation or the aggravating circumstances of the case. "The combined effect of these statements tended to undermine the impartiality of the presentence report and constituted error. It would have been better procedure to have stricken the statements from the report." [372]

Although 2929.03(D)(1) provides that the presentence report is to be submitted for the jury's evaluation, the trial court in its discretion, may properly delete erroneous matters that would have the potential to mislead the jury. Such as an erroneous conclusion as to how the victim died.[373]

---

[371] *State v. Broom,*. 40 Ohio St. 3d 277, 533 N.E. 2d 682 (1988).

[372] *State v. Glenn*, 28 Ohio St. 3d 451, 504 N.E. 2d 701 (1986).

[373] *State v. Greer*, 39 Ohio St. 3d 236, 530 N.E. 2d 382 (1988).

30. Resentencing Upon Remand.

In the case of a jury trial where a sentence of death is vacated and remanded on appeal because of error at the penalty phase, the trial court, in resentencing, cannot sentence the defendant to death.[374] The *Penix* court found prejudicial error because of improper jury instructions. The court held that because R.C.2929.03(C)(2)(b) provides that the trial jury and trial judge shall sentence a defendant, "* * * that the recommendation must be made by the same jury that convicted the offender at the guilt phase of this bifurcated trial." The court reasoned that, although the United States Supreme Court suggested in *Skipper v. South Carolina*,[375] resentencing of a death penalty may be permitted if authorized by statute, since Ohio's death penalty statute does not provide for a second jury to be impaneled for a resentencing, resentencing of a death sentence is not authorized. See also, *State v. Zuranski* [376]

31. Trial Court's Failure to Articulate Its Reasoning in Its Weighing Duties.

In *Maurer, supra.*, the court held that where the trial court does not fully comply with R.C. 2929.03(F), by properly weighing the aggravating circumstances against the mitigating

---

[374] *State v. Penix,* 32 Ohio St. 3d 369, 513 N.E. 2d 744 (1987).

[375] *Skipper v. South Carolina,* 476 U.S. 1, 90 L. Ed. 2d 1 (1986).

[376] *State v. Zurans,* 32 Ohio St. 3d 379, 513 N.E. 2d 753 (1987).

circumstances and articulating the reasoning, there is not necessarily error.

"The panel of three judges * * * shall state* * * the reasons why the aggravating circumstances the offender was found guilty of committing were sufficient to outweigh the mitigating factors. * * *" 2929.03(F)

Where it is shown that the defendant was not prejudiced by the omission of the court's reasoning in the weighing process, reversal in not necessarily required. Where the trial court fails to "specify either what evidence it found to be mitigating or its rationale for stating that such evidence did not outweigh the aggravating circumstances it is not error unless it can be shown that the defendant was prejudiced.[377]

---

[377] *State v. Johnston*, 39 Ohio St. 3d 48, 529 N.E. 2d 898 (1988).

CHAPTER 32

Aggravated Assault and Felonious Assault

In defining the elements of aggravated assault R.C. 2903.12 (1) states that no person shall cause serious physical harm to another or another's newborn. R.C. 2903(2) states that no person shall cause or attempt to cause physical harm to another or another's newborn by means of a deadly weapon. The above prohibitions are identical to the elements of felonious assault, under R.C. 2903.11 except that facts that would normally establish felonious assault are reduced to aggravated assault if the actor is "under the influence of sudden passion or in a sudden fit of rage, either of which is brought on by serious provocation occasioned by the victim that is reasonably sufficient to incite the person in to using deadly force." R.C. 2903.12(A).

Felonious assault also includes offenses of a sexual nature including sexual contact with another if the offender is HIV positive and sexual conduct with a minor.

1. Provocation

The court in *State v. Deem* [378] adopted the language defining serious provocation announced by the court of appeals in *State v. Mabry.* [379]

"Provocation, to be serious, must be reasonably sufficient to bring on extreme stress and the provocation must be reasonably sufficient to incite or to arouse the defendant into using deadly force. In determining whether the provocation was reasonably sufficient to incite or arouse the defendant into using force, the court must consider the emotional and mental state of the defendant and the conditions and circumstances that surrounded him at the time."

Aggravated assault is an offense of inferior degree to felonious assault. It is not technically a lesser-included offense. However, it is properly charged to the jury in the same manner as a lesser-included offense. If, "in a trial for felonious assault, where the defendant presents sufficient evidence of serious provocation (such that a jury could both reasonably acquit the defendant of felonious assault and convict the defendant of aggravated assault), an instruction on aggravated assault must be given." *Deem, supra.*

In an aggravated assault prosecution where the defendant was convicted of two separate parts of R.C. 2903.12(A)(1) and (2), and where there was only one animus behind the stabbing of the victim, the defendant can only be convicted of one count of aggravated assault. It should be noted that the defendant can be tried on both counts, but can only be convicted of one count. After conviction, for sentencing purposes, the state must choose which charge will merge into the other.[380]

---

[378] *State v. Deem* 40 Ohio St. 3d 205, 533 N.E. 2d 294 (1988).

[379] *State v. Mabry,* 5 Ohio App. 3d 13, 449 N.E. 2d 16 (1982).

[380] *State v. Brown*, 119 Ohio St. 3d 447, 895 N.E. 2d 149 (2008).

Felonious assault can be a lesser included offense of attempted murder. This court previously held that felonious assault is not a lesser included offense of murder. *State v. Barnes*, 94 Ohio St.3d 21, 759 N.E.2d 1240, this ruling however was based on the strict statutory-elements test set forth in *Deem.*

That ruling has not been disturbed, however in regard to R.C. 2903.11(A)(1), causing serious physical harm, felonious assault is a lessor included offense.

When the charge is an attempt to commit a crime, the normal analysis that has been used to determine lesser included offenses cannot help. Because an attempt charge means that the primary charge has not been completed. As result, the test to be used is whether the charge gives notice of the proposed lesser included offenses. "Since the desire to physically harm is a subset of, and necessarily included in, the desire to kill, and since one cannot intend to kill without also intending to cause physical harm, we conclude that felonious assault through causing serious physical harm is a lesser included offense of attempted murder."[381]

---

[381] State v. Deanda, 136 Ohio St.3d 18, 2013-Ohio-1722

CHAPTER 33

Burglary and Aggravated Burglary.

The three breaking and entering offenses, aggravated burglary, burglary, and breaking and entering, are distinguishable according to the potential of harm to persons present and the type of habitation involved.

1. Aggravated Burglary in General.

The aggravated burglary statute, R.C. 2911.11 provides that no person by force, stealth, or deception shall trespass in an occupied structure or in a separately secured or separately occupied portion of an occupied structure, when another person other than an accomplice of the offender is present with purpose to commit in the structure or in the separately secured or separately occupied portion of the structure any criminal offense, if any of the following apply:

The offender inflicts, or attempts to inflict physical harm on another; the offender has a deadly weapon or dangerous ordnance on or about the offender's person under the offender's control.

2. Burglary in General.

The burglary statute, R.C. 2911.12, the violation of which although is threatening to the inhabitants, presents a lesser threat than aggravated burglary; it does not require any threat or attempts to inflict physical harm, or the possession of a deadly weapon or dangerous ordnance

3. Allied Offenses.

Due to the nature of these breaking and entering offenses, that is, entering a dwelling house, with purpose to commit a crime, the likelihood of other crimes being committed in addition to the breaking and entering is high. This is especially true where the offender encounters the occupants of the dwellings. As a result, it is not unusual for an indictment to contain other counts in addition to the primary charge of burglary or breaking and entering.

Because of the potential of other counts in the indictment, courts are often required to decide whether the offenses charged in addition to the burglary charges are allied offenses of similar import, or whether they are committed with a separate animus so that multiple convictions are warranted.

A leading case is *State v. Frazier*, this case is important not only because it discusses allied offenses of similar import in the context of burglary where two crimes are committed almost simultaneously, it also discusses the element of a "purpose to commit a felony."[382]

It does not matter under this section whether the offender actually commits a crime as long as it can be proven that the purpose for breaking and entering was to commit a crime. In *Frazier,* the court held that the offender could be found guilty of both aggravated burglary and aggravated robbery predicated on his forcing the door of the house open and subsequently beating the occupants. The aggravated burglary and aggravated robbery were committed separately because, once the door was forced open, the crime of aggravated burglary was complete, and the remaining acts of the defendant were properly considered as aggravated robbery.

"Whether an intended felony is actually committed is irrelevant to the burglary charge * * * But where the intended felony is actually committed, a new crime arises for which the defendant may be convicted."

The court of appeals erroneously determined that the acts constituting aggravated burglary and aggravated robbery could not be separated. However, this court found the harm to the victim constituted the aggravated robbery, which was separate from the aggravated burglary.

Aggravated burglary and theft are separate offenses even though they share common elements. "The completion of the theft offense is not necessary [to prove aggravated burglary] and that the purpose to commit any felony will suffice to supply the requisite intent."

---

[382] *State v. Frazier,* 58 Ohio St. 2d 253, 389 N.E. 2d 1118 (1979).

The court in *State v. Mitchell*, held that after applying the two-step test for allied offenses, the next step is to look at the defendant's conduct to see if the offenses were committed with a separate animus as to each. The court focused its analysis on the fact that it is not necessary to complete the theft offense in order to be found guilty of aggravated burglary. Further, R.C. 2913.02 (theft) concerns nonconsensual taking, while R.C. 2911.11 is focused toward potential harm to persons and, accordingly the general assembly intended to distinguish aggravated burglary and theft, and make them separately punishable. [383]

4. Present or Likely to be Present.

The question of whether a person is *likely to be present* depends more on the owner's intention and purpose for maintaining the home than on whether that person would be home at any particular time.

In the case of a permanent dwelling house where the family was in and out of the house throughout the day, the fact that they were in and out of the house is sufficient evidence to show that they were likely to be present in the home any time of the day, " * * * and that such house was burglarized when the family was temporarily absent, the state has presented sufficient evidence to support a charge of aggravated burglary under R.C. 2911.11." [384]

A person who is not home can be "likely to be present." The court in *State v. Kilby* stated "From the facts [that is being in and out of the house during the day] a permissive inference could have been drawn by the jury regarding the likelihood of [the victims] being present in the residence at the time of the burglary."[385]

It should be noted, under the current R.C. 2911.11 a conviction of aggravated burglary requires a person to be present in the occupied structure. Under the new burglary statute, the "likely to be present" language remains.

---

[383] *State v. Mitchell,* 6 Ohio St. 3d 416, 453 N.E. 2d 593 (1983).

[384] *State v. Fowler*, 4 Ohio St. 3d 16, 445 N.E. 2d 1119 (1983).

[385] *State v. Kilby,* 50 Ohio St. 2d 21, 361 N.E. 2d 1336 (1977).

5. Jury Charge on the Underlying Crime.

In an aggravated burglary prosecution where the charge to the jury fails to define the underlying crime, other than to state there must be a finding that *any criminal offense* has been committed, is proper

Although this court would prefer that the trial court instruct on the underlying crime it is not required in every case. This is true even if the indictment incorrectly states the underlying crime as long as the defendant has notice that the indictment incorrectly states the underlying crime.

The trial court is permitted to conform the jury instructions to the facts presented at trial which point to the correct underlying crime.[386]

It is up to the trial judge to decide whether the underlying crime is an alternative-means or multi-act crime.

Where the trial judge did not give a more thorough instruction on the need for unanimity in the verdict for the underlying crime other than stating that all jurors must agree on the verdict, there is no error because there is no due process right to a unanimous verdict in state court only by court rule pursuant to Crim. R. 31(A).

There was no plain error because the verdict was not against the manifest weight of the evidence because the act of entering forcibly can be reasonably construed as entering with criminal intent.[387]

---

[386] State v. Lynn, 129 Ohio St. 3d 146, 2011-Ohio-2722.

[387] State v. Gardner, 118 Ohio St. 3d 420, 889 N.E. 2d 995 (2008).

CHAPTER 34

Breaking and Entering

R.C. 2911.13, the breaking and entering statute states that no person by force, stealth, or deception, shall trespass in an unoccupied structure, with purpose to commit therein any theft offense, or any felony. In addition, no person shall trespass on the land or premises of another, with purpose to commit a felony.

1. Trespass.

Trespass may not be proven where the person has privilege to enter the land of another, even if that person enters the land to commit a felony. In *State v. Barksdale,* the defendant did not commit breaking and entering trespass where he entered a used car lot in order to steal a car because the element of trespass cannot be proven where the car lot was open to the public. The defendant's entrance was privileged and he not did relinquish this privilege because of his purpose to commit a felony. "The statute was not meant to function so as to enhance every criminal violation occurring on property not owned by the defendant." [388]

However, where the offender enters a lot open to the public contingent upon a fee being paid, the grant of privilege is contingent upon payment. In *State v. Lyons*, where the defendant attempted to steal car on a "honor park" lot, the court held: "* * * we hold for purposes of R.C. 2911.13(B), an otherwise unauthorized entry onto property restricted to those who pay a fee constitutes trespass where the person entering the property manifests no intention to pay the fee." [389]

---

[388] *State v. Barksdale* , 2 Ohio St. 3d 126, 443 N. E. 2d 501 (1983).

[389] *State v. Lyons*, 18 Ohio St. 3d 204, 480 N.E. 2d 767 (1985).

CHAPTER 35

Domestic Violence.

1. Cohabitation.
2. Temporary Protection Order.
3. Prior Convictions.
4. Reluctant Victim Testimony

The elements that constitute the crime of domestic violence are identical to those of assault, with the exception of an added element contained in R.C. 2919.25(C): "No person by threat of force, shall knowingly cause a family or household member to *believe* that the offender will cause imminent physical harm to *family or household member*. The remainder of the statute states: "no person shall knowingly cause or attempt to cause physical harm to a family or household member" R.C. 2919.25(A); and "No person shall recklessly cause serious physical harm to a family or household member. R.C. 2919.25(B)

Under R.C. 2919.25(C), a violation is a misdemeanor of the fourth degree.(this is commonly referred to as domestic violence threats) A violation under (A) or (B) is a misdemeanor of the first degree, with certain exceptions. An offender who has a previous conviction for domestic violence, or for one of other specified felonies, can be convicted of a felony of the fourth degree. Two or more convictions of Domestic Violence can subject the offender to a felony of the third degree.

A family or household member includes a spouse; one living as a spouse; a former spouse; a parent or child; a person related by consanguinity or affinity to the defendant; a parent or child of a spouse, or a common-law spouse, or a former spouse. See the statute for other relationships that apply.

Also included are spouses or former spouses who no longer live with the offender if they have lived with the offender within five years prior to the offense.

Finally, household member also includes the natural parent of the offender's spouse. Consult the statute for all of the specifics.

The domestic violence statute is not vague and not unconstitutionally overbroad because it prohibits a person from causing or attempting to cause physical harm to a family or house hold member.

It does not prohibit a person from using corporal punishment to discipline a child. The prohibition being only that the parent may not cause physical harm as defined in R.C. 2901.01. Physical harm under the statute means "any injury." The court held "injury" means the invasion of a legally protected interest of another: "A child does not have a legally protected interest which is invaded by proper and reasonable parental discipline." Accordingly, under the statute an offender is properly apprised of all of the elements of the offense.[390]

R.C. 2919.25(A) permits reasonable parental discipline. The court found discipline to be unreasonable where a drunken parent dragged an eight-year-old child from bed, ordered him to stand at attention, punched him in the stomach, pushed him to the floor, ordered him to stand at attention, and then pounded his head against the wall until the other parent rescued the child. The parent was not "disciplining" the child in a proper and reasonable manner contemplated by RC 2919.22. [391]

1. Cohabitation.

One definition of family or household member includes those who cohabitate. The parties do not have to share the same address to "cohabitate."

In this regard, "Having considered the above definitions of "cohabitant" and "family or household member," we conclude that the essential elements of "cohabitation" are (1) sharing of familial or financial responsibilities and (2) consortium. Possible factors establishing shared familial or financial responsibilities might include provisions for shelter, food, clothing, utilities, and/or commingled assets. Factors that might establish consortium include mutual respect, fidelity, affection, society, cooperation, solace, comfort, aid of each other, friendship, and conjugal relations. These factors are unique to each case

390 *State v. Suchomski* , 58 Ohio St. 3d 74, 567 N.E. 2d 1304 (1991).

391 *Ibid.*

and how much weight, if any, to give to each of these factors must be decided on a case-by-case basis by the trier of fact."[392]

This holding is significant because the parties were not living together. The court stated the relationship is determinative and not necessarily the living arrangements.

The court has recently further commented on the evidence necessary to establish cohabitation. Where the defendant and the victim have lived together or are currently living together. However, this factor is not determinative. It is also possible to establish with factors such as consortium, and affection. The current sharing of living expenses is not a crucial factor[393]

2. Temporary Protection Order.

Where a temporary protection order is in place, the protected person cannot be prosecuted for complicity in violating the order where the protected person invites the defendant to have contact with the protected person. [394]

A divorce decree can modify a civil protection order so that a prosecution for violation of the order is improper. A divorce decree that is imprecise as to how visitation may be accomplished implies that some contact is required for the parties to arrange visitation. So, that a divorce decree that does not spell out precisely the conditions in which a person can have contact with his children does not subject that person to a criminal prosecution for violation of a previous civil protection order. The divorce decree provides a presumption that the CPO has been modified to accomplish visitation. [395]

In a domestic violence prosecution in which the degree of the crime depends on proving prior convictions the state has two options:

1. It may use a judgment entry pursuant to R.C. 2945.75(B)(1) if so, "the judgments must comply with

Crim.R. 32(C). In that event, the judgment entry must set forth

---

[392] *State v. Williams*, 79 Ohio St.3d 459, 683 N.E.2d 1126 (1997).

[393] State v. McGlothen, 138 Ohio St. 3d 146, 2014-Ohio-85.

[394] *State v. Lucas*, 100 Ohio St.3d 1, 795 N.E.2d 642 (2003).

[395] *State v. Price*, 118 Ohio St. 3d 144, 886 N.E. 2d 852 (2008).

(1) the fact of a conviction, (2) the sentence, (3) the judge's signature, and (4) the time stamp indicating the entry upon the journal by the clerk."

This is not the only way to establish a prior conviction, the defendant can stipulate to the prior conviction. However, if the state does choose to use a judgment entry it must comply with all of the above (4) requirements.[396]

A defendant must be served a civil protection order in order to be convicted of a criminal violation for failure to comply. It is not sufficient that the protected person merely "show" the order to the person who is the subject of the order." R.C. 2903.214(F)(1) requires that the delivery be the result of the court order. "The court shall cause the delivery of any protection order," before a violation of R.C. 2919.27(A)(2) can be charged."[397]

3. Prior Convictions (Stipulations).

Pursuant to R.C. 2919.25(D)(3), and (D)(4) a prior conviction of misdemeanor domestic violence causes the current charge to be either a forth degree felony or third degree felony respectively.

In order to prove a prior conviction, either a certified copy of the conviction must be entered into evidence or the defendant must stipulate to the prior conviction.[398]

4. Reluctant Victim Testimony.

Where a victim of domestic violence tries to invoke her 5th amendment rights not to testify and where the court nevertheless orders her to read her statement to the jury, the defendant does not have standing to challenge the

---

396 *State v. Gwen*, Slip Opinion No. 2012-Ohio-5046

397 *State v. Smith,* 136 Ohio St.3d 1, 2013-Ohio-1698

398 *State v. Tate*, 138 Ohio St. 3d 139, 2014-Ohio-44.

admission of the victim's testimony. Further there is no evidence that the witness was in danger of self-incrimination.

Although the trial court did not inquire into the reason for the invoking of the privilege it was harmless beyond a reasonable doubt because the remaining evidence established the defendant's guilt beyond a reasonable doubt.[399]

[399] State v, Arnold, 147 Ohio St. 3d 138, 2016-Ohio-1595.

CHAPTER 36

DUI

(Driving While Under the Influence of Alcohol)

1. Subpoena by the State of Blood Test Results.
2. Horizontal Gaze Nystagmus Test.
3. Breathalyzer Tests.
4. Probable Cause to Administer a Breathalyzer Test.
5. Operating a Motor Vehicle, defined.
6. Farm Tractors.
7. Arrest of Person Not Observed Driving.
8. Citation for DUI.
9. Under the Influence, defined.
10. Availability of Testing Equipment.
11. Offender's right to have own test performed.
12. Breath Test admissibility.
13. Senior Operator.
14. Admission of out-of-court tests.
15. Accuracy of the Instruments
16. Admission of Routine Calibration Logs.
17. Storage of Urine Samples.
18. Maintenance Logs.
19. Delay in Drawing Blood.
20. Refusal give Consent to Blood Alcohol Test.
21. Defense Expert Testimony.
22. Relevant Factors under "per se" Defense.
23. Uncounseled Defense and Enhanced Sentence.
24. Aggravated Vehicular Assault and DUI.

1.Subpoena by the State of Blood Test Results.

Where an accident victim is taken to a hospital and is administered a blood-alcohol test, not at the request of a police officer, the state cannot subpoena the results of the blood test because revealing the results would be a violation of the physician patient privilege R.C. 2317.02(B).

The court held that in order to allow the results of the test, it would have to create a "public policy limitation on the statutorily created physician-patient privilege * * *." The court does not have the power under its rule making authority to modify privileges. Evid. R. 501, "The rule clearly states that the matter of privilege is controlled by statute or common law." [400]

Pursuant to R.C. 4511.191(A), one who drives on Ohio's Highways is deemed to consent to the test. (If the test is refused, a one-year driver's license suspension is mandated.

2. Horizontal Gaze Nystagmus Test.

A police officer may testify to the results of a horizontal gaze nystagmus test as being relevant to probable cause to arrest. Expert testimony of the test is not required. The test results are admissible as long as a proper foundation is laid in regard to the testifying officer's training, and ability to administer the test

An officer may not, however, testify what he or she believes the offender's blood alcohol level is, this could present due process problems because: (1) the test cannot be verified or duplicated; (2) the margin of error;

[400] *State v. Smorgala,* 50 Ohio St. 3d 222, 553 N.E. 2d 672 (1990).

(3) the circumstance of the test may affect its reliability; (4) Nystagmus may be caused by other conditions; (5) More accurate chemical tests are available.[401]

3. Breathalyzer Tests.

Where one wishes to challenge the results of a breathalyzer test, a pretrial motion to suppress followed by a no contest plea is a proper method. There is no waiver at the time of the no contest plea because the court's ruling on the admissibility of the test is not a liminal ruling because, in effect, the defense to a charge under R.C. 4511.19(A)(3) is "destroyed where the breathalyzer test is declared valid after a pretrial challenge.

If the defendant pleads no contest after such a ruling, judicial economy will be served by appeal of the pivotal issue rather that forcing the defendant to go through a futile trial."[402]

4. Probable Cause to Administer a Breathalyzer Test.

Concerning the administration of a breathalyzer test, the state has the burden of going forward with evidence to show probable cause if there is a warrantless search and the defendant alleges the lack of probable cause. Where the state does not prove probable cause, the test result will be suppressed. The question of probable cause can be presented even where it is not specifically raised.

In a motion to suppress the test, defense counsel met his burden even though his motion did not specifically raise the issue of probable cause to administer the test. It was sufficient to allege the test was illegally obtained, there was no warrant authorizing the test, and there was no probable cause to arrest defendant:

---

[401] *State v. Bresson,* 51 Ohio St. 3d 123, 554 N.E. 2d 1330 (1990).

[402] *Defiance v. Kretz*, 60 Ohio St. 3d 1, 573 N. E.2d 32 (1991).

"Therefore, we find that the defendant met the requirement that he place the prosecution on notice to the grounds upon which he challenged the administration of the breathalyzer test." Here the state did not present argument and as result, did not prove probable cause. *Xenia v. Wallace.*[403]

5. Operating a Motor Vehicle, Defined.

An intoxicated person found sleeping in a car parked on private property with the key in the ignition, is operating a motor vehicle while intoxicated in violation of R.C. 4511.19(A)(1) and (3).

Driving a motor vehicle and operating a motor vehicle are not the same. In *State v. Cleary*, the court held operating a vehicle is broader than driving. A person sitting in the front seat of an automobile with the key in his possession is operating the vehicle. [404]

See also, *State v. McGlone*, "*McGlone* was sitting in the driver's seat of his car with the motor running. The car was under his control. He could have moved the car whenever he wanted and, in fact, admitted he had been driving the car. * * * *McGlone* urges us to * * * consider him both reasonable and prudent because he drove from a public highway into the driveway of a private residence and fell asleep." R.C. 4511.19 prohibits operating a motor vehicle anywhere in this state while under the influence of alcohol or drugs. This includes private driveways. [405]

6. Farm Tractor.

The defendant's operator's license was improperly suspended for operating a farm tractor because a farm tractor is not a motor vehicle and R.C. 4507.16(B) provides for the suspension of a person operating a motor vehicle. R.C. 4507.03 provides that an operator's license is not required to drive a farm tractor upon a highway, and since R.C. 4501.01(B) excludes

---

[403] *Xenia v. Wallace,* 37 Ohio St. 3d 216, 524 N.E. 2d 889 (1988).

[404] *State v. Cleary,* 22 Ohio St. 3d 198, 490 N.E. 2d 574 (1986).

[405] *State v. McGlone,* 59 Ohio St. 3d 122, 570 N.E. 2d 1115 (1991).

farm tractors from the definition of motor vehicles, R.C. 4507.16(B) is not applicable for suspending a license for driving a tractor.

However, the trial court properly found the defendant guilty of driving a farm tractor while intoxicated because the local statute prohibits the driving of "any vehicle" while intoxicated.[406]

7. Arrest of Person Not Observed Driving.

A police office may arrest and charge a person for driving under the influence of alcohol even if the officer did not see the person operating the vehicle. Where there was an accident on a public street and the defendant admits to driving the vehicle, and is visibly under the influence of alcohol, the officer can reasonably conclude the person was driving the vehicle while under the influence of alcohol. *Oregon v. Szakovits.*[407]

8. Citation for DUI.

A uniform traffic ticket charging the offender with "DUI" which refers to the ordinance that gives rise to the offense is not required to indicate the substance by which the person charged is intoxicated. A complaint in a traffic procedure "simply needs to advise the defendant of the offense with which he is charged, in a manner that can be readily understood by a person making a reasonable attempt to understand" (citations omitted).

A defendant can always ask for a bill of particulars if he does not understand the crime with which he was charged.[408]

9. Under the Influence Defined.

It is reversible error where the trial court improperly instructs the jury as to the meaning of "under the influence. It was improper to charge the jury that

---

[406] *Wauson v. Badenhop*, 9 Ohio St. 3d 152, 459 N.E. 2d 867 (1984).

[407] Oregon v. Szakovits ,32 Ohio St. 2d 271, 291 N.E. 2d 742 (1972).

[408] *Barberton v. O'Connor*, 17 Ohio St. 3d 218, 478 N.E. 2d 803 (1985).

"under the influence" meant that the alcohol had "some influence" on the defendant because: "Such a charge would be included and make actionable such influences as the minuscule alteration of an accused's heartbeat, breathing rate, perspiration, salivation - or even humor or good spirits." This erroneous part of the charge was read along with the proper definition. However, the court found that the jury could have taken the incorrect definition for the controlling law; as a result, the conviction was reversed. *State v. Hardy* [409]

10. Availability of Testing Equipment.

It is not unconstitutional for a municipality to choose not to have available the means for the defendant to take the blood alcohol tests provided for under R.C. 4511.191(A). The implied consent statute and the statute prohibiting the operation of a motor vehicle while under the influence of alcohol are separate and distinct.

Appellant was told he could have a test taken at his own expense, but he did not request it. Nothing under the statute entitles anyone to the administration of the tests, "We conclude that, although the submission of sobriety tests is not mandatory upon the arresting authority, nor is the failure to provide the galaxy of tests enumerated in R.C. 4511.191(A) unconstitutional." [410]

11. Where Offender is not advised of His Right to His Own Test.

Where a person tested for a determination of percentage of alcohol in his blood is not advised, pursuant to R.C. 4511.19(B), that he may have a test administered on his own, the test results are not necessarily inadmissible, it must be determined whether that person is prejudiced thereby. R.C. 2945.83 provides that there shall be no reversal of a lower court's decision, "unless it affirmatively

[409] State v. Hardy, ,28 Ohio St 2d 89, 276 N.E. 2d 247 (1971).

[410] *Kettering v. Baker*, 42 Ohio St. 2d 351, 328 N.E. 2d 805 (1975).

appears on the record that the accused was or may have been prejudiced thereby." [411]

12.Breath Tests.

"Before the results of a breathalyzer test are admissible, it is incumbent on the state to show that the instrument was in proper working order and the manipulator had the qualifications to conduct the test." [412]

13. Senior Operator.

It is not necessary that a senior operator be present during a test as long as the operator is under the general direction of a senior operator.[413]

14. Trial Court's Discretion to Admit Out of Court Tests.

The trial court did not abuse its discretion in refusing to admit the results of an out-of-court simulated test of the defendant on a BAC Verifier machine. The test took place three months after his arrest. "The admission or rejection of out-of--court experiments is particularly within the sound discretion of the trial court, and reviewing courts will not interfere absent an abuse of discretion.[414]

15. Accuracy of the Instruments.

The court of appeals improperly reversed the convictions of two defendants where the reversal was based on reliance by the court of appeals on the

---

[411] *State v. Myers*, 26 Ohio St. 2d 190, 271 N.E. 2d 245 (1971).

[412] *Mentor v. Giordano,* 9 Ohio St. 2d 140, 224 N.E. 2d 343 (1967).

[413] *Aurora v. Kepley,* 60 Ohio St. 2d 73, 397 N.E. 2d 400 (1979).

[414] *Columbus v. Taylor*, 39 Ohio St. 3d 162, 529 N.E. 2d 1382 (1988).

Department of Health's Manual. The manual stated the accuracy of the instruments is no better than plus or minus .01 percent, which would make the possible range of the percentage of alcohol in the blood of one defendant 097 to 117, and of the other .095 to .115 percent.

The evidence supported the convictions because the level of error could be verified by a calibration check. In addition, when the most recent calibration check was done, the range of both defendants' blood alcohol level put them in the range of the statutory limit of .10 percent.[415] The current limit is now .08.

16. Admission of Routine Calibration Logs.

The officer who calibrates the intoxilyzer equipment is not required to testify at trial notwithstanding Evid. R. 803(8), which prohibits the introduction of reports regarding an officer's observation of criminal activity. Evid. R. 803(8) does not prohibit "records of routine, intra-police, or machine maintenance nature, such as intoxilyzer calibration logs. Such routine records are highly likely to be reliable, and are precisely the type contemplated as admissible by the public records exception to the rule against hearsay." [416]

17. Strict Compliance of Storage of Urine Samples.

In order to admit a urine sample in a prosecution for driving under the influence, strict compliance with Ohio Adm. Code 3701-53-05(F) is not required; substantial compliance is sufficient. Therefore, where the suspect's urine sample was not refrigerated at the required temperature, there was no showing of prejudice by this fact alone. There is also some evidence that refrigeration reduces vapor loss, the lack of refrigeration could have benefited the defendant.[417]

---

[415] *State v. Schuck*, 22 Ohio St. 3d 296, 490 N.E. 599 (1986).

[416] *State v. Ward,* 15 Ohio St. 3d 355, 474 N.E. 2d 300 (1984).

[417] *State v. Plummer,* 22 Ohio St. 3d 292, 490 N.E. 2d 902 (1986).

The requirement of Ohio Adm. Code 3701-53-05(F) that blood and urine specimens be refrigerated when not in transit can also be met with substantial compliance. See State v. Plummer [418] and State v. Mayl. [419] Even where substantial compliance has been shown, the defendant is permitted to show prejudice as is expressed in the burden shifting test:[420]

1. Motion to suppress must be filed or is waived. (If waived, the state requirement to lay a foundation for admissibility is waived.)
2. The state then has the burden to show substantial compliance, if met then:
3. The defendant has the burden to demonstrate prejudice.[421]

18. Maintenance Logs.

" * * * Certified copies of pages from a permanent log book maintained by a police department in accordance with regulations promulgated by the Director of Health pursuant to R.C. 3701.143, are admissible in evidence as an exception to the hearsay rule under R.C. 2317.42" [422]

19. Delay in Drawing Blood.

Where a suspect's blood is not withdrawn for testing to determine the concentration of alcohol in her blood within two hours of the time of the alleged violation of the ordinance, the test cannot be used as evidence relating to the violation of R.C. 4511.19, concerning operating a vehicle with a prohibited concentration of alcohol in her blood. However, the evidence may be admitted under 4511.19(A) (1) (a) for operating a vehicle under the influence of alcohol and/or drugs.

Because of the per se rule and the presumption of 4511.19(A) (2), (3), or (4), it is important that a solid foundation for the admission of the test be

[418] 22 Ohio St. 3d 292, 490 N.E. 2d 902.

[419] 106 Ohio St. 3d 207, 2005-Ohio-4629, 833 N.E. 2d 1216.

[420] State v. Burnside, 100 Ohio St. 3d 152, 2003-Ohio-5372, 797 N.E. 2d 71.

[421] State v. Baker, 146 Ohio St. 3d 456, 2016-Ohio-451.

[422] *State v. Walker*, 53 Ohio St. 2d 192, 374 N.E. 2d 132 (1978).

established. Admission of the results in a per se charge that were taken more than two hours later, "would defeat the legislative purpose and produce confusing, unreliable and inconsistent verdicts."

20. Refusal to Give Consent to Blood Alcohol Test.

Where a defendant initially refused to give consent to submit to a chemical test but gave permission within two hours of his arrest, his license was nevertheless properly suspended for refusal to take the test, pursuant to R.C. 4511.191.

The defendant's subsequent permission does not affect the initial refusal. The court implied, however, where the suspect immediately retracts his refusal, and then has been denied the test; the refusal may not be used against him.

Here the defendant gave permission a half-hour after given the opportunity to have the blood alcohol test. "We concluded herein that the time limits of R.C. 4511.91 * * * is only a restriction on the admission in evidence of the results of such tests, and does not have the effect of extending the time within which an arrested person may choose to submit or refuse to submit to a chemical test under the provisions of R.C. 4511.191(D).[423]

A defendant's refusal to submit to a blood alcohol test is admissible. *South Dakota v. Neville*.[424]

There is no fourth amendment or Section 14 Article 1 of the Ohio Constitution violation where defendant refuses to consent to chemical testing. It makes no difference if the refusal would have subjected the defendant to an enhanced sentence due to a prior dui conviction.[425]

21. Defense Expert Testimony.

Where the trial court refuses to allow a defense expert witness to testify generally to the reliability of the intoxilyzer, the accused in not denied his

---

[423] *In re Brooks*, 27 Ohio St. 2d 66, 271 N.E. 2d 810 (1971).

[424] *South Dakota v. Neville,* 459 U.S. 553, 74 L. Ed. 2d 748, 105 S. Ct. 916 (1983).

[425] *State v. Hoover*, 123 Ohio St. 3d 418, 2009-Ohio-4993.

constitutional right to present a defense. The legislature has resolved the question of the device's reliability and relevancy. The presumption of R.C. 4511.19 does away with the necessity of the prosecution to prove the effect of alcohol on the individual.

The defendant is still able to present evidence in rebuttal of the presumption he was under the influence of alcohol, "such as a video tape or testimony * * * concerning the accused's sobriety * * * as well as technical evidence, such as additional chemical tests and the completion of field sobriety tests." He may attack the reliability of specific testing procedure and the qualifications of the operator" and "defense expert testimony as to the weight, not admissibility is allowed." He "may not make a general attack on the reliability and validity of the breath testing equipment * * *" [426]

22. Relevant Factors Under Per Se Defense.

In *State v. Boyd*, the trial court correctly excluded evidence in a prosecution under R.C. 4511.19(A)(3), where the defendant attempted to introduce his manner of speech and of walking.

The only relevant factors were whether: (1) He was operating a vehicle within the state; and (2) At the time, he had a blood alcohol level of ten-hundredths of one gram or more by weight of alcohol per two hundred liters of his breath. "Standing alone, appellee's appearance, manner of speech and walking, and lack of any symptoms of intoxication are not relevant evidence and therefore, not admissible." [427]

23. Uncounseled Defense and Enhanced Sentence

Where a DUI defendant's degree of crime is enhanced pursuant to R.C. due to prior convictions of DUI, and the defendant attacks the prior convictions on the grounds that they were uncounseled, the burden of producing prima facie evidence that the conviction was uncounseled is on the defendant.

---

[426] *State v. Vega,* 12 Ohio St. 3d 185, 465 N.E. 2d 1303 (1984).

[427] *State v. Boyd,* 18 Ohio St. 3d 30, 479 N.E. 2d 850 (1985).

It is not enough that the defendant show that he was not represented by counsel at the time of his convictions he must make a prima facie showing that he was *uncounseled* and that he did not waive counsel. The fact that one is not represented by counsel does not, by itself, invalidate a conviction.

Only after such prima facie evidence is produced by the defendant does the burden shift to the state to prove the convictions were valid by showing a waiver of counsel from the record.

When presenting its case in chief, the state can meet its burden by presenting certified copies of the judgments of prior convictions. The burden is not on the state to prove defendant was represented by counsel unless the defendant first makes a prima facie showing that he was uncounseled. [428]

24. Aggravated Vehicular Assault and DUI.

Cumulative Sentences (Aggravated Vehicular Assault and DUI) A violation of R.C. 4511.19 (operating a vehicle under the influence) is a predicate offense of Aggravated Vehicular Assault (R.C. 2903.08(A)(10(a) And though one may be convicted of aggravated vehicular assault if one is in violation of R.C. 4511.19 the OVI statute, the offenses are not of similar import requiring a merging of convictions or sentences.

Aggravated Vehicular assault and OVI are offenses of dissimilar import. OVI simply prohibits a person from operating a vehicle wile under the influence of alcohol, a drug of abuse or a combination thereof. A conviction for Aggravated vehicular assault requires the causing of serious physical harm to another person or an unborn person. Accordingly, consecutive sentences may be imposed. [429]

25. Juvenile Convictions (as enhancements)

Where the defendant had four adult OVI convictions and one uncounseled juvenile OVI equivalent juvenile adjudication, it was improper to enhance the present DUI under the theory that the defendant has 5 prior DUI convictions. The

[428] *State v. Thompson* 121 Ohio St. 3d 250, 2009-Ohio-314.

[429] State v. Earley, Slip Opinion 2015-Ohio-4615.

state used the juvenile adjudication to give the defendant five OVI's making the prosecution a 4th degree felony.[430] State v. Brooke, 113 Ohio St. 3d 199, 2007-Ohio-1533 applies to uncounseled juvenile delinquency findings as well as to adult uncounseled convictions and cannot be used to enhance the penalty for DUI.

26. Sentencing.

Where a defendant has been convicted of OVI as a 3d degree felony with repeat offender specifications the trial court must sentence the defendant to a mandatory 1,2,3,4, or 5-year sentence for the repeat offender specification. The court at its option can also sentence the defendant to 9,12, 18, 24, 30, or 36 months for the OVI conviction.[431]

The equal protection violation found by this court in State v. Wilson[432] which implies that identical criminal offenses that provide for different penalties always violate the equal protection clause does not apply to a dui prosecution in which different penalties are authorized for the same conduct because R.C. 4511.19(G) (1) (d) and R.C. 2941.1413 are penalty enhancements based on prior conduct.

R.C. 4511.19(G)(1)(d) is a fourth-degree felony if the defendant has five OVI convictions in the previous 20 years. R.C. 2941.1413 provides for repeat offenders.

Mere sentence enhancements based on a defendant's prior OVI convictions is not in violation of the equal protection in the sense that the same conduct has different penalties. The enhancement of the above is based on a rational progression penalty that was enacted to deal with recidivism.[433]

27. Adequacy of Evidence of Drug Influence.

Under an adequacy of evidence analysis test the issue is: is the evidence sufficient to sustain a verdict. In a OVI prosecution where the testimony of the

[430] State v. Bode, 2015-Ohio-1519

[431] State v. South

[432] 58 Ohio St. 2d 52, 388 N.E. 2d 745 (1979).

[433] State v. Klembus, 146 Ohio St. 3d 84, 2016-Ohio-1092.

police office at a traffic accident is that the defendant admitted to taking drugs that can Impair his driving and his testimony as to the defendant's demeanor is sufficient to sustain a conviction for OVI.

"When the effects of a drug are sufficiently well known—as they are with hydrocodone—expert testimony linking ingestion of the drug with indicia of impairment is unnecessary."[434]

29. 28. Driving Privileges

30.

28 A person given a lifetime license suspension may have driving privileges after three years. The granting of driving privileges is not a modification or termination of the suspension which requires a 15-year waiting period pursuant to R.C. 4510.54 . R.C. 4510.13 controls the issuance of driving privileges and permits a court to grant limited driving privileges for any of the designated purposes.[435]

29

CHAPTER 37

Endangering Children

1. Culpable Mental States.
2. Failure to Protect.
3. Knowledge of Proper Mental State.
4. Amendment of the Indictment to include Serious Physical Harm.
5. Child Enticement

[434] State v. Richardson, Slip Opinion No. 2016-Ohio-8448

[435] State v. Manocchio, 138 Ohio St. 3d 345, 2014-Ohio-785.

1. Culpable Mental States.

Endangering children is not a strict liability offense; recklessness is sufficient culpability for conviction.

It is permissible to amend the indictment to include the element of recklessness in an endangering children prosecution because the amendment does not change the name or identity of the crime pursuant to Crim. R. 7(D), because: (1) the name of the crime remained the same, and the identity of the crime was not changed by adding the culpable mental state of recklessness. [436]

(Where the identity of the offense is changed such as where the trial court amends the indictment that changes the penalty or the degree of the crime such amendment is not permissible.[437]

It should be noted, that recklessness is an essential element of the crime of endangering children, without a showing of recklessness a conviction will not stand. *State v. McGee.*[438]

2. Failure to Protect

Endangering children not only prohibits affirmative acts against the child, but also prohibits failures to protect the child. "An inexcusable failure to perform one's duty to protect a child, where such failure to act results in a substantial risk to the child's health or safety, is an offense under R.C. 2919.22." [439]

3. Knowledge of Proper Mental State.

The accused was not misled or prejudiced even though an amendment was made to the substance of the indictment pursuant to Crim. R. 7(D).

---

[436] *State v. Adams,* 62 Ohio St. 2d 151, 404 N.E. 2d 144 (1980).

[437] *State v. Davis, 121 Ohio St. 3d 239, 903 N.E. 2d 609 (2008).*

[438] *State v. McGee,* 79 Ohio St. 3d 193, 680 N.E. 2d 975 (1997).

[439] *State v. Kamel*, 12 Ohio St. 3d 306, 466 N.E. 2d 860 (1984).

Defendant's knowledge of the proper mental state was evidenced by his motion to dismiss the indictment for not containing the proper mental state. [440]

4. Amendment of the Indictment to include Serious Physical Harm.

An indictment can be amended at any time if the amendment does not change the name or identity of the crime. If the amendment changes the penalty or degree of the crime it necessarily changes the identity of the crime.

Where the amendment to the indictment charging child endangering is challenged alleging that the failure to include the factor of serious physical harm in the indictment, the court found the amendment was proper because the elements were properly delineated and fairly informed the defendant of the crime. The indictment before amendment stated the crime was a third-degree felony which requires serious physical harm. [441]

5. Child Enticement.

The child enticement stature R.C. has been declared unconstitutional as being overbroad as it criminalizes otherwise protected behavior concerning normal interaction with a child by someone other than the designated persons in the statute.[442]

---

[440] *State v. O'Brien*, 30 Ohio St. 3d 122, 508 N.E. 2d 144 (1987).

[441] *State v. Pepka*, 125 Ohio St. 3d 124, 2010-Ohio-1045.

[442] State v. Romage, 138 Ohio St. 3d 390, 2014-Ohio-783.

CHAPTER 38

Escape.

1. Acts Constituting a Valid Arrest.
2. Common Law Defense.
3. Post Release Control.

To be convicted of escape the defendant must know he or she is under detention, or at least be reckless in regard thereto. Escape includes a break from detention, as well as from arrest. It also includes a failure to return to detention where the detainee is granted temporary leave. R.C. 2921.34.

This section reviews those cases where the defendant was under questionable custody. Detention has been defined by in *State v. Reed*, "A person is under 'detention' as that term is used in R.C. 2921.34, when he is arrested and the arresting officer has established control over his person."[443]

1. Acts Constituting a Valid Arrest.

An arrest requires on the part of the arresting person: (1) an attempt to arrest, (2) real or pretended authority to arrest, and (3) actual or constructive seizure of the person.[444]

In *Reed, supra.*, the defendant fatally shot a police officer after the officer stopped the defendant's car. The defendant was not guilty of escape because the police officer had not established control over him. "A person is under 'detention' as that term is used in R.C. 2921.34 when he is arrested and the arresting officer has established control over his person, in the case at bar such

[443] *State v. Reed*, 65 Ohio St. 2d 117, 418 N.E. 2d 1359 (1981).

[444] *State v. Barker*, 53 Ohio St. 2d 135, 372 N.E. 2d 1324 (1978).

control was not established. Officer Burdsall had only approached the car with his gun drawn and ordered the occupants out of the car when he was shot."

Similarly, In *State v. Claytor*, the defendant shot and killed two security guards who stopped him while he was trespassing on the grounds of a hospital. The court held that the stopping of a person and asking for identification does not establish an arrest. Even though it could be argued that the officers had established control over the defendant, the establishment of control, by itself does not amount to an arrest without a showing of *intent to arrest.*

"There is no evidence that could even be inferred from Gagliardo's [guard supervisor] testimony that he wanted * * * [the guards] to place the two men in custody or detain them in any way, even though he knew * * * [the guards] had found the men and stopped to talk to them. Claytor may have feared that he was about to be arrested. But there is simply nothing in the record to support a finding that the guards intended to arrest the two men when they asked for identification or that the two men understood the request to be tantamount to being placed in custody." [445]

2. Common Law Defense.

There is a common-law defense to escape. In *State v. Cross*, the court held that the common law affirmative defense of necessity or duress has not been abrogated by the escape statute. The court made it clear that for one to prevail in a defense of necessity or duress, it must be established that there is a "present, imminent, immediate, and impending death or bodily injury." [446]

The situation could be one where the inmate was fleeing from a burning building, or where an "inmate must choose between death, beating or homosexual advances, citing *People v. Lovercamp*.[447]

In *Cross*, the reasons giving for escape did not meet the standard of "present, imminent, immediate * * *." Here the defendant escaped because the

---

[445] *State v. Claytor,* 61 Ohio St. 3d 234, 574 N.E. 2d 472 (1991).

[446] *State v. Cross*, 58 Ohio St. 2d 482, 391 N.E. 2d 319 (1979).

[447] *People v. Lovercamp,* 43 Cal. App. 3d 823, 118 Cal. Rptr. 110 (1974).

jail was cold and he caught a cold. In addition, since the escapee did not turn himself in for three weeks after visiting Mexico, his credibility was suspect.

3. Post Release Control.

The State must prove the defendant was under detention. Detention includes post release control See R,C, 2921.01(E).

R.C. 2929.19(B)(3) requires the sentencing court to inform the defendant orally that there is a possibility of post release control. If the court fails to orally inform the defendant, he is nevertheless subject to being prosecuted for escape if the court's sentencing entry indicates that his sentence includes post release control. This principal does not go to the issue of whether the sentence is valid without the oral notification of post release control.[448] For a challenge of the validity of such sentences see State v. Bezak[449]

---

[448] *State v. Jordan*, 124 Ohio St.3d 397, 2010-Ohio-281.

[449] *State v. Bezak*, 114 Ohio St. 3d 94, 2007-Ohio-3250.

CHAPTER 39

Ethnic Intimidation

Ohio's ethnic intimidation statue R.C. 2927.12, was, at first, declared unconstitutional by the court in *State v. Wyant*,[450] the statute provided: "(A) No person shall violate [cited sections] * * * by reason of the race, color, religion, or national origin of another person or group of persons. Under section (B) of the statute, a conviction of ethnic intimidation subjects the defendant to a penalty of the next higher degree of the offense that was committed.

Because the enhanced penalties are based only on the actor's reason or his motive for acting, the court held that a person's motive for committing a crime could not support either a separate crime or an enhanced penalty. "Conduct motivated by racial or religious bigotry can be constitutionally punished under the criminal code without resort to constructing a thought crime. In fact, the behavior which is alleged in each case before us can be punished under the criminal statute identified in R.C. 2927.12." The court made it clear there is a distinction between an act of discrimination, which is properly prohibited, and the motive of the discrimination.

The danger in such a statute is that the state may punish a person or enhance a penalty based on that person's viewpoint. The court concluded that though there is a constitutional protection of thoughts, this protection does not "shield a citizen from punishment for proscribed acts." The court upheld the underlying convictions of aggravated menacing. This ruling was appealed. In the interim, as a result of the United States Supreme Court's ruling in *Wisconsin v. Mitchell* [451] [which upheld the constitutionality of a similar statute] the court reversed its holding in *Wyant* and subsequently found Ohio 's Ethnic Intimidation statute constitutional.[452]

---

[450] *State v. Wyant,* 64 Ohio St. 3d 566, 597 N.E. 2d 450 (1992).

[451] *Wisconsin v. Mitchell,* 508 U.S. 476 (1993).

[452] *State v. Wyant*, 68 Ohio St.3d 162, 624 N.E.2d 722 (1994).

CHAPTER 40

Gambling

1. **Gambling Devices and Criminal Tools.**
2. **Mere Possession of Gambling Devices not Illegal.**
3. **Illegal Gambling by a Non-Profit Corporation.**
4. **Book Making.**
5. **Evidence of the Existence of a Gambling House.**

R.C. 2915.02 prohibits gambling for profit. The prohibitions include bookmaking, and those activities that facilitate gambling such as the transmission or exchange of information used to establish odds. Betting or engaging in a scheme of chance is prohibited if it is a substantial source of income for the participant. Gambling for charitable purposes is permitted if the charity qualifies as a true charitable organization.

The committee comment to this statute states that penny-ante poker games and office football pools are permitted unless some profit is taken other than the gain accruing to a winner. Where there is a charge for admission to a game or a percentage of the pot is taken by the house, or the house takes an edge in the odds, it is evidence that the game is one for profit, and thereby is prohibited.

1. Gambling Devices and Criminal Tools.

Because of the principal that specific statutory provisions prevail over general statutory provisions, it was improper to indict a person for the felony of possession of criminal tools under R.C. 2923.24, a felony of the fourth degree, where the defendant possessed gambling devices, the possession of which was made a misdemeanor under R.C. 2915.02(A)(5).

"Given that the General Assembly clearly enacted R.C. 2915.02(A)(5) to reach criminal possession of a gambling device and classified such conduct as a misdemeanor of the first degree under R.C. 2915.02(F), we hold the R.C. 2923.24, a general statute prohibiting the possession and control of criminal tools and classifying such conduct as a fourth degree felony, cannot be used to charge and convict a person of possessing and controlling a gambling device."[453]

2. Mere Possession of Gambling Devices not Illegal

"In order for a gambling device to be illegal, it must be acquired, possessed, controlled, or operated with the purpose to 'establish, promote, or operate, or knowingly engage in conduct that facilitates any scheme or game of chance conducted for profit.' R.C. 2915.02(A)(2) and (5)." [454] Poker is a game of chance. Because an element of skill is involved does not mean the game is not a game of chance. Poker or other video machines can be gambling devices per se under R.C. 2915.01(F). However, mere possession of these machines does not give rise to a violation of the gambling laws. Here the machines were illegally

---

[453] *State v. Volpe*, 38 Ohio St. 3d 191, 527 N.E. 2d 818 (1988).

[454] *Garona v. State*, 37 Ohio St.3d 171, 524 N.E. 2d 496 (1988).

confiscated because "* * * no one was charged with the commission of an offense and there is also nothing inherently illegal about appellee's possession of the machines."

3. Illegal Gambling by a Non-Profit Corporation.

A non-profit organization can be convicted of gambling for profit under R.C. 2915.02. A Fraternal Order of Eagles Post possessed electronic draw poker machines. Although the defendant was a charitable organization under R.C. 2915.01(H), it was not exempt from prosecution under R.C. 2915.02 merely because it was a nonprofit organization. Though the Post is a non-profit institution for tax purposes, the income received by its use of gambling devices is profit. In order to be exempt as a charitable organization and to have certain gambling activities exempt from prosecution, under R.C. 2915.02(D)(1), the money or assets received must be "used by, or given, donated, or otherwise transferred to any organization * * * that is tax exempt * * *" [455]

Here the organization was operated for the benefit of its members. When any organization is operated exclusively for the benefit of members, it does not qualify for the exemption.

4. Book Making.

Book making is a strict liability offense.[456]

[455] *State v. Posey*, 40 Ohio St. 3d 420, 534 N.E. 2d 61 (1988).

[456] *State v. Wac*, 68 Ohio St. 2d 84, 428 N.E. 2d 428 (1981).

5. Evidence of the Existence of a Gambling House.

Sufficient probable cause is present to issue a search warrant for a gambling house under the following facts: (1) the telephone of the premises was listed to a fictitious business; (2) the persons operating the business were known gamblers with prior gambling arrests; (3) the information was from the personal observations of law enforcement officers.[457]

[404] *State v. Thomas*, 61 Ohio St. 2d 223, 400 N.E. 2d 401 (1980).

CHAPTER 41

Kidnapping

1. Kidnapping in General.

The Kidnapping statute, R.C. 2905.01 contains two major sections. Both sections prohibit a person by force, threat, or deception from removing a person from where he was found or from restraining him of his liberty. In the case of a victim under the age of thirteen, or a mentally incompetent person the removal or restraint by itself is sufficient to establish kidnapping, without the necessity of showing of force, threat or deception.

The kidnapping charge is often indicted with other crimes, most typically rape, murder, robbery, and burglary. During trial, as well as, during appellate proceedings the question often arises as to whether the kidnapping charge is a separate distinct offense, or whether it is merely incidental to the primary underlying crime. This question is important for sentencing considerations, and determines whether the defendant will be sentenced solely on the kidnapping charge or also on the underlying crime.

2. Kidnapping and Rape.

In *State v. Mitchell*, the court held that kidnapping is "implicit within every forcible rape, and kidnapping and rape are allied offenses of similar import, and where the kidnapping is merely incidental to the underlying crime there can be but one conviction." [458]

The following cases are illustrative of this principal:

In *State v. Price*,[459] the defendant was charged with rape and kidnapping. The court determined that kidnapping was not established where the movement of the victim was merely from the back seat of a car to the ground where she was raped. In other words, the movement was incidental to the underlying crime of rape. A similar holding was found in *State v. Logan*, where the kidnapping was found to be incidental to the underlying crime of rape where the victim was taken down an alley and raped.[460] The court found that this movement of the victim was also incidental to the underlying crime of rape.[461]

---

[458] 6 Ohio St. 3d 416, 453 N.E. 2d 593 (1983).

[459] *State v. Price,* 60 Ohio St. 2d 136, 398 N.E. 2d 772 (1979)

[460] *State v. Logan,* 60 Ohio St.2d 126, 397 N.E. 1345 (1979).

[461] See also, *State v. Donald,* 57 Ohio St. 2d 73, 386 N.E. 2d 1341

Contrast the above with the following where the circumstances of the kidnapping, rape and murder were each clearly committed with a separate animus. "The restraint and asportation of the victim at gunpoint, in a car, to a location over a mile away can hardly be considered as merely incidental to the rape and murder of the victim." [462]

3. The Two-Tier Test

In order to assist the trial courts, the court has developed a "two-tier test" to determine whether a kidnapping has been committed as a separate crime. This test arose from the dictates of R.C. 2941.25, the multi-count provision, which was enacted to prevent what has been described in the Legislative Committee Comment as "* * * 'shotgun' convictions."

The two-tier test was described in *State v. Blankenship* where the defendant was charged with kidnapping and felonious assault. The court held: "* * * first, if it is determined that the elements of the two crimes correspond so that the commission of one will result in the commission of the other they are allied offenses of similar import. In the second tier, the conduct of the defendant is reviewed as to whether the defendant possessed a separate animus for each crime." [463]

(1979).

[462] *In re State v. Broom*, 40 Ohio St. 3d 277, 533 N.E. 2d 682 (1988).

[463] *State v. Blankenship,* 38 Ohio St. 3d 116, 526 N.E. 2d 816 (1988).

In *Blankenship*, several inmates overcame a prison guard. They choked him until he lost consciousness, and tied his legs together. Later, the guard was hit in the head with a piece of body building equipment. The court found that, under these facts, the kidnapping and felonious assault were committed separately. "* * * the kidnapping occurred when the guard was rendered unconscious and then bound with a rope. * * * The felonious assault * * *occurred after the kidnapping had taken place."

4. Subjecting the Victim to a Substantial Risk of Harm.

Where the victim was subjected to a substantial risk of harm, even if the kidnapping was incidental to the underlying crime, kidnapping may be found to be a separate offense.

In *State v. Powell*, the defendant lured the victim to a house, led her to the fourth floor in order to rape her. He then threw her from the window, killing her as rescuers were entering the house. [464]

The taking of the victim to the fourth floor made it possible for him to throw her out of the window to her death thereby substantially increasing the risk of harm to the victim. As a result, the kidnapping was a separate offense.

In *State v. Maurer*, kidnapping was established separately from the primary aggravated murder and rape charges where the defendant picked up the victim from school drove her to a wood where he raped and killed her. Citing as authority *State v. Jenkins*,[465]

---

[464] *State v. Powell,* 49 Ohio St. 3d 255, 552 N.E. 2d 191 (1990).

[465] *State v. Jenkins,* 15 Ohio St. 3d 164, 473 N.E. 2d 264 (1984).

the court held, "In Jenkins, we required prolonged restraint, secretive confinement, or significant movement apart from that involved in the underlying crime in order to justify the application of the aggravating circumstance of kidnapping under R.C. 2929.04(A)(7)." [466]

5. Asportation by Deception.

In *State v. Ware,* the facts would normally lead one to conclude that the rape was an allied offense of similar import where the victim was forcibly moved from a lower level to the upstairs of a house. However, the court found asportation by deception, independent of the rape. The deception occurred when the defendant told the victim she could use his telephone, (he did not have one) after which she followed him several blocks to the house in which she was raped.[467]

In *State v. Morales*, even though the establishment of force was not essential because the offense involved the kidnapping of a victim under the age of 13, kidnapping by deception was established because the defendant lured the victim into a house by telling him that he wished to discuss a problem in his family. [468]

---

[466] *State v. Maurer,* 15 Ohio St. 3d 239, 473 N.E. 2d 768 (1984).

[467] *State v. Ware,* 63 Ohio St. 2d 84, 406 N.E. 2d 1112 (1992).

[468] *State v. Morales,* 32 Ohio St. 3d 252, 513 N.E. 2d 267 (1987).

6. Restraint Sufficient to Establish Kidnapping.

An abduction is not necessary for a kidnapping conviction, a *restraint* for any of the specified purposes is sufficient.

In *State v. Seiber*, the court, in finding that a restraint without an abduction can be a kidnapping, also discussed the factor of creating a substantial risk of serious physical harm:

"Appellant clearly killed Norris in the course of kidnapping the Schoenbergers and Norris, while restraining them for the purpose of terrorizing the Schoenbergers (R.C. 2905.01(A)(3). He also kidnapped Norris and the Schoenbergers by restraining then of their liberty when the circumstances created "a substantial risk of serious physical harm" to the victims (R.C. 2905(B)(2).[469]

7. Aggravated Robbery as an Allied Offense.

The court found that kidnapping and aggravated robbery are allied offenses of similar import. The defendant while committing a robbery caused the victim to remain in the bedroom while pointing a gun at the victim. The court focused on the fact that the presence of the handgun had the tendency to "forcibly restrain" the victim this being also an element of kidnapping. This was a 4-3 decision and should be read narrowly and not as a broad concept. There are certainly many instances in which this holding should not apply. Chief Justice Moyer's dissent seems to be the better view.[470]

---

[469] *State v. Seiber,* 56 Ohio St. 3d 4, 264 N.E. 2d 408 (1990).

[470] *State v, Winn*, 121 Ohio St. 3d 413, 2009-Ohio-1059.

CHAPTER 42

Possessing Criminal Tools.

R.C. 2924.23 prohibits the possession of an item, substance, device, instrument, or article with the purpose to use it criminally. It is prima facie evidence of criminal purpose to possess dangerous ordnance unless it can be shown the possession is for legitimate purposes. Articles or devices designed or adapted for criminal use as well as used for criminal purposes are also prohibited.

The court has made many decisions under this statute. The major issue however, has been where a defendant has been charged with possessing criminal tools even though there has been a specific statute of a lesser degree that prohibits the same conduct.

In *State v. Volpe,* the appellant was charged with violations of R.C. 2915.02 (gambling), R.C. 2915.03 (operating a gambling house), 2923.24 (possession of criminal tools). The crime of possession of criminal tools cannot be charged where there is a specific statute that prohibits the identical conduct. Here possession of the gambling device was a first-degree misdemeanor, but possession of criminal tools was a fourth-degree felony. This resulted in different penalties for the same conduct. The court held: "Therefore, since R. C. 2915.02 and

2923.24 provide for different penalties for the same conduct, they cannot be construed to give effect to both." [471]

"Given that the General Assembly clearly enacted R.C. 2915.02(A)(5) to reach criminal possession and control of a gambling device and classifying such conduct as a fourth-degree felony, cannot be used to charge and convict a person of possessing and controlling a gambling device. Accordingly, we reverse the judgment of the court of appeals and remand these two cases to the trial court for disposition consistent with this opinion."

The use of criminal tools does not have to involve only state law. A person can be prosecuted under state law for possessing criminal tools that were used to violate federal law and although the defendant is not being prosecuted under federal law the use of the tools to violate the law is sufficient for a conviction under the statue. For instance, as in the prosecution concerning copyright violations.[472]

---

[471] *State v. Volpe,* 38 Ohio St. 3d 191, 527 N.E. 2d 818 (1988).

[472] *State v. Chappell*, Slip Opinion No. 2010-Ohio-5991.

CHAPTER 43

Aggravated Robbery and Robbery.

1. **Threat or Use of Force.**
2. **Serious Physical Harm.**
3. **Attempt to Inflict Serious Physical Harm.**
4. **Deadly Weapon or Ordnance.**
5. **Unloaded Firearm.**
6. **Property.**
7. **Circumstantial Evidence of the Theft.**
8. **As an Allied Offense of Kidnapping.**
9. **Fleeing Immediately after the Theft.**

Both aggravated robbery and robbery are theft offenses that include the element of the use, or attempted use of, force against a person. In aggravated robbery, that force must result in serious physical harm, or it must be an attempt to inflict serious harm. In the alternative, the offender may be convicted of aggravated robbery if the offender has under his or her control a deadly weapon or dangerous ordnance.

In robbery, the elements are the use of, or threat to use, force coupled with theft or attempted theft.

Robbery is, at least under R.C. 2911.01 (A)(1), is not a lesser included offense of aggravated robbery because under (A)(1) all that is required is that a deadly weapon be on or about the offender's person or control. It does not require the use or threatened use of force. "Irrespective of how broadly 'force' is defined under the robbery statute it remains that an accused can be convicted of aggravated robbery under R.C. 2911.01(A)(1) without having used or threatened to use any force, as long as the accused merely possesses a deadly weapon or dangerous ordnance during the commission of the theft." [473]

The court has not yet decided whether robbery is a less-included offense of aggravated robbery under R.C. 2911.01(A)(2). It could be that "Inflict or attempt to inflict serious physical harm on another would include as a lesser included offense "use or threaten the immediate use of force against another" as is stated in the robbery statute.

1. Threat or Use of Force.

The current robbery statute requires an objective standard in evaluating the nature of the threat. "This requirement is satisfied if the fear of the alleged victim was of such a nature as in reason and common experience is likely to induce a person to part with property against his will and temporarily suspend his power to exercise his will by virtue of the terror impressed." [474]

The threat to use immediate force can be established even where the offender assures the victim that he has no intention to use force. For instance, where the defendant held his right hand under his shirt while demanding money from a cashier at a convenience store, and stated: "I am not going to hurt you, this is

---

[473] *State v.Merriwether*, 64 Ohio St. 2d 57, 413 N.E. 2d 790 (1980).

[474] *State v. Davis*, 6 Ohio St. 3d 91, 451 N.E. 722 (1983).

all I want, I'm not going to hurt you." The court, in affirming the conviction for aggravated robbery, held that the above statement "could be interpreted to reinforce the threat, conveying the implication that the statement remains applicable only so long as no resistance is offered." [475]

2. Serious Physical Harm.

Serious physical harm is defined in R.C. 2901.01(E) (1)-(5). To prove serious physical harm it is not necessary to produce medical records or medical testimony. In footnote 10 of *State v. Spikes* the court held, in regard to 2901.01(E)(5): "Any physical harm which involves acute pain of such duration as to result in substantial suffering or which involves any degree of protracted or prolonged pain" can be proved by the testimony alone of the victim. [476]

3. Attempt to Inflict Serious Physical Harm.

An attempt to inflict serious physical harm can be shown even though the offender of his own volition ceased attacking the victim after the offender took the money that was the subject of a struggle between him and the victim. Even though there was no evidence presented that the offender intended to inflict serious

---

[475] *State v.Davis*, 6 Ohio St.3d 91, 451 N.E.2d 772 (1983).

[476] *State v. Spikes,* 67 Ohio St. 2d 405, 423 N.E. 2d 1122 (1981).

physical harm,"[F]rom the evidence a jury could reasonably conclude beyond a reasonable doubt, that the assailant attempted to inflict whatever harm was necessary to incapacitate Levy. Furthermore, a jury could reasonably find that the attacker would not have stopped short of serious physical harm, had the victim failed to let go of the money bag." [477]

4. Deadly Weapon or Ordnance.

R.C. 2911.01(A)(1) requires that the offender have on his person or in his control a deadly weapon or dangerous ordnance.

R.C. 2923.11 defines a deadly weapon: "* * * any instrument, device, or thing capable of inflicting death, and designed or specially adapted for use as a weapon, or possessed, carried used as a weapon."

In the case of a handgun, it is not necessary for the state to produce the handgun. It is sufficient if the testimony establishes that the offender was seen holding the gun or that shots were heard.

In *State v. Vandenburg*, the court held: "where there is credible evidence that there was a gun used in a robbery, and when that gun is not available for testing, it is not necessary for the state to prove that the gun could actually fire a projectile in order to sustain a conviction for aggravated robbery." [478]

---

[477] *State v. Eley* , 56 Ohio St. 2d 169, 383 N.E. 2d 132 (1978). (superseded on other grounds by constitutional amendment)

[478] *State v. Vandenburg,* 61 Ohio St 2d 285, 401 N.E. 2d 437 (1980).

5. Unloaded Firearm.

The firearm does not have to be loaded, a gun used in a robbery is "as a matter of law a deadly weapon; whether it is loaded or unloaded." [479] The court in *Meek*, although, basing its holding on R.C. 2923.11 (B), which defines firearm to include an unloaded firearm, discussed the harm that can be caused by a gun unloaded or loaded, it can create a "highly charged atmosphere" in which harm to a victim may occur in many ways.

6. Property.

It is not necessary that the property, which is the subject of a theft or an attempted theft, be in the possession or control of the victim. Where a kidnap victim was ordered to call the store where he was employed so that the offender could collect a ransom, the court held, "Through the anticipated kidnapping, appellant moreover conspired, and eventually attempted, to exert control over the property of Busch [victim] had he succeeded, the requirements of R.C. 2913. 02(A) (1), (4) would have been met. Similarity the victim is not required to be the owner of the property.[480]

---

[479] *State v. Meek*, 53 Ohio St. 2d 35, 372 N.E. 2d 341 (1978).

[480] *Vaugh v. Maxwell*, 2 Ohio St. 2d 299, 209 N.E.2d 164 (1965).

7. Circumstantial Evidence of the Theft.

Aggravated robbery may be established by circumstantial evidence. Hence, where it was shown that the kidnap/murder victim was wearing certain clothing and jewelry, and those items were later seen in the possession of the defendant, this circumstantial evidence was sufficient to establish the crime, even though there was no evidence to show that the primary motivation of the offender was to commit a theft offense. [481]

---

481. *State v. Durr*, 58 Ohio St. 3d 86, 568 N.E. 2d 674 (1991); See also, *State v. Johnson*, 46 Ohio St. 3d 96, 545 N.E. 2d 636 (1989).

8. As an Allied Offense of Kidnapping.

The court found kidnapping and aggravated robbery to be allied offenses of similar import. The defendant while committing a robbery caused the victim to remain in the bedroom while pointing a gun at the victim. The court focused on the fact that the presence of the handgun had the tendency to "forcibly restrain" the victim, this being also an element of kidnapping. This was a 4-3 decision and should be read narrowly and not as a broad concept. There are certainly many instances in which this holding should not apply. Chief Justice Moyer's dissent seems to be the better view.[482]

9. Fleeing Immediately after the Theft.

After the theft is complete or after the defendant abandons the property that was the object of the theft. A subsequent use of force to escape does not necessarily elevate the theft to a robbery.[483]

[482] *State v. Winn*, 121 Ohio St. 3d 413, 2009-Ohio-1059.

[483] State v. Thomas, 106 Ohio St. 3d 133, 2005-Ohio-4106.

CHAPTER 44

Rape

1. In General.
2. Force.
3. Force in Rape and Force Sufficient to Constitute a Separate Crime of Kidnapping.
4. Kidnapping by Deception.
5. Rape and Prolonged Restraint.
6. Force and a Pattern of Sexual Abuse.
7. Rape Shield Law.
8. Past Sexual Relations with the Victim.
9. In Camera Hearing.
10. Sexual Activity with Another.
11. Where the Victim is a Prostitute.
12. Sexual History as Admissible Evidence.
13. Sufficiency of Evidence.
14. Evidence of Possible Civil Suit.
15. Type of Rape.
16. Multiple Offenses.
17. Circumstantial Evidence of Rape and Attempted Rape.
18. Adult Prosecuted for Rape that occurred when he was a Juvenile.

1. In General

Rape is an aggravated felony of the first degree. The rape of a person under 13 accompanied by force or the threat force requires a sentence of life imprisonment.

R.C. 2907.02 provides that no person shall engage in sexual conduct with another, not the spouse of the offender or the spouse of the offender living separate and apart from the offender. Rape also is established where the victim's judgment is impaired by the defendant's administering of any drug by force or surreptitiously, or by threat of force or deception; lastly, as stated above, the victim is less than thirteen years of age regardless of whether the defendant knows the age of the victim.

2. Force.

There is no minimum threshold by which to measure force. The existence of force is relative, depending upon the physical, as well as, the relational status of the parties. Where there is a family relationship, as in the case of a parent offender and a child victim, the traditional definition of force or threat of force is not necessarily relevant.

In *State v. Eskridge*, the offender was convicted of raping his four-year old daughter. The record revealed a minimal amount of physical force. The victim testified:

"He took off my panties, and did the nasty stuff * * * He put his thing in me." The court found the offender used "at least minimal force in committing the rape." "In light of all the circumstances, i.e., the child's tender age, and the relationship of parental authority * * * we find substantial evidence from which the trial court could have found beyond a reasonable doubt that [the offender] committed the acts with force." [484]

The court in *Eskridge*, further discussed force as follows: "Force need not be physically brutal, but can be subtle and psychological." See *State v. Labus*, "with the filial obligation of obedience to the parent, the same degree of violence would not be required upon a person of such tender years, as would be required were the parties equal in size, age and strength." [485]

3. Force in Rape and Force Sufficient to Constitute a Separate Crime of Kidnapping.

Because the act of rape necessitates at least some degree of restraint upon the victim, it is not unusual for an indictment to also charge the offender with kidnapping. Therefore, it is important to examine the difference in restraint inherent in kidnapping, and how it differs from the restraint that is merely incidental to the rape.

If in committing the rape, the offender does not commit a separate act of asportation there can be no finding of the separate crime of kidnapping. Where the offender, for instance, moves the

---

[484] *State v. Eskridge,* 38 Ohio St. 3d 56, 526 N.E. 2d 304 (1988).

[485] *State v. Labus*, 102 Ohio St 26, 130 N.E. 161 (1921).

victim from the back seat of a car to behind a bush for engaging in sexual conduct this, standing by itself, is insufficient evidence to sustain a kidnapping charge.

Under those facts, the court held:

"The force by which appellant removed Christa from the car to behind a nearby bush to engage in sexual conduct, as required under the rape statue, is indistinguishable from the force by which appellant restrained Christa of her liberty as required under the kidnapping statute."

"There was no act of asportation distinct from the rape either in time or in function." *State v. Price.*[486]

In *State v. Donald*, the court, in making a general finding that kidnapping and rape can be allied offenses of similar import, held that where the offender forced his victim from a stockroom office to a men's locker room, he did not commit the separate act of kidnapping because both crimes were motivated by a single purpose and both convictions relied upon identical conduct and the same evidence. [487]

4. Kidnapping by Deception.

In *State v. Ware,* the offender committed the separate crimes of kidnapping and rape where he lured the victim to his home telling her she could use a telephone. Once in his home, as she resisted his advances, he carried her upstairs and raped her. The court held that the act of carrying the victim upstairs

---

[486] *State v. Price,* 60 Ohio St. 2d 136, 398 N. E. 2d 772 (1979).

[487] *State v. Donald,* 57 Ohio St 2d 73, 386 N.E. 2d 1341 (1979).

was not sufficient to constitute a separate offense of kidnapping, but the deception of lying to the victim concerning using his telephone was sufficient to establish kidnapping by deception. "[W]e conclude that there was an act of asportation by deception significantly independent from the asportation incidental to the rape." In other words, the offender kidnapped the victim by deception, by having her accompany him several blocks to his home. [488]

5. Rape and Prolonged Restraint.

In *State v. Brown*, the court found that kidnapping and rape were committed separately and with a separate animus where the offender not only raped the victim, but also restrained her for several hours. The offenses occurred after a party, where the victim awoke to find the offender in bed with her, he engaged in sexual conduct with her for several hours and thereafter restrained her of her liberty for several hours more. [489]

The court held: "[A]ppellant's victim suffered a prolonged restraint, approximately an eight-hour ordeal, and was held secretively * * * he bound and gagged his victim upon completion of his sexual attacks upon her which indicates that this particular restraint, was performed to facilitate appellant's escape, that being the case, the separate animus necessary to sustain the conviction for kidnapping, * * * was present."

---

[488] *State v. Ware,* 63 Ohio St. 2d 84, 406 N.E. 2d 1112 (1980).

[489] *State v. Brown,* 12 Ohio St. 3d 147, 465 N.E. 2d 889 (1984)

6. Force and a Pattern of Sexual Abuse.

A pattern of sexual abuse is insufficient to establish the element of force. Of significance is the victim's testimony: "He didn't force me, but he – it had started from such a long time back, that the way he had started with me, I felt like if I didn't do it that I would be punished, 'cause every time that he asked me to do something and I wouldn't, it would be held against me. I wouldn't be able to go out. I would be limited. So, I felt like if I didn't do it, I would be punished for it." [490]

7. Rape Shield Law.

R.C. 2907.02(D) and R.C. 2907.05(D), the so-called rape shield provisions prohibits the admission of evidence regarding the reputation and prior sexual activities of the victim or the defendant unless the evidence involves the origin of semen, pregnancy, or disease, or the victim's past sexual activity with the offender, and only to the extent that the court finds that the evidence is material to a fact at issue in the case, and that its inflammatory or prejudicial nature does not outweigh its probative value.

8. Past Sexual Relations with the Victim.

Where the offender attempted to introduce evidence of past sexual conduct with the victim, such evidence was properly

---

[490] *State v. Schaim*, 65 Ohio St.3d 51, 600 N.E.2d 661 (1992).

excluded because the offender's defense was not that the victim consented, but that he was not present.[491]

This holding was based on R.C. 2907.02 (D)'s requirement that the proffered evidence be "material to a fact at issue in the case, and that its inflammatory or prejudicial nature does not outweigh its probative value." The court held: "In this posture, [attempted admission of a past sexual relationship where the defense was that he was not present] appellant's proffered evidence of his alleged past sexual relationships with the victim did not tend to prove or disprove a disputed fact of consequence in the cause." The proffered evidence was simply not material to an alibi defense.

9. In Camera Hearing.

Although R.C. 2907.02(E) requires an in-camera hearing before testimony can be received regarding past sexual history of the victim or the defendant. This right to a hearing can be waived if not asserted prior to trial, or during trial with good cause shown. A failure by the trial court to hold the hearing can also be non-prejudicial where the testimony is merely corroborative or cumulative.[492]

---

[491] *State v. Graham*, 58 Ohio St. 2d 350, 390 N. E. 2d 805 (1979).

[492] *State v. Acre*, 6 Ohio St 3d 140, 451 N.E. 2d 802 (1983).

10. Sexual Activity with Another.

The admissibility of evidence of sexual activity with another is similarly not allowed even though the hospital records contradict the victim's testimony during voir dire, pursuant to R.C. 2907.02(E)

In *State v. Ferguson,*[493] the victim's hospital records revealed that she had sexual intercourse with another person approximately two days before she was raped. During voir dire, she testified that she did not have sexual relations with anyone for 10 days prior to the rape. Since, in this case, there was no issue as to origin of semen, pregnancy or disease, the trial court properly refused to allow the introduction of the evidence of the victim's past sexual activity. This court held: "In the case a bar appellee is seeking to introduce evidence of the victim's prior sexual activity with one other than appellee in an attempt to impeach her credibility. R.C. 2907. 02 clearly prohibits such an impeachment technique * * *." The issue in this case was whether the victim consented to sexual relations with the offender. Whether or not she had sexual relations with another 2 or 10 days later was not material."

11. Where the Victim is a Prostitute.

In *State v. Gardner,* the defendant was not permitted to introduce evidence that the victim was a prostitute. "Evidence that the complainant had a reputation as a prostitute is not sufficiently probative of consent to outweigh the state's legitimate interest in excluding the testimony, at least where there is no suggestion in the record that financial arrangements were entered into for sexual activiti~~es in this instance." Since t~~he fact of prostitution was a

[493] *State v. Ferguson,* 5 Ohio St. 3d 160, 450 N. E 2d 265 (1983).

collateral matter, the defense was not permitted to use it for impeachment. [494]

12. Sexual History as Admissible Evidence.

Where the contested proffered sexual history evidence is not admitted to merely impeach the victim's credibility, it may, in some instances, be admissible.

In *State v. Williams*,[495] appellant's defense was consent. On direct examination, the victim testified that she never had previous sexual intercourse with the appellant. She further testified that she did not have sex with men because she was gay. Appellant attempted to introduce evidence through a defense witness who would testify that he had sex with the victim in the past. In finding that the trial court erred in not allowing the evidence, the court distinguished Gardner, supra., "* * *[In Gardner] the excluded evidence was designed to merely impeach the victim' credibility, and thus had no probative value as to the alleged rape itself. However, here * * * the proffered evidence has a more important purpose, which is to <u>negate the implied establishment of an element of the crime charged.</u> For this reason, the probative value of the testimony outweighs any interest that state has in exclusion." (Emphasis added)

Since the state introduced this testimony inferring lack of consent, the defense is permitted to counter it. The court further allowed the introduction of this evidence per Evid. R. 608 (B)

---

[494] *State v. Gardner,* 59 Ohio St. 2d 14, 391 N.E. 2d 337 (1979).

[495] *State v. Williams,* 21 Ohio St. 3d 33, 487 N.E. 2d 560 (1986).

where specific instances of the conduct of witness, for the purpose of attacking or supporting his credibility * * * may not be proved by extrinsic evidence. However, since the rule is intended to prohibit the introduction of non-probative evidence, "* * * the proffered evidence in this case was probative of the factual issue of consent, and is offered for more than mere impeachment of credibility, Evid. R. 608 (B) does not bar its admissibility."

13. Sufficiency of Evidence.

Because of the state's burden of proof in rape prosecutions, it is impermissible to draw inferences as to the establishment of the elements of rape where the victim's testimony regarding the sexual act was: "* * * and then we had intercourse a couple of times." The court found this evidence insufficient because "the victim did not testify we had *sexual* intercourse, nor did the victim testify as to any degree of penetration.

"In order to sustain a conviction on rape charges predicated on either vagina or anal intercourse, the state is required to establish beyond a reasonable doubt that the accused and the victim actually engaged in vaginal or anal intercourse under R.C. 2901.01(A), the state may establish vaginal or anal intercourse by proving the slightest degree of penetration." [496]

14. Evidence of Possible Civil Suit.

Evid. R. 611(B) provides that cross-examination shall be permitted on all relevant matters and matters affecting credibility."

[496] *State v. Ferguson*, 5 Ohio St. 3d 160, 450 N.E. 2d 265 (1983).

"Trial court abused its discretion in refusing to allow evidence of the contemplated civil suit. We hold: accused is permitted to cross-examine the prosecuting witness as to the witness' pending or contemplated civil action * * *" [497]

15. Type of Rape.

The trier of fact is not required to make a specific finding as to what type of rape was committed, vaginal, anal, fellatio, or cunnilingus. "The fact that some jurors might have found that appellant committed one, but not the other type of rape in no way reduces that reliability of appellant's conviction, because a finding of either type of conduct is sufficient to establish the fact of rape in Ohio." [498]

Here appellant argued that the jury should have been given a specific instruction as to whether appellant committed vaginal rape, anal rape, or both.

16. Multiple Offenses.

If a victim is raped vaginally as well as by way of fellatio, the offender can be properly convicted of two separate offenses of rape. "* * * each defendant by engaging in fellatio followed immediately by vaginal intercourse committed 'two * * * offenses of * * * similar animus as to each * * *' within the meaning of division one of R.C. 2941.25." [499]

[497] *Ibid.*

[498] Ibid.

[499] *State v. Barnes*, 68 Ohio St. 2d 13, 427 N.E. 2d 517 (1981). See also *State v. Ferguson, supra.*

17. Circumstantial Evidence of Rape and Attempted Rape.

In *State v. Heinish*, the court found insufficient evidence of attempted rape where the murder victim was found with her blue jeans partially unzipped, her blouse partially up from her waist, and where she was wearing no underwear or shoes. A saliva stain was found on the outside of her blue jeans, which could have been placed by the defendant as well as by 32% of the Caucasian population.

"There is no evidence by itself sufficient to reach the threshold of a separate crime of attempted rape as opposed to gross sexual imposition." [500] But see, *State v. Durr*, where the victim's body was found nude from the waist down with no other physical evidence that a rape occurred due to the decomposition of the body.

There was however additional circumstantial evidence. The victim had been seen by the girlfriend of the defendant tied up in the back seat of his car. He told his girlfriend he had her in the back of his car tied up because "she would tell."

This additional evidence was sufficient so that "a rational trier of fact could have found the appellant guilty of rape beyond a reasonable doubt." [501]

---

[500] *State v.Heinish,* 50 Ohio St. 3d 231, 553 N.E. 2d 1026 (1990)

[501] *State v. Durr,* 58 Ohio St.3d 86, 568 N. E. 2d 674 (1991).

18. Adult Prosecuted for Rape that occurred when he was a Juvenile.

There is no violation of due process to try as an adult and sentence to life imprisonment a defendant who as a juvenile committed the crime at the age of 15, but was not prosecuted until reaching the age of twenty-one.

Hence, a juvenile offender who committed forcible rape of a child under the age of 13 was properly prosecuted as an adult and sentenced to life in prison.[502]

R.C. 2152.02 (C)(3) provides: any person, who while under eighteen years of age, commits an act that would be a felony if committed by an adult and who is not taken into custody or apprehended for that act until after the person attains twenty-one years of age is not a child in relation to that act."

Because of the clear intent of the above statute, a crime committed by a fifteen-year-old and not prosecuted until the offender was over twenty-one years old did not violate due process.

19. Sexual Predator Law Retroactivity.

Where a person convicted of rape is several years later classified, as a sexual predator, pursuant to the Sexual Offender Registration and Notification Law (SORN), there is no violation of

---

[502] *State v. Warren*, 118 Ohio St. 3d 200, 887 N.E. 2d 1145 (2008).

the Ex Post Facto Clause. SORN is civil in nature and it was the legislature's intent to make it retroactive.[503]

There is a violation of the double jeopardy clause where the trial court for the first time, classifies a defendant as a sex offender ten months after the original sentence. When a defendant is classified as a sex offender this classification by itself is punitive and hence raises double jeopardy issues if it is later added to a final sentence.

Hence where there is a disagreement as to whether a sexual act was consensual a hearing to determine this cannot be commenced ten months after the sentencing.

The trial courts original sentence was a final judgment that incorporated all of the relevant factors in regard to the punishment, including any possible classifications.[504]

Where a defendant has been convicted of a violation of R.C. 2950.05 for failure to notify the sheriff of a change of address. The law in effect at the time of the conviction controls the degree of felony for such failure. Hence, a defendant who has been convicted of the offense pursuant to Megan's law (a fourth-degree felony) cannot be charged with the penalty of the subsequent Adams Walsh Act (a first-degree felony).[505]

---

[503] *State v. Ferguson*,120 Ohio St. 3d 7, 896 N.E. 2d 110 (2008).

[504] State v. Raber, 134 Ohio St.3d 350, 2012-Ohio-5636.

[505] State v. Howard, 134 Ohio St.3d 467, 2012-Ohio-5738

If an offender who fails to register pursuant to Megan's Law and is indicted for a failure to register under the AWA even though the reclassification requirements were held unconstitutional. Since requirements in regard to giving 20 days' notice is the same under both acts, the defendant was properly indicted.[506]

20. Confrontation Clause.

Where a child rape victim is interviewed for the purpose of medical diagnoses and treatment and the victim is unavailable at trial the interviewer may testify as to the child's statement for this purpose. However, where the child has been interviewed pursuant to a criminal investigation, the confrontation clause comes into effect and the interviewer may not testify as to the child's statements. If the interview is of a dual purpose, the statement for medical diagnosis and treatment must be separated from the statements that are of a forensic capacity with the medical statements being admitted and the forensic portions excluded.[507]

A teacher has a dual role in regard to inquiring into possible child abuse. If the inquiry is of a non-emergency nature, the teacher becomes an agent of law enforcement and, as a result, any hearsay testimony of that teacher becomes a confrontation clause issue.[508]

---

[506] State v. Brunning, 134 Ohio St.3d 438, 2012-Ohio-5752

[507] State v. Arnold, 126 Ohio St.3d 290, 2010-Ohio-2742

[508] State v. Clark, Slip Opinion No. 2013-Ohio-4731

21. Preindictment delay.

As a result of recent dna analysis of cold cases several indictments have be secured for cases that were over twenty years old. This court has articulated the criterial to be used to determine if such prosecutions can go forward or whether such delays are a due process violation.

This case found that the court of appeals that dismissed such a case used an improper standard in analyzing these cases.

Preindictment delay violates due process only when 1. It is unjustified and 2. Where actual prejudice is present.

As a result, the defendant has the burden of showing actual prejudice, if so the state then must show a justifiable reason for delay.

The court of appeals erred in focusing on the prosecution delay instead of first determining if actual prejudice existed.

The loss of witnesses, the possibility that memories will fade, or that evidence may be lost "is not sufficient to establish actual prejudice." Per se but may be as in the case State v. Luck, 15 Ohio St. 3d 150, 472 N.E. 2d. 1097.[509]

22. Children Issues.

Although this court in State. v. Young held used a narrower definition of nudity That R.C. 2907.323(A)(1). In which it must be shown that there was focus on the genital and a lewd depiction, the broader definition of R.C. 2907.323(A)(1). Applies in a prosecution for the use of children in nude videos etc.[510]

---

[509] State v. Jones, Slip Opinion No. 2016-Ohio-5105.

[510] State v. Martin, Slip Opinion No. 2016-Ohio-7196.

CHAPTER 45

Trafficking in Drugs

1. Where the Drugs Sold are not Controlled Substances.
2. Failure of the indictment to Name the Controlled Substance.
3. Trafficking by a Physician.
4. No duty to Separate Portions of Marijuana before Weighing.
5. Selling Counterfeit Substances.
6. Improper Amendment of the Indictment.
7. Waiver of Testimony of Lab Analyst.
8. Transporting Drugs into a Detention Facility.

1. Where the Drugs Sold Are Not Controlled Substances.

One can be convicted of trafficking in drugs even though the drugs sold were not actually controlled substances. In *State v. Scott*, the defendant arranged a drug transaction with an uncover agent, the drugs sold were found to contain no controlled substances. The court focused on the language of R.C.

2925.03(A)(1) which prohibits sales as well as "offers to sell." The court rejected appellant's argument that a transfer must actually occur: "By using the phrase 'offer to sell' in the disjunctive with 'sell' throughout R.C. 2925.03, the General Assembly expressly and properly prohibited appellant's conduct as a form of trafficking in drugs." [511]

The court read the intent of R.C. 2925.03 to prohibit commerce in drugs and that "commerce" may consist of elements other than actual transfers. This is because other acts that are not transfers are prohibited such as financing, R.C. 2945.03(A)(8), production R.C. 2925.03(A) and transportation and distribution R.C. 2925.03(A)(2). Since the above are trafficking offenses so is an offer to sell. Further evidence to support this ruling is that “offer to sell” is used in the disjunctive with “sell” illustrating a separate prohibition.

In *State v. Patterson*, the defendant who represented he was selling a controlled substance where he knew that it was not, failed in his argument that he could not have been convicted because he did not have the intent to sell a controlled substance. "One's understanding of the nature of the substance does not necessarily determine whether he or she knowingly offered to sell a controlled substance. We will not read the additional element of knowledge of the nature of the substance into R.C. 2925.03 (A)(1), (5), or (7)." [512]

The crucial factor is whether the offender knowingly offered to sell a controlled substance, not whether he had knowledge of the actual composition of the substance.

---

[511] *State v. Scott,* 69 Ohio St. 2d 439, 432 N.E. 2d 798 (1982).

[512] *State v. Patterson,* 69 Ohio St. 2d 445, 432 N.E. 2d 802 (1982).

2. Failure of the indictment to Name the Controlled Substance.

Where an indictment fails to name the controlled substance, that indictment is defective and cannot be corrected by the trial court under Crim. R. 7(D) because it would be an improper change in the name or identity of the crime. This is so because under R.C. 2925.03(A)(8) the severity of the crime is dependent upon the type of drug involved. As such, the type of controlled substance involved constitutes an essential element of the crime, which must be included in the indictment.

However, where an indictment for drug trafficking does not name the specific drug involved but names the correct schedule thereby informing he defendant of the severity of the crime such as whether or not a trafficking offense is alleged, such indictment is sufficient. Further, with the availability of a bill of particulars the defendant has an opportunity to be adequately informed of the specific drug involved.[513]

Where the jury verdict form does not specify the drug of which the defendant is charged with possessing, but where the indictment, jury instructions, and the evidence presented at trial correctly specify the drug, the defendant has sufficient notice and can be properly convicted of the crime.[514]

---

[513] *State v. Jackson*, 134 Ohio St.3d 184, 2012-Ohio-5561

[514] *State v. Efford*, 132 Ohio St.3d 159, 2012-Ohio-2224

R.C. 2925.11E(1)(a) imposes a mandatory fine for certain drug trafficking violations that are first, second or third degree felonies. And R.C. 2929.18(B)(1) imposes a mandatory fine for certain felonies in general. Both statutes provide for waivers of this mandatory fine. This mandatory fine can be waived if the defendant files an affidavit of indigency prior to sentencing. Where the trial court waives the fine before an affidavit of indigency is filed that part of the sentence is void. This does not mean however that the entire sentence is void and may be appealed. Only the failure to properly waive the mandatory fine can be appealed.[515]

3. Trafficking by a Physician.

Even though a physician may not actually sell a controlled substance, he is in violation of R.C. 2925.03(A) (1) if he unlawfully issues a prescription for a controlled substance not in the course of bona fide treatment of a patient. Sale as defined in R.C. 3719.01(E)(E) includes delivery, barter, exchange, transfer, gift, or offer thereof. "When a doctor sells a prescription for the drug or sells the drug itself, the result is the same: Unlawful commerce of a controlled substance." [516]

In *State v. McCarthy*, the trial court erred in refusing to give a requested jury instruction that would have permitted the jury to consider the subjective state of mind of the defendant physician when determining whether the drugs administered were for "bona fide" medical treatment of a patient. The court held that the jury instruction given by the trial court had the effect of limiting its

[515] State v. Moore, 135 Ohio St.3d 151, 2012-Ohio-5479

[516] *State v. Sway*, 15 Ohio St 3d 115, 472 N.E. 2d 1065 (1984).

inquiry as to whether the physician had complied with the statutes and rules governing the distribution of controlled substances.

Had the instruction included a definition of "bona fide" the subjective state of mind of the defendant could have been considered in determining whether his conduct was criminal. In other words, a crime is not necessarily committed merely by the defendant's deviation from the statute and rules. The court held that the definition of the term *bona fide* is as legally important as are the terms "knowingly," intentionally" and "purposely." [517]

The *McCarthy* court further stated: "Consequently, inasmuch as the trial court did not charge the jury with the proposed instruction proffered by defendant, which would have permitted the jury to consider defendant's subjective state of mind in considering the criminality, or lack thereof, of defendant's conduct, the court of appeals correctly reversed the multiple convictions rendered against defendant."

Where a health care provider is charged with trafficking in drugs the burden of proof that he did not follow the guidelines for distributing drugs is on the prosecution and it is not an affirmative defense that the defendant must establish. [518]

4. No duty to Separate Portions of Marijuana before Weighing.

When determining the weight of marijuana, the state has no duty to separate any portion of the plant.[519]

---

[517] *State v. McCarthy,* 65 Ohio St. 3d 589, 605 N.E. 2d 911 (1992).

[518] *State v. Nucklos*, 121 Ohio St. 3d 322, 2009-Ohio-742.

The affirmative defense of personal use may not be asserted where the defendant possesses more than three times the bulk amount since there is a presumption that the possession of three times the bulk amount cannot be for personal use. [520]

In cocaine possession offenses, the weight of the substance must be separated from fillers.[521]

5. Selling Counterfeit Substances.

Where a person knowingly sells a counterfeit substance, that person may be charged with knowingly selling or offering to sell a controlled substance under 2925.02(A)(1) *and* also knowingly selling or offering to sell a counterfeit controlled substance under R.C. 2925.37(B) since these offenses are not allied offenses of similar import. In the case of a person who was found to knowingly offer to sell Percodan, a controlled substance, he violated (A)(1), and also since it was shown that he knew the substance was counterfeit he violated 37(B).[522]

Where a defendant has been convicted of selling a controlled substance analog before such sales were illegal under Title 29, The defendant was nevertheless properly convicted. R.C.

[519] *State v. Wolpe,* 11 Ohio S t. 3d 50, 463 N.E. 2d 384 (1984).

[520] *State v. Davis*, 16 Ohio St. 3d 34, 476 N.E. 2d 655 (1985).

[521] State v. Gonzales, Slip Opinion No. 2016-Ohio-8319.

[522] *State v.Mughni*, 33 Ohio St. 3d 65, 514 N.E. 2d 870 (1987).

3719.013 enacted prior to the above has treated analogs as controlled substances.[523]

6. Improper Amendment of the Indictment.

A trial court cannot amend the indictment in a prosecution for possession of controlled substances where the amendment changes the identity of the crime. In *State v. Davis*, the court amended the indictment from a charge alleging the defendant possessed less than the bulk amount to possession of five times but less than fifty times the bulk amount of Oxycontin. This amendment changed the identity of the crime and had the effect of convicting the defendant of a crime of which the grand jury did indict him. Not only was this a violation Crim. R. 7(D), it was also plain error.[524]

7. Waiver of Testimony of Lab Analyst.

Where a laboratory analysis of drugs possessed by the defendant was admitted into evidence pursuant to.R.C. 2925.51 and where defense counsel failed to demand the testimony of the

---

[523] State v. Shalish, Slip Opinion No. 2016-Ohio-8358.

[524] *State v. Davis*, 121 Ohio St. 3d 239, 903 N.E. 2d 609 (2008).

analyst within seven days of receiving the report pursuant to the requirements R.C. 2925.51(C), the report is properly admitted and is prima facie evidence of the identity and weight of the drugs.

The failure to demand the testimony of the lab analyst constitutes a waiver of the right to cross-examine the analyst. This waiver of confrontation rights pursuant to the 6th amendment can be made by defense counsel. It does not have to be made directly by the defendant. There is a presumption that defense counsel is acting in the best interest of the client and the failure to demand may be the result of trial strategy.

Further, records of scientific tests are not testimonial implying confrontational rights as defined by Crawford v. Washington. State v. Crager 116 Ohio St. 3d 369, 2007-Ohio-6840, 879 N.E. 2d 745. [525]

8. Transporting Drugs into a Detention Facility.

A person in custody who is taken into a detention facility with drugs of abuse on his person is deemed to have voluntarily taken the drugs into the facility. Here the defendant denied when asked if he had any drugs on him before he was taken into the facility. [526]

---

[525] *State v. Pasqualone* 2009-Ohio-315, 121 Ohio St. 3d 186.

[526] *State v. Cargile*, 123 Ohio St. 3d 343, 2009-Ohio-4939.

CHAPTER 46

Theft

Under the principal that possession in property is the interest that is protected by the theft statute, pursuant to R.C. 2913.02(D),* * * "a thief can steal from another thief." "Title ownership in a specific person other than the defendant is not an element of a theft offense." * * * "The identity of the holder of a certificate of title is not the controlling issue. The issue is whether the defendant had lawful possession of the vehicle" [527]

1. Theft by Deception.

A theft does not have to occur by the traditional method of taking property from another. A theft can occur by deception. For instance, in the case of a construction contractor, theft by

[527] *State v. Rhodes*, 2 Ohio St. 3d 74, 442 N.E. 2d 1299 (1982).

deception can be committed where the contractor fails to complete the work he agreed to perform; and who also uses inferior materials and charges for nonexistent items or otherwise has failed to repair as contracted. "In the case at bar, the state's witnesses testified that Eliott represented to the city that he had completed work under a contract with the city which in fact, was not completed and received payment for." [528]

2. Determination of Value.

The determination of value of the object of the theft is important because the degree of the crime, and hence the penalty is dependent on the value of the item stolen.

In determining the value of stolen goods R.C. 2913.61 (D) (1), (2), and (3) describe three methods that correspond to the type of item stolen. (D)(1) covers heirlooms, collector's items, which are to be valued in regard to the amount of money that would compensate the owner for the loss. (D)(2) covers personal effects. Their value is the cost of replacing the stolen item with new property of like kind and quality. (D)(3) covers real or personal property not covered under the previous sections. Its value is the fair market value.

In a robbery prosecution where the defendant was found guilty of the lesser included offense of theft. It was proper for the trial court to find the defendant guilty of a fifth-degree felony based on its determination that the value of the stolen property was

[528] *State v. Jacobozzi,* 6 Ohio St. 3d 86, 451 N.E. 2d 749 (1983).

$500.00 or more. This is true even though the indictment did not specify the value of the subject of the theft. The determination of the value of the stolen goods is a special finding and is not an element of theft.[529]

The relationship between the value of the property and the degree of the crime has been amended; values that were once felonies are now misdemeanors[530]

3. Personal Effects.

Where the defendant was indicted for the theft of automobile parts from the car of the victim, it was error to calculate the value of the stolen goods under (D)(2) as personal effects since the definition of personal effects "is not intended to cover all items of tangible property having some personal use, but is

limited to articles having an intimate association with the owner. It does not encompass batteries, radiators or other equipment removed from the owner's automobile." [531]

4. Sales Tax.

Sales tax may be added when determining the cost of replacement of stolen household goods. A stolen radar detector was found to be a personal effect for replacement purposes, but it was error to add the sales tax since the cost of replacement of the radar detector was 295.00,

---

[529] *State v. Smith*, 121 Ohio St. 3d 409, 2009-Ohio-787.

[530] State v. Taylor, 138 Ohio St. 3d 194, 2014-Ohio-460.

[531] *State v. Chaney*,11 Ohio St. 3d 208, 465 N.E. 2d 53 (1984).

which would make the theft a misdemeanor, but adding the sales tax made it a felony. [532]

The use of state sales tax would be unconstitutional because the Ohio Constitution requires that all laws have a uniform operation throughout the state, and since the tax is subject to several exemptions, its application would be inconsistent.

5. Theft by Threat.

Theft by threat is a crime of lesser degree of robbery and under the right circumstances, in a robbery prosecution, the jury can be instructed to consider theft by threat. "It was possible for the jury to find appellee not to have threatened the immediate use of force but to have employed a threat of a lesser degree * * * under these circumstances the trial court was required to give the instruction on the lesser included offense." [533]

6. Aiders and Abettors.

An aider and abettor can be convicted of theft by deception even though there is no proof that the principal committed the crime. Aiding and abetting is a separate substantive offense.[534]

---

[532] *State v. Adams*, 39 Ohio St. 3d 186, 529 N.E. 2d 1264 (1988).

[533] *State v. Davis*, 6 Ohio St.3d 91, 451 N.E.2d 772 (1983).

[534] *State v. Graven*, 52 Ohio St. 2d 112, 369 N.E. 2d 1205 (1977).

7. Attempted Theft.

It is reasonable to assume that an attempted theft occurred where the victim's bedroom was in disarray, her purse and wallet were open, and the bedroom closet was open and in disorder.[535]

[535] *State v. Davis*, 56 Ohio St. 2d 51, 381 N.E. 2d 641 (1978).

CHAPTER 47

Voluntary Manslaughter

1. Passion or Rage.
2. Extreme Emotional Stress.

R.C. 2903.03 provides that no person, while under the influence of sudden passion or in a fit of rage, either of which is brought on by serious provocation occasioned by the victim that is reasonably sufficient to incite the person into using deadly force, shall knowingly cause the death of another.

1. Passion or Rage.

"Where one inflicts a mortal wound in a sudden affray or in heat of blood or passion, without time for reflection or the passion to cool, that person is guilty of manslaughter. If, however, it appears that the accused reflected, deliberated, or cooled between the time of provocation, and the time the fatal stroke was given, or if in legal presumption there was time of opportunity for cooling, the killing was done with malice and intent to kill." [536]

---

[536] *State v. Robinson,*161 Ohio St. 213, 118 N.E. 2d 517 (1954).

It is a question for the trier of fact to determine whether a killing was done in the heat of passion, or whether there has been sufficient time elapsed for a period of reflection before the killing.

2. Extreme Emotional Stress.

In State v. Pierce, the court ruled that, as a matter of law, extreme emotion stress was not established. Here the defendant killed his ex-wife's boyfriend the day after they had a telephone conversation in which the defendant supposedly agreed to fight the victim. "Given the period of time which elapsed between these telephone conversations and the killing on the next morning * * *such killing was not, as a matter of law, committed under extreme emotional stress, since no finder of fact could possibly conclude that the killing was performed under the influence of sudden passion or in the heat of blood, without time and opportunity for reflection or for passions to cool." [537]

Extreme emotional stress is not an element of voluntary manslaughter "it is a circumstance which mitigated a defendant's culpability." *Pierce, supra.*

Extreme emotional stress need not be established beyond a reasonable doubt or by a preponderance of evidence in order for a jury to consider it. Where <u>some</u> evidence is produced to show extreme emotional stress, the lesser-included offense of voluntary manslaughter <u>must be charged</u>.

The committee comment to this statute states that emotional stress built up over a period of time can be sufficient to establish voluntary manslaughter, contrary to the committee comment the court held:

---

[537] *State v. Pierce,* 64 Ohio St. 2d 281, 414 N.E. 2d 1038 (1980).

"To treat a deliberate, calculated homicide as voluntary manslaughter because extreme emotional stress brought on by the requisite provocation caused the laying of plans for the killing, as well as the killing itself, is a grave step which we do not believe the General Assembly meant to take. It is clear that a reading of the statute and the history of voluntary manslaughter the requirement has always been a killing under the heat of passion from immediate provocation. A killing brought about by prolonged stress and provocation is simply a planned murder which would be prior calculation and design."

Where there is some evidence that the defendant was "panicked" at the time he killed, coupled with the knowledge that his adversary had brought a gun into the fray, and the gun was fired was sufficient evidence to charge a jury to consider the element of extreme emotional stress.[538]

---

[538] *State v. Soloman*, 66 Ohio St. 2d 214, 421 N. E. 2d 139 (1981).

CHAPTER 48

Gross Sexual Imposition and Sexual Battery.

Gross sexual imposition is a lesser-included offense of rape. However, where the defendant denies participation in the offense of rape he or she is not entitled to a charge of gross sexual imposition. Otherwise, it would become necessary for the jury to disbelieve the victim as to conduct but to find contact.

"* * * [T]he state's entire case depended on the credibility which the jury attached to the girl's testimony as to penetration." There was testimony separate of gross sexual imposition that was not charged. However, this testimony was not connected with any of the specific acts of penetration. [539]

1 .Sufficiency of Evidence.

There is sufficient evidence for a conviction of gross sexual imposition where the victim testified that her father touched her buttocks, "although barely so." This testimony was coupled with testimony from another daughter that the father used backrubs as a prelude to sexual contact.[540]

---

[539] *State v. Johnson* 36 Ohio St.3d 224, 522 N.E.2d 1082 (1988).

R.C. 2907.03(A) (13) is unconstitutional violation of equal protection. In that it imposes strict liability on peace officers even off-duty acts.

Sexual battery prosecutions are authorized where there is an authoritarian relationship, but where an off-duty peace officer is subject to strict liability for engaging in sex with a minor where there is no authoritarian relationship is unconstitutional.[541]

The mens rea requirement of gross sexual imposition pursuant to R.C. 2907.05 is "purpose." The statute is one of strict liability and therefore it is not necessary for the indictment to state the mens rea.[542]

---

540 *State v. Schaim*, 65 Ohio St.3d 51, 600 N.E.2d 661 (1992).

541 State v. Mole, Slip Opinion No. 2016-Ohio-5124.

542 *State v. Dunlap*, 129 Ohio S. 3d 461, 2011-Ohio-4111.

CHAPTER 49

Disruption of Public Services.

A conviction under R.C. 2909.04(A)(3) for the disruption of public services may be obtained by the simple act of damaging a private telephone or cell phone. There is no requirement that a "large scale" disruption occur. If an individual is in the process of calling for help or assistance to a public service agency anyone who, in attempting to prevent that person from connecting to the agency, destroys the phone, is liable. [543]

[543] *State v.Robinson*, 124 Ohio St. 3d 76, 2009-Ohio-5937.

CHAPTER 50

Intimidation of a Witness.

A successful prosecution for witness intimidation must establish that the intimidation occurred after the commencement of criminal proceedings, not merely after the criminal act. Where witnesses to a crime are threatened before the crime has been reported and no prosecution or investigation has been initiated, the person who made the threats cannot be convicted under this statute. However, these facts do not prevent the defendant from being convicted of aggravated menacing (See R.C. 2903.21).

It is important to contrast this holding with the intimidation of a victim of a crime. Threats to a victim of a crime are a violation immediately after the crime is committed.[544]

A police officer who uses his position to intimidate a witness with false arrests and lies is guilty of intimidation.

Here the police office took into custody a person he knew to not be guilty. The officer threatened the person that his mother would be charged with a crime if he did not confess to the crime. The officer then took the false confession and used it to arrest the

[544] State v. Malone, 122 Ohio St. 3d 244, 2009-Ohio-310. See also State v. Davis, 132 Ohio St.3d 25, 2012-Ohio-1654.

person. The police officer then used the false confession to pursue the mother of the accused and told her that if she complied with his request for sex he would release her son.

"R.C. 2921.03 makes it unlawful for a person to knowingly take certain actions to influence, intimidate, or hinder a witness, a party official, or a public servant in the discharge of a duty. R.C. 2921.03(A). The ways in which it is illegal to exert such improper influence are by knowingly (1) using force, (2) unlawfully threatening harm against any person or property, or (3) using a materially false or fraudulent writing in any way with malice, bad faith, wantonness, or recklessness."[545]

---

545 *State v. Steele,* Slip Opinion No. 2013-Ohio-2470

PART FOUR: DEFENSES

CHAPTER 51

Accident as A Defense.

"How should a man be held to contemplate the consequences of an act when he did not contemplate the act itself?" Thus, the court in *Jones v. State*, summarized the theory of accident as a defense. This lack of contemplation of the "act" on the part of the accused is directly related to whether that person possessed *criminal intent.* [546]

Where a defendant asserts accident as a defense, the burden of proof does not shift to the defendant. By asserting this defense, the defendant is, in effect, alleging that the state has not proved the essential element of criminal intent.

In *Jones*, the court, in reversing the murder conviction, held that the following jury instruction should have been given: "The burden of proof is not in this case upon the defendant to show that the gun was discharged by accident, or force exerted by other persons than the defendant, but that it is incumbent upon the state to establish, to the satisfaction of the jury, and beyond a reasonable doubt, that the defendant deliberately discharged the gun with premeditation and motive before you can find him guilty of murder in the first degree."

[546] *Jones v. State*, 51 Ohio St. 331, 38 N.E. 79 (1894).

Accident therefore is not an affirmative defense that must be proven by a preponderance of the evidence. The trial court committed reversible error where it charged the jury that the defense of accident must be proven by a preponderance of the evidence.[547]

This court has, in the past, been liberal in allowing the defendant to prove the defense of accident. In *Jones, supra.* The defendant was indicted for shooting his son to death. The defendant attempted to admit evidence of the bad character of a married woman with whom his son was allegedly involved. This evidence was intended to show the natural feelings of love the father had towards his son. Such feelings would be contrary to intent to kill his son. In addition, the trial court should have allowed evidence of the character of the woman's husband to support the reason the defendant brought the gun to the confrontation: not to kill his son, but because he feared the husband would resist him. Because the above evidence would tend to show the defendant's state of mind at the time of the homicide, it could have supported his accident defense.

---

[547] See also, *State v. Poole*, 33 Ohio St. 2d 18, 294 N.E. 2d 888 (1973) where the trial court erred by requiring the defendant to prove accident by a preponderance of evidence.

CHAPTER 52

Alibi

1. **Alibi Procedurally.**
2. **Good Faith Failure to File Notice.**
3. **Bad Faith in filing Notice.**

Where a defendant raises the defense of alibi, he "tenders proof that the place at which he was at the time of the commission of the alleged crime at least raises a reasonable doubt that he committed the crime, either as a principal, or as an aider and abettor." [548]

The defendant is not required to established an alibi by any specific burden of proof. It is sufficient only that *some* evidence be presented, in the trial court's view, that tends to establish the alibi. Once sufficient evidence is presented, the burden shifts to the state, which is required to show the defendant's presence at the scene of the offense.

Accordingly, it is error where a trial court charges the jury that, in order to consider the defense of alibi, the evidence supporting the claim must outweigh the evidence opposing it.[549]

---

[548] *State v. Norman* 103 Ohio St. 541, 134 N. E. 474 (1921).

[549] *Walters v. State*, 39 Ohio St. 215 (1883).

The Walters court held: 1. the burden of proof does not change when alibi is presented. 2. The jury may acquit the defendant because of the alibi evidence *even if it finds that alibi was not fully established.*

Alibi Procedurally.

"The purpose of pretrial discovery rules such as the alibi notice requirement of Crim. R. 12.1 is to insure a fair trial for both the state and the defendant." *State v. Smith.*[550]

Crim. R. 12.1 requires a defendant, as a prerequisite to an attempt to establish an alibi, to file in writing not less than seven days before trial and serve on the prosecution a notice of alibi stating the place he or she claims to have been at the time of the offense.

2. Good Faith Failure to File Notice.

A good faith failure to give notice of alibi is not necessarily fatal to a defendant's ability to present an alibi defense. Where the defendant has failed to file the notice within the rule's time period, a trial court's denial of the defendant's presentation of alibi evidence can, in some circumstances, constitute an abuse of discretion.

In *Smith, supra,* the trial court abused its discretion in excluding evidence of the proffered alibi defense where the exclusion did not serve the "interest of justice." As the result *of Smith,* the principal emerges that where there is no showing of bad

[550] *State v. Smith*, 50 Ohio St. 2d 51, 362 N.E. 2d 988 (1977).

faith on the part of defense counsel in filing a timely notice of alibi, and where the prosecution was not surprised by the assertion of the alibi defense, the defense should be allowed to proceed with an alibi defense.

In *Smith*, the defendant attempted to introduce evidence of his whereabouts on the date of the crime. The trial court abused its discretion by not allowing the alibi testimony because it was clear that the state had foreknowledge that the testimony of the proposed alibi witnesses would be crucial because the state's evidence placed all of the witnesses at the scene of the crime.

In addition, there was no evidence that the state would have presented its case differently. The trial court also could have granted the defendant's request for extra time for the prosecution to prepare for these witnesses.

As a result of this ruling, the defendant and his girlfriend were only allowed to testify that they were not at the scene of the drug sale. Because they were not allowed to testify where they were at the time of the crime, this partial alibi testimony left the defendant in a position that was no better, or probably worse than if he had not asserted the alibi defense.

The court-imposed silence as to their whereabouts damaged the defendant's chances for a fair trial.

"[S]ince the alibi evidence was not withheld from the prosecution in bad faith, since it would not have surprised or otherwise prejudiced the prosecution, and since its admission was necessary under the facts of the instant cause to insure the defendant a fair trial, we find that the trial court's exclusion of that alibi testimony defeated the policy of justice and fair play."

3. Bad Faith in Filing Notice.

On the other hand, in another *Smith* case, the failure of defense counsel to file a notice of alibi was probably the result of a trial tactic, and the testimony of the alibi witnesses was properly excluded. "In this case, the prosecution was unaware of the identity of the alibi witnesses, it had no opportunity or motive to question these witnesses or to investigate the facts, and it would have suffered prejudice by the introduction of alibi testimony. Furthermore, there is some indication of proof that the alibi defense was withheld from the prosecution in bad faith, as a planned trial tactic." [551]

To conclude, although, the trial court has discretion to allow the presentation of an untimely alibi defense, that discretion must be tempered with the consideration of the interests of justice. Where the state is not surprised and not unduly burdened by a tardy alibi defense, the trial court may allow the presentation of the defense. On the other hand, any bad faith on the part of the defense should result in a denial of the opportunity to present the untimely alibi defense.

---

[551] *State v. Smith*, 17 Ohio St. 3d 98, 477 N.E. 2d 1128 (1985).

CHAPTER 53

Discriminatory Prosecution.

The defense of discriminatory prosecution may be established where it can be shown: "(1), that, while others similarly situated have not generally been proceeded against because of conduct of the type forming the basis of the charge against him (2), he [the defendant] had been singled out for prosecution, and (3), that the government's discriminatory selection of him for prosecution has been invidious or in bad faith, i.e., based upon such impermissible considerations as race, religion, or the desire to prevent his exercise of constitutional rights."[552]

In *Flynt*, pursuant to the above prerequisites, the defendant was indicted for, inter alia, pandering obscene magazines in violation of R.C. 2907.32(A)(2). The defendant failed to establish discriminatory prosecution even though those possessing other similar magazines were not indicted.

Legitimate reasons for not prosecuting all of the similar offenders can include the desire of the prosecutor to use the first prosecution as a test case. Further, there were other legitimate and nondiscriminatory reasons; one being that the defendant was an in-state business, because it was easier to prosecute an in-state business.

---

[552] *State v. Flynt*, 63 Ohio St. 2d 132, 407 N.E. 2d 15 (1980), quoting *United States v. Barrios* (C.A. 2, 1974), 501 F. 2d 1207.

To establish discriminatory prosecution the defendant must show that he or she alone would be prosecuted. "In order to sustain their burden, the defendants need to present testimony from those individuals responsible for dealing the intended course of future prosecutions."

CHAPTER 54

Entrapment.

"The defense of entrapment is established where the criminal design originates with the officials of the government, and they implant in the mind of an innocent person the disposition to commit the alleged offense and induce its commission in order to prosecute.[553] Entrapment is an affirmative defense.

1. Tests to Determine Entrapment.

There are two basic tests to determine whether entrapment has occurred, the *objective test* and the *subjective test*. This court has chosen to adopt the subjective test that the United States Supreme Court adopted in *Sorrells v. United States*,[554] and *Sherman v. United States*.[555] This subjective approach is known as the *Sherman-Sorrells* doctrine.

In the objective test, the conduct of the law enforcement person or its agent is examined in order to determine if such

[553] *State v. Doran*, 5 Ohio St.3d 187, 449 N.E. 2d 1295 (1983).

[554] *Sorrells v. United States,* 287 U.S. 435, 53 S. Ct. 210 (1932).

[555] *Sherman v. United States,* 356 U.S. 369, 2 L.Ed.848, 78 S.Ct. 819 (1958).

conduct would induce an ordinary law abiding citizen to commit a crime.

The subjective test focuses on the defendant's predisposition. The following factors are to be considered when applying the subjective test:

(1) the accused's previous involvement in criminal activity of the nature charged, (2) the accused's ready acquiescence to the inducements offered by the police, (3) the accused's expert knowledge in the area of the criminal activity charged, (4) the accused's ready access to contraband, and (5), the accused's willingness to involve himself in criminal activity.

The classic definition of entrapment can be found in" *Sorrells, supra.* "Entrapment is the conception, and it's planning of an offense by an officer, and his procurement of its commission by one who would not have perpetrated it except for the trickery, persuasion, or fraud of the officer.

Entrapment is an affirmative defense wherein the defendant has the burden of going forward, and of proving entrapment by a preponderance of the evidence.

Sherman and *Sorrells* both involved repeated attempts to induce the defendant to commit crimes by either an informant, or a law enforcement officer.

In *Sherman*, a government informer met the defendant at a doctor's office where he was receiving treatment for a drug addiction, the informant made many requests until the defendant agreed to sell him drugs. In *Sorrells* a prohibition agent repeatedly solicited the defendant.

In *Doran, supra.*, the leading Ohio case on entrapment, the defendant met a woman hitchhiker who repeatedly told him she needed money to hire an attorney in order to regain the custody of her children from her husband. She told him if he could obtain drugs for her to sell that she could secure the funds she needed. She even introduced him to an undercover narcotics agent who posed as her boyfriend. After continuing to beg Doran to sell her drugs, so she could sell them herself, he finally agreed and sold her and her "boyfriend" drugs, on six occasions.

CHAPTER 55

Self Defense

Self-defense is an affirmative defense.[556] In order to established self-defense, the defendant must show:"(1) The slayer was not at fault in creating the situation giving rise to the affray; (2) The slayer had a bona fide belief that he was in imminent danger of death or great bodily harm and his only means of escape from such danger was in the use of such force; (3) the slayer must not have violated any duty to retreat or avoid the danger.[557]

In *Robbins*, the trial court properly refused to charge on self-defense where the appellant was the aggressor, striking the first blow and, even though the victim eventually began to choke the defendant, the defendant had several opportunities to retreat, but chose not to.

"The evidence in the record is clear that the appellant was at fault in creating the situation giving rise to the affray and nowhere in the record is there evidence indicating an attempt on

[556] *State v. Nolton*,19 Ohio St.2d 133, 249 N.E.2d 797 (1969).

[557] *State v. Robbins*, 58 Ohio St 2d 74, 388 N.E. 2d 755 (1979).

the part of the appellant to withdraw from the conflict and his intention of abandoning his action to do harm to the victim." [558]

In *State v. Martin*, the defendant argued that if self-defense is proved it would negate an essential element of *mens rea* of aggravated murder, and placing the burden of proof of self-defense on the defendant would require him to prove his innocence. [559]

This court held that R.C. 2901.05(A) places the burden of proving all elements of the offense charged, including the *mens rea* on the prosecution. The court has adopted the reasoning in *Patterson v. New York* where it was held that it would be too "onerous" to require the state to disprove the existence of self-defense, since the facts would be peculiarly within the knowledge of the defendant. See R.C. 2901.05(C)(2).

Self-defense is more than a denial or contradiction of the evidence, rather it admits the facts, and then asserts other facts claimed to eliminate the defendant's guilt. "The elements of the crime and the existence of self-defense are separate issues. Self-defense seeks to relieve the defendant from culpability rather than to negate an element of the offense charged." *Martin, supra.*

1. The Duty to Retreat.

One does not have a duty to retreat in his or her home, business, or automobile. A failure to give a special instruction

---

[558] *Robins, supra.*

[559] *State v. Martin,* 21 Ohio St. 3d 91, 488 N. E. 2d 166 (1986).

on the duty to retreat, however, can be harmless error under Crim. R. 52(A).

A duty to retreat does not apply to *any* place a person has a right to be.[560]

The trial court did not err in requiring the defendant to testify before he would charge the jury on self-defense. At the point in the trial when the request was made the court stated that the defendant had not established the defense. Since the defendant has the duty to offer evidence of self-defense, if necessary, he is required to waive his right to silence because he is in the best position to provide the evidence. *State v. Seliskar*.[561] See also *State v. Williford*, where the trial court should have charged the jury on self-defense of family members. [562]

The facts do not support a request to charge self-defense where the defendant does not present sufficient evidence that he feared assault from the victim, or where there was no overt act by which the defendant could "reasonably believe he was in imminent danger of death or great bodily harm." *State v. Rogers*.[563]

An aggressor may still claim self-defense if, after having provoked the action, withdraws in good faith as far as

---

[560] *State v. Jackson*, 22 Ohio St. 3d 281, 490 N.E. 2d 893 (1986).

[561] *State v. Seliskar,* 35 Ohio St. 2d 95, 298 N.E. 2d 582 (1973).

[562] *State v. Williford*, 49 Ohio St. 3d 247, 551 N.E. 2d 1279 (1990).

[563] *State v. Rogers,* 43 Ohio St. 2d 28, 330 N.E. 2d 674 (1975).

he can and clearly announces his withdrawal. *State v. Melchior*.[564]

[564] *State v. Melchior,* 56 Ohio St. 2d 15, 381 N.E. 2d 195 (1978).

CHAPTER 56

Battered Woman Syndrome.

Where a woman kills, or uses deadly force against her husband and asserts the affirmative defense of self-defense, that woman may, if the evidence supports it, claim she is a battered woman whereby she may introduce evidence in support of her claim of self-defense that, at the time she used the deadly force, she suffered from battered woman syndrome.

In *State v. Koss*, the defendant stated she killed her husband after she returned home around midnight, and while she was undressing, her husband "hauled off" and hit her. She remembers hearing a "noise or something," left the house and drove to another state.

At trial, several witnesses testified that her husband had beaten her in the past. She testified to various beatings including one where her husband attempted to smother her with a pillow, and another where he put a radio in the bathtub while she was taking a bath. She testified that she dropped a domestic violence charge against him three years ago, because he threatened to kill her children. She stated that she could not remember what happened after he hit her, but testified the killing was an accident. [565]

---

[565] *State v. Koss,* 49 Ohio St. 3d 213, 551 N.E. 2d 970 (1990).

The trial court prevented her from presenting evidence of battered woman syndrome. She was charged with murder, but was convicted of the lesser-included offense of voluntary manslaughter, and was sentenced to eight to twenty-five years in prison.

The court in reversing the conviction, overruled its decision in *State v. Thomas* [566] (in *Thomas*, the court held that battered wife syndrome cannot be admitted into evidence in support of a claim of self-defense.) In *Koss*, the court held, "Where the evidence establishes that a woman is a battered woman, and when an expert's qualified to testify about battered woman syndrome, expert testimony may be admitted to assist the trier of fact in determining whether the defendant acted in self-defense."

This court previously rejected this defense in *Thomas, supra.*, under the theory that the defense was not related to a science, profession or occupation to be "beyond the ken of an average person." However, expert testimony concerning battered wife syndrome has been found to be relevant to assist the trier of fact to determine whether the defendant had reasonable grounds to believe she was in imminent danger since self-defense in Ohio is based on the subjective test. See *State v. Smith.*[567]

Of significance is the court's finding that expert testimony can be used to rebut the general misconception of a battered woman. The misconceptions include:" she is free to leave the man," and, "she enjoys the beatings." This court referred to the New Jersey Supreme Court's opinion in *State v. Killy*, [568] [this

---

[566] *State v. Thomas,* 66 Ohio St. 2d 518, 423 N.E. 2d 137 (1981).

[567] *State v. Smith,*10 App. 3d 99, 460 N.E. 2d 693 (1983).

[568] *State v. Killy,* 97 N.J.178, 478 A. 2d 364 (1984).

evidence] "It is aimed at an area where the purported common knowledge of the jury may be very much mistaken, an area where juror's logic, drawn from their own experience may lead to a wholly incorrect conclusion, an area where expert knowledge would enable the jurors to disregard their prior conclusions as being common myths rather that common knowledge."

The battered woman syndrome is not a new defense, but is helpful in assisting the trier of fact to determine whether the defendant possessed a belief of imminent danger or great bodily harm causing her to believe that the use of deadly force was her only option.

It must be kept in mind that in order to admit testimony of battered syndrome, there must be: (1) a history of abuse, and (2) an imminent danger of death or great bodily harm under the subjective test, " * * * in that it [the history of abuse] formed the basis for the woman's perception of being in imminent danger of severe bodily harm or death at the hand of her partner', Brown, When Battered Woman Kill (1987), 175." [569]

Battered Woman Defense has since been codified in R.C. 2901.06.

Where the defendant introduces expert psychiatric testimony to support a batter-woman syndrome defense, the state is permitted to rebut that testimony with testimony of its own psychiatrist. There is no violation of the right against self-incrimination because by putting such evidence in its case in chief the defendant has thereby waived its right to silence because its own psychiatrist would have testified as to the defendant's statements thereby opening the door for rebuttal testimony.

---

[569] See also, *State v. Thomas*, 77 Ohio St. 3d 323, 673 N.E. 2d 1339 (1997).

When this defense becomes apparent the court may order the defendant to submit to a psychiatric examination.

Caveat, the state's psychiatrist may only testify in regard to whether he or she has an opinion as to whether the syndrome is present. He may not testify as to the veracity of the defendant. [570]

[570] *State v. Goff*, Slip Opinion No. 2010-Ohio-6317.

CHAPTER 57

Diminished Capacity.

1. Lack of Mental Capacity.
2. Diminished Capacity Evidence in Death Penalty Cases.

The diminished capacity defense, that the defendant lacked the mental capacity to form the specific mental state required for a particular crime is not recognized in Ohio. Accordingly, no expert testimony may be admitted in an attempt to establish this defense.[571]

This court has adopted the definition of diminished capacity as articulated by the court in United States v. Brawner (C.A.D.C. 1972) 471 F. 2d 969 at 998: "expert testimony as to defendant's abnormal mental condition may be received and considered, as tending to show, in a responsible way, that the defendant did not have the specific mental state required for a particular crime or degree of crime - even though he was aware that his act was wrongful and was able to control it, and hence was not entitled to complete exoneration."

The Wilcox decision was based primarily on the perceived inability of the jury to understand such testimony that oftentimes would consist of overly technical "line drawing" in which various

[571] *State v. Wilcox*, 70 Ohio St. 2d 185, 436 N.E. 2d 523 (1982).

degrees of fine-tuning as to capacity or incapacity of particular defendants would be presented. (But see the following section regarding intent.)

1. Lack of Mental Capacity.

A defendant may, however, present evidence that he lacked the mental capacity to form the required intent to commit the crime. This can be shown by evidence that the defendant was intoxicated, or mentally ill.[572]

"We hold therefore, that the partial defense of diminished capacity is not recognized in Ohio * * * and consequently, a defendant may not offer expert psychiatric testimony, unrelated to the *insanity defense*, to show that the defendant lacked the mental capacity to form the specific mental state required for a particular crime or degree of crime."

2. Diminished Capacity Evidence in Death Penalty Cases.

Diminished capacity expert testimony can be received in the mitigation portion of a death penalty prosecution. "Except in the

[572] See *State v. Fox*, 68 Ohio St. 2d 53, 428 N.E. 2d 410 (1981), and *State v. Jackson* (1972), 32 Ohio St. 2d 203. [note the burden on the defendant is not to show insanity by a preponderance of the evidence, but only to raise the issue. See Jackson re this burden] and *State v. Humphries*, 51 Ohio St.2d 95, 364 N.E.2d 1354 (1977).

mitigation phase of a trial, a defendant may not offer expert psychiatric testimony, unrelated to the insanity defense, to show that he lacked the mental capacity to form the specific mental state required for a particular crime."[573]

Where the defendant asserts a defense that is in the nature of a diminished capacity defense the trial court may not instruct the jury on diminished capacity unless there is a claim of not guilty by reason of insanity. It is well-established in Ohio that the diminished capacity defense is not viable.[574]

---

[573] *State v. Cooey* 46 Ohio St. 20, 544 N.E. 2d 895 (1989).

[574] *State v. Fulmer*, 117 Ohio St. 3d 319, 883 N.E. 2d 1052 (2008).

CHAPTER 58

Citizen Arrest Defense.

R.C. 2935.04 authorizes an arrest by "any person without a warrant: * * * whom he had reasonable cause to believe is guilty of the offense, and detain him until a warrant can be obtained." R.C. 2935.07 requires the person to "inform the person to be arrested of the intention to arrest him and the cause of the arrest."

The defense of using reasonable force to effect a citizen arrest necessarily involves, an allegation of excuse or justification, and is therefore, an affirmative defense * * * and must be proved by a preponderance of the evidence." [575]

---

[575] *State v. Rogers*, 43 Ohio St.2d 28, 330 N.E. 2d 674 (1975).

PART FIVE: CRIMINAL EVIDENCE

CHAPTER 59

The Common Law and the Rules of Evidence.

Pursuant to Evid. R.102, the Ohio Rules of Evidence are to be interpreted in accordance with the Common Law of Ohio, and are not to be a vehicle for expansive Interpretations. This philosophy is more limiting than Fed R. of Evid. 102, which was enacted to promote the growth and development of the law of evidence.[576]

This conservative stance is lessened, however with the principal that the common law is to be followed unless it clear that the particular rule of evidence shows that a change from the common law is intended.[577]

Further, the rules of evidence should not have the effect of impinging constitutional or statutory rights. This can be seen in State *v. Spikes*, where the court discussed the principal that rights

---

[576] *State v. Boston*, 46 Ohio St. 3d 108, 545 N.E. 2d 1220 (1989) (overruled on other grounds).

[577] See Also *State v. Ward*, 15 Ohio St. 3d 355, 474 N.E. 2d 300 (1984).

must not be impinged by the rules of evidence. *Spikes* contrasted the right to confrontation with the admission of medical records permitted by the Rules. [578]

[578] State *v. Spikes,* 67 Ohio St.2d 405, 423 N.E. 2d 1122 (1981).

CHAPTER 60

Challenge of Evidentiary Rulings.

Evid. R. 103 delineates the requirements that must be fulfilled to challenge an erroneous ruling by the trial court where the court either admits or excludes evidence. The key to this rule is that not all errors by the trial court in ruling on evidentiary matters are grounds for reversal unless a *substantial right* of the party has been affected. Nevertheless, even though a substantial right has been affected, the party affected must have objected to the admission of the contested evidence, and have stated the grounds for objection, unless it is apparent from the context.

Where the court excludes evidence, the party seeking to introduce the evidence must make an *offer of proof* unless the substance of the evidence was apparent from the context of the questions. The requirements of this rule do not apply where it can be established that the trial court's ruling constituted plain error that affected the substantial rights of the party.

CHAPTER 61

Offer of Proof.

Unless a trial court's error in denying admission of evidence is apparent on the record, no review will be permitted unless the proponent of the evidence has made an offer of proof, pursuant to Evid. R. 103(A)(2).

In *State v. Unger,* the defendant failed to apprise the trial court of the importance of the needed testimony by an offer of proof. The trial court refused to grant a continuance, and since the alleged error was not apparent on the record, and because the grant or denial of a continuance in left to the sound discretion of the trial court, the defendant's failure to apprise precluded review of this issue on appeal. [579]

"Evid. R. 103(A)(2) requires an offer of proof in order to preserve any error in excluding evidence, unless the excluded evidence is apparent in the record." [580] This rule requires a timely objection, or motion to strike, in the case of a ruling that allows the *admission* of evidence.

---

[579] *State v. Unger,* 67 Ohio St. 2d 65, 423 N.E. 2d 1078 (1981).

[580] *State v. Brooks*, 44 Ohio St. 3d 185, 542 N.E. 2d 636 (1989).

CHAPTER 62

Character Evidence.

Evid. R. 404 delineates the criteria to be used to determine the admission of character evidence. In general, the admission of a person's character is not permitted to prove the person acted in conformity with his character.

The defendant may offer evidence of his good character as part of his defense to a crime charged. However, once the defendant has "opened the door" to character evidence, the prosecutor is permitted to rebut this evidence of good character by introducing evidence of the accused "bad character."

In regard to the victim of the crime, Evid. R. 404(A)(1) permits the defendant to introduce into evidence character traits of the victim, with the prosecutor having the right to rebut this evidence. It should be noted that there are statutory exceptions to the admission of character evidence concerning rape, gross sexual imposition, and prostitution. Accordingly, the relevant statutes should be consulted.

Evid. R. 404(B) is probably given the most attention. This rule governs the admission of "other crimes, wrongs, or acts."

1. Initial Introduction of Bad Character.

"Generally, the prosecution is forbidden to introduce initially evidence of the accused's bad character, unless and until the accused gives evidence of his good character. Although character is not irrelevant, the danger of prejudice outweighs the probative value of such evidence. The danger of prejudice is highest when character is shown by other criminal acts, and hence the rule that the prosecution may not introduce evidence of other criminal acts of the accused unless the evidence is substantially relevant for some purpose other than to show a probability that the individual committed the crime because he is a man of criminal character." [581]

In *State v. Mann*, the trial court committed reversible error in admitting evidence that the defendant violated a civil injunction. The admission of the violation inferred that the defendant had a propensity to commit the crime charged. Here it was admitted to show the defendant was crime prone, and not for any of the enumerated purposes of Evid. R. 404(B), which allows admission of the evidence for proof of motive, opportunity, intent, preparation, plan, knowledge, identity, or absence of mistake or accident. [582]

Pursuant to R.C. 2945.59 and Evid.R. 404(B). It is proper to admit evidence of a defendant's prior criminal sexual activities with another person as long as the jury is instructed that the evidence cannot be used to prove character in violation of the rule.

---

[581] *State v. Lytle,* 48 Ohio St. 2d 391, 358 N.E. 2d 623 (1976), vacated, in part, on other grounds, 438 U.S. 910.

[582] *State v.Mann,* 9 Ohio St. 3d 34, 482 N.E. 2d 592 (1985).

In State v. Curry[583] this court held that the admission of this evidence is limited to the immediate background of the crime and the identity of the defendant. However, the above statute and rule were enacted after Curry. Whose language only spoke of the above limiting situations. Now, however the Court states that other allowable reasons exist to admit such evidence.

Specifically, in this case another victim of the defendant was permitted to testify that the defendant also sexually assaulted him in a similarly manner as the victim in the present case.

When considering admitting such evidence a trial court must use a three-step approach:

1. Determine relevancy. [Here the court found the evidence relevant because it showed the defendant's motive and plan].
2. Determine whether it is being admitted for a legitimate purpose or that it improperly tends to prove character of the defendant and that he acted in conformity with his bad character. [Here the court found that the limiting instruction was sufficient.]
3. 3. Determine whether the probative value outweighs the possible prejudice. [Here again the court found the limiting instruction sufficient.[584]
    a. Where under this rule improper evidence of other acts is admitted the standard of review for

[583] 43 Ohio St.2d 66, 330 N.E.2d 720 (1975)

[584] State v. Williams, 134 Ohio St.3d 521, 2012-Ohio-5695.

determining harmlessness is abuse of discretion of the trial court.

1. Criminal Rule 52(A) states that the error is harmless if it does not affect substantial rights. The burden is on the State to so prove. Once there is a finding that the evidence is prejudicial it must be determined is the testimony contributed to the defendant's conviction. If so, then it must be determined after the prejudicial is excised if the remaining evidence is sufficient for conviction. In a weak case, such admission of evidence my improperly convict the defendant. [585]

[585] State v. Morris, Slip Opinion No. 2014-Ohio-5052.

CHAPTER 63

Identity

1. Admission of Other Crimes to Prove Identity.

It is not improper to admit testimony of possible other crimes committed by the defendant, pursuant to Evid. R. 404(B), to show identity.

In State v. Lott, an identification witness testified that she noticed the defendant and his car, in an unrelated incident, outside of the house of a neighbor who was burglarized and assaulted. The witness was able to identify the defendant because she saw his face and took his license plate number. [586]

"Evidence of other acts, is admissible for various purposes such as identity, Evid. R. 404(B). The relatively brief, benign and muted evidence about Lott's other similar crimes, present here, constituted neither error not prejudice to Lott's rights." [587]

---

[586] *State v. Lott*, 51 Ohio St.3d 160, 555 N.E.2d 293 (1990).

Corroboration of a state's witness's testimony that the defendant owned several guns and a machine that made driver's licenses, was properly admitted under 404(B) since the witness testified the defendant hit the victim with a gun and the ownership of the machine tied the defendant to the ownership of other relevant evidence. This evidence was properly admitted and, even though the evidence could have been interpreted to show criminal propensity, it nevertheless had legitimate evidentiary purposes.

Appellate review of the admission of similar act evidence as permitted by Evid.R. 404(B). requires the court to use an abuse of discretion standard. An appellate court is not to do a de novo review in which it considers whether it would have admitted the evidence. The standard to be applied is a *deferential review* and should only be reversed where an abuse of discretion is found.[588]

2. Limiting Instructions.

To legitimize the admission of such evidence it is necessary that the jury be given a limiting instruction that the use of the other acts evidence is for the purpose of identification and is not to be considered as representative of the defendant's bad character.[589]

---

[587] *Lott,supra.*

[588] *State v. Morris*, 132 Ohio St.3d 337, 2012-Ohio-2407

[589] *State v. Wickline*, 50 Ohio St. 3d 114, 552 N. 2d 913 (1990).

In *State v. Smith*, evidence of the death of an acquaintance of the victim that occurred in similar circumstances as the victim in the present case was properly admitted to prove the identity of the defendant. The state's theory was that the defendant gave drugs to both of the victims and that each victim did not accidentally ingest the drugs.

The death of the two victims was nearly identical, both died in the defendant's trailer, and the defendant stated they both used drugs that he did not supply. They both died of acute morphine intoxication. [590]

For evidence to be admitted as an other act, it is not required that the acts be similar to the crime charged "* * * If such other acts do in fact 'tend to show' any of those things, they are admissible notwithstanding they may not be 'like' or 'similar' to the crime charged." In addition, it is error for a jury to be instructed that evidence of other acts cannot be considered as evidence of guilt because only material evidence is allowed to be admitted pursuant to R.C. 2945.59.

If the evidence is not material to guilt, it cannot be admitted. *State v. Flonnery*.[591] In *Flonnery*, the trial court properly admitted the facts of seven other robberies as other acts evidence to show identity of the perpetrator. All of the robberies occurred in the downtown area of the city and there was strong evidence the defendant committed the other robberies. Some of the robberies were committed somewhat differently than most of them, but this did not affect their admissibility. "Such differences do affect the relative value of these events but not their admissibility. The

---

[590] *State v. Smith,* 49 Ohio St. 3d 137, 551 N.E. 2d 190 (1990).

[591] *State v. Flonnery,*.31 Ohio St. 2d 124, 285 N.E. 2d 726 (1972).

relative weight to be given the evidence is for the jury to determine." [592]

3. Convictions as Similar Acts.

Evidence of a similar criminal plan was properly admitted in *State v. Coleman*. Approximately ten other similar acts of the defendant were introduced into evidence. The admission of the similar acts was compelling, the majority of the victims were young black females who were killed by ligature strangulation; the bodies were generally left in abandoned buildings or areas where they would not be found for some time; and appellant and his accomplice normally fled in a stolen car. The above facts were properly admitted because they revealed, "*a unique identifiable plan of criminal activity*." [593]

4. Similar Acts as a Principal Offender.

Although, generally, evidence of other crimes points toward the identity of the defendant; such evidence can also be used where the contested issue is whether the defendant is a *principal offender*. Evidence may be admitted, for instance, showing that the defendant took the lead in the crime and possessed a knife used in a similar robbery. [594]

---

[592] *Flonnery*, supra.

[593] *State v. Coleman,* 45 Ohio St. 3d 298, 554 N.E. 2d 622 (1989).

[594] *State v. Byrd*, 32 Ohio St. 3d 79, 512 N.E. 2d 611 (1987).

5. Similar Acts in Rape Prosecutions.

It was proper to admit similar act evidence of a prior rape from another jurisdiction where the facts were almost identical concerning the manner in which the crime was committed and the age of victim. The *identity* of the offender was an issue, and the evidence of the first rape tended to show the identity of the perpetrator of the second.[595] This evidence of similar acts is admissible under both Evid. R. 404(B) and R.C. 2945.59 (although 2925.59 does not refer to *identity*, identity is included under the umbrella of scheme, plan or system.[596]

In *Shederick*, a prosecution of aggravated murder predicated upon a rape, a prior rape victim testified that defendant pulled her panties down and turned them inside out, and stabbed her in the neck. The murder victim's panties were turned inside out and she was also stabbed in the back.

CHAPTER 64

---

[595] *State v. Shederick*, 59 Ohio St.3d 146, 572 N.E. 2d 59 (1991).

[596] *State v. Broom*, 40 Ohio St. 3d 277, 533 N.E. 2d 682 (1988).

Use of a Firearm While Committing a Crime.

1. Operability

2. Firearm Specification in Indictment

R.C. 2929.14(D)(1)(a)(ii) (formally R.C. 2929.71) requires the offender who is convicted of, or pleads guilty to a specification charging him with having a firearm on or about his person, to serve three years' incarceration for this specification in addition to his sentence for the substantive crime.

1. Operability

The establishment of a firearm specification requires proof that the firearm is operable. The operability of the firearm can be proven beyond a reasonable doubt with direct or scientific evidence. Operability of a firearm must be proven in order to impose a term of actual incarceration. This court held in *State v. Gaines* that proof the defendant possessed a "deadly weapon" pursuant to R.C.2911.01 is not sufficient to prove the defendant possessed a "firearm" pursuant to R.C. 2929.71(A), it is necessary to show operability even if with circumstantial evidence. [597]

The court suggested proof of operability could be established by way of testimony of gunshots, smell of gunpowder, bullets or bullet holes.

[597] *State v. Gaines,* 46 Ohio St. 3d 65, 545 N.E. 2d 68 (1989).

The court subsequently modified *Gaines* in regard to evidence necessary to prove the firearm specification, holding that the state may rely on all of the "surrounding facts and circumstances in establishing whether a firearm was used in the commission of a felony." *State v. Murphy.* [598]

In *Murphy,* the defendant, while robbing a convenience store, pointed a gun at a customer, and announced if not given money that he would kill the clerk.

The court found these facts sufficient to establish beyond a reasonable doubt the defendant possessed a firearm pursuant to R.C. 2923.11(B). The operability of the firearm can be proven "* * * by the testimony of lay witnesses who were in a position to observe the instrument and the circumstances surrounding the crime." The state is not required to introduce the firearm at trial.

In *State v. Thompkins*, the court found implicit threats sufficient to show operability of a handgun. In *Thompkins*, the defendant pointed the gun and told the clerk to "be quick." The court held: "However, the fact that Thompkins did not explicitly threaten Brinkman does not take away from the fact that Brinkman thought her life was in danger. Even absent any explicit verbal threats on the part of Thompkins, the trier of fact in this case could have reasonably concluded, based on the totality of the circumstances, that Thompkins was in possession of a firearm at the time of the offense, that is a deadly weapon capable of expelling projectiles by an explosive or combustible propellant." [599]

---

[598] *State v. Murphy,* 49 Ohio St. 3 206, 551 N.E. 2d 932 (1990).

[599] *State v. Thompkins* ,78 Ohio St. 3d 380, 678 N.E. 2d 541 (1997).

The new R.C. 2923.11(B)(2) allows the establishment of the operability of a firearm by the use of circumstantial evidence. "When determining whether a firearm is capable of expelling or propelling [projectiles] * * * the trier of fact may rely on circumstantial evidence* * *"

Where the defendant is indicted for felonious assault a felony of the second degree with a firearm specification, and was later convicted of the lesser-included offense of aggravated assault a felony of the fourth degree. The requirements of R.C. 2929.11(G), R.C. 2929.71(C), R.C. 2929.141(A) and R.C. 2941.143 requiring the indictment to contain a deadly weapon specification, does not mean that the lesser included third or fourth degree felony must be in a separate count of the indictment with a firearm specification for R.C. 2929.11(B)(7) to apply. "* * * if this * * * indictment, count in the indictment, or information charg[es] him with * * *the offense * * * ' (emphasis added) of a greater degree than a third or fourth degree felony the indictment or count necessarily and simultaneously charges the defendant with lesser included offenses as well." [600]

Where a burglar enters a dwelling unarmed, and acquires a firearm from the burglarized home, this act of acquiring the firearm is sufficient evidence to find the defendant guilty of having a firearm in possession during the commission of a felony.[601]

R.C. 2941.146(A) is a firearm specification that requires an additional five-year sentence to anyone convicted of discharging a

[600] *State v. Lytle*, 49 Ohio St. 3d 154, 551 N.E. 2d 950 (1990).

[601] *State v. Powell*, 59 Ohio St. 3d 62, 571 N.E. 2d 125 (1991).

firearm from a vehicle if that defendant is knowingly causing or attempting to cause death or physical harm to another. This statute does not apply to one who was not in the vehicle and who was standing on the ground between the driver's door and the automobile and who has no "substantial contact" with the vehicle.[602]

2. Firearm Specification in Indictment

Firearm Specification (Law enforcement officer)

R.C. 2941.145 is the firearm specification often contained in an indictment which causes the underlying crime to be enhanced either by an additional three year or five-year sentence. This specification does not apply to an on-duty police officer working within the scope of his employment even though the police officer may have been involved in a wrongful shooting.

USE OF DEADLY FOR BY POLICE.

This case reviews the law of the use of deadly for by a police officer. These cases are to be analyzed under a 4th amendment reasonableness standard. The law in Ohio is the result of several federal court rulings. In regard to a fleeing felon deadly force is not justified unless the flight poses a serious danger to the officer or to others.[603]

---

[602] *State v. Swidas*, Slip Opinion No. 2012-Ohio-4638

[603] State v. White, 142 Ohio St. 3d. 277, 2015-Ohio-492.

CHAPTER 65

Competency

1. Competency of a Spouse.
2. Competency of a Child Witness.

A person is competent to testify unless it can be established that the person is of unsound mind or is a child under the age of ten who appears "incapable of receiving just impressions of the facts and transactions respecting which they are examined or relating them truly" Evid. R. 601.

1. Competency of a Spouse.

Evid. R 601(B) was amended July 1, 1991, a spouse is now permitted to testify against the other spouse who is charged with a crime against the testifying spouse, a child of either spouse, or where the spouse elects to testify. The confidential privilege of R.C. 2317.02 (C), R.C. 2945.42, and Evid. R. 501 remain in effect however.

There is a distinction between *spousal privilege* and *spousal competency.* A defendant may prevent a spouse from testifying regarding private acts or communications unless a third person was present. However, the spouse is nevertheless not *competent* to testify to those acts or privileges unless the spouse *elects* to testify.

The spouse must be informed by the court that he or she does not have to testify, and that it must be his or her choice to testify. A trial court cannot order a spouse to testify unless that crime is against the spouse or a child of either spouse. [604]

Where a spouse testifies against the other spouse and the trial court has failed to inform the spouse the she does not have to testify in violation of Evid. R. 601(B), the trial court has erred. A reviewing court must then perform a plain-error analysis to determine whether plain error has occurred and whether manifest injustice in present, that is would the defendant have been convicted but for the admission of the spousal testimony.[605]

2. Competency of a Child Witness.

In *State v. Frazier*, the appellant challenged the trial court's ruling that a seven-year-old witness, who saw the defendant kill his mother and stepfather, was incompetent because he did not understand the nature of an oath, and because there was no showing that he had the capacity to relate the events. The court held that the determination of competency is within the trial court's discretion. Further, the trial court must take into consideration the following five factors:

1. The child's ability to receive accurate impressions of fact or to observe acts about which he or she will testify.
2. The child's ability to recollect those impressions or observations.

---

[604] *State v. Adamson,* 72 Ohio St. 3d 431, 650 N.E. 2d 875 (1995).

[605] *State v. Davis*, Slip Opinion No. 2010-Ohio-5706.

See also *State v. Brown*, 115 Ohio St.3d 55, 2007-Ohio-4837, 873 N.E.2d 858.

3. The child's ability to communicate what was observed.

4. The child's understanding of truth and falsity.

5. The child's appreciation of his or her responsibility to be truthful.

In *Frazier*, the child witness was able to relate the facts. Concerning his duty to tell the truth, he stated he would receive a "whopping" if he did not tell the truth. The court further held that if the witness did not understand the meaning of an oath, it was sufficient that the trial court was satisfied the child *knew his duty to tell the truth.* [606]

In order for an unavailable child declarant to testify concerning child abuse pursuant to Evid.R. 807, the child's competency does not have to be established. This court previously held in *State v. Said* that such competency must be established. In limiting that holding, the court emphasized the plain language of Evid. R. 807(B)(3)(a). Which does not require a competency hearing.[607]

---

[606] *State v. Frazier,* 61 Ohio St. 3d 247, 574 N.E. 2d 483 (1991).

[607] *State v. Silverman*, 121 Ohio St. 3d 581, 2009-Ohio-1576.

CHAPTER 66

Circumstantial Evidence.

Ballantine's Law Dictionary defines circumstantial evidence as "Facts and circumstances surrounding a transaction from which the jury or trier of fact may infer other connected facts which reasonably follow, according to the common experience of mankind."

In 1991, The Ohio Supreme Court overruled its longstanding rule concerning the use of circumstantial evidence in criminal trials. The prior law was known as the *Kulig* rule for *State v. Kulig.*[608] In *Kulig*, the court held: "Circumstantial evidence relied on to prove an element of a crime must be irreconcilable with any reasonable theory of an accused's innocence in order to support a finding of guilt."

In *State v. Jenks*,[609] the court reviewed the standard to be used by an appellant court in reviewing a conviction based on circumstantial evidence, as well as the jury instruction to be given. The prior standard of review required an appellant court to reverse

---

608 *State v. Kulig,* 37 Ohio St. 2d 157, 309 N.E. 2d 897 (1974).

609 *State v. Jenks* ,61 Ohio St. 3d 259, 574 N.E. 2d 492 (1991). (superseded by constitutional amendment for unrelated issue)

a conviction based solely on circumstantial evidence, "* * * where the evidence does not as a matter of law, preclude all reasonable theories of innocence."[610]

This court concluded that circumstantial evidence, as well as, direct evidence inherently possesses the same probative value, "Hence we can discern no reason to continue the requirement that circumstantial evidence must be irreconcilable with any reasonable theory of an accused innocence in order to support a finding of guilt ** *all that is required of the jury is that it weigh all of the evidence, direct and circumstantial, against the standard of proof beyond a reasonable doubt." [611]

Concerning appellate review, the *Jenks* court held where circumstantial evidence was considered by the trier of fact, the standard of review is now the same whether the conviction was based on circumstantial evidence or direct evidence. "* * * an appellate court's function when reviewing the sufficiency of evidence to support a criminal conviction is to examine the evidence admitted at trial to determine whether such evidence, if believed, would convince the average mind of the defendant's guilt beyond a reasonable doubt."

The court's holding is the result of an examination of the reliability of circumstantial evidence. There were other holdings of the court that pointed toward this decision. For instance, in *State v. Nicely*, the court found that circumstantial evidence is not necessarily of less probative value than direct evidence, and is in some instances very reliable. [612]

---

[610] *State v. Sorgee*, 56 Ohio St. 2d 438, 384 N.E.2d 290 (1975).

[611] *Jenks, supra.*

CHAPTER 67

Expert Testimony.

1. **Witness Veracity.**
2. **Testimony as to the credibility of a witness.**
3. **Basis of Opinion Testimony.**
4. **Testimony on the Ultimate Issue.**
5. **Trial Court's Errors in Evaluating Expert Testimony.**
6. **Testimony by a Non-Testing Expert.**

Evid. R. 702 permits expert testimony if it will aid the trier of fact in determining a fact in issue or in understanding the evidence. The fact in issue must be beyond the jurors' common experience. The testimony may be presented in the form of an opinion, and is not limited to scientific or technical knowledge; it can consist of specialized experience, training or education.

1. Witness Veracity.

An expert in not permitted to testify as to the veracity of a witness. In *State v. Boston*, the court found that the trial court improperly allowed testimony from an expert witness as to the veracity of a child victim of sexual abuse. A doctor testified that the

[612] *State v. Nicely,* 39 Ohio St. 3d 147, 529 N.E. 2d 1236 (1988).

victim had not fabricated her allegations of abuse, and had not been programmed to make accusations. This testimony was, in effect, a declaration that the victim was telling the truth. [613]

This evidence is inadmissible. Reversible error occurred because the expert testimony infringed on the duty of the fact finder in "making determinations of veracity and credibility* * *In our System of justice it is the fact finder not the so-called expert or lay witness who bears the burden of assessing the credibility and veracity of witnesses." (Justice Brown's concurring opinion adopted by the court.) It should be noted that the experts were, of course, permitted to give their opinion as to whether sexual abuse had occurred.

In the same vein, an expert is not permitted to testify as to whether a witness is lying. The court held in *State v. Moreland*, "For the reasons we stated in *Boston*, we hold that an expert may not testify as to the expert's opinion of the truth or falsity, or accuracy or inaccuracy, of the statements of a child declarant." [614]

2. Testimony as to the Credibility of a Witness.

There may be, however, a special need for expert testimony as to the credibility of a witness where it can be established that the witness possesses some mental or physical problem that could affect his ability to observe and relate events.[615] In *Brown*, the court held, although it is proper under a court's discretion to allow

---

[613] *State v. Boston* ,46 Ohio St. 3d 108, 545 N.E 2d 1220 (1989).

[614] *State v. Moreland* ,50 Ohio St. 3d 58, 552 N.E. 2d 894 (1989).

[615] *State v. Brown*, 40 Ohio St. 3d 277, 533 NE 2d 682 (1988).

expert testimony as to eyewitness identification of a typical eyewitness, the opinion of an experimental psychologist as to the credibility of a particular witness must be supported by a particularized need of that witness, such as a physical or mental impairment. [616]

In the prosecution's case in chief it is a violation of the defendants' rights under the 5th amendment and Article 1, Section 10 of the Ohio Constitution for a psychologist to testify that a defendant is feigning mental illness after the defendant abandons his previous defense of NGRI.[617]

3. Basis of Opinion Testimony.

Evid. R. 703 states that an expert may base his or her opinion either on what he or she has perceived, or on what has been admitted into evidence.

In *State v. Solomon*, the testimony of an expert psychiatrist as to the mental state of the defendant was properly admitted into evidence even though it was based, in part, on evidence not in the record. If the testimony is based solely on records not in evidence and the psychiatrist did not examine the defendant, the expert may not testify. The court held that Evid. R. 703 is to be read in the disjunctive; the rule is satisfied where the expert opinion is based on perceptions *or* facts *or* data admitted in evidence.[618] *State v. Chapin* further illustrates this principal. [619]

---

[616] *State v. Beull*, 22 Ohio St. 3d 124, 489 N.E. 2d 795 (1986).

[617] State v. Harris, _2015-Ohio-166.

[618] *State v. Solomon* , 59 Ohio St. 3d 124, 570 N.E. 1118 (1991).

4. Testimony on the Ultimate Issue.

Evid.R.704 provides that opinion testimony of an expert may be admitted even if it goes to the ultimate issue to be decided by the trier of fact. This rule must be applied in conjunction with Evid. R. 701 and Evid. R. 702, in that it must be *helpful* to assist the trier of fact in the determination of a factual issue.[620]

In *Cleveland v. Cleveland, Elec. Illm. Co.*, a prosecution for air pollution violations, air pollution inspectors were permitted, pursuant to Evid. R. 704, to testify that the emissions exceeded the legal level, making it a violation of the law, "Thus, the testimony of the air pollution inspectors, as expert witnesses, may include the ultimate issue of fact in the form of a conclusory opinion concerning the existence or nonexistence of an element of the criminal offense to be proven beyond a reasonable doubt." [621]

---

[619] *State v. Chapin* , 67 Ohio St. 2d 437, 424 N.E. 2d 526 (1981).

[620] See *State v. Boston*, *supra.*, and *Shephen v. Midland Mutual Life Ins.Co.*, 152 Ohio St. 6, 87 N.E. 2d 156 (1949).

[621] *Cleveland v. Cleveland Elec. Illm. Co.,* 4 Ohio St 3d 184, 448 N.E. 2d 130 (1983).

5. Trial Court's Errors in Evaluating Expert Testimony.

In a death penalty prosecution where the defendant asserts a mental retardation defense, which if successful would preclude the state from putting him to death, pursuant to Atkins v. Virginia,[622] the trial court abused its discretion in evaluating psychiatric evidence where it ignored and substituted its own opinion as to what the experts should use in evaluating the evidence.

This error included the mistaken belief that a retarded person cannot appear to be normal in everyday life. The expert testimony from both sides agreed that the defendant was retarded. In addition, although there is no requirement to accept blindly expert testimony, there must be some objective reason for ignoring such testimony. This opinion contains a thorough discussion of the factors and procedures that mental health experts utilize in evaluating mental capacity. [623]

6. Testimony by a Non-Testing Expert.

DNA testimony of an expert who did not personally perform the test is properly admitted as a business record under Evid. R.803(6). There is no Confrontational Clause issue because the DNA results are non-testimonial business records and accordingly, are not in violation of the United States Supreme Court's Crawford

---

[622] *Atkins v. Virginia*, 536 U.S. 304, 122 S.Ct. 2242, 153 L.Ed. 2d 335 (2002).

[623] *State v. White*, 118 Ohio St. 3d 12, 885 N.E. 2d 905 (2008).

decision.[624] Further, the testifying expert was capable of being cross-examined as to the procedures used and the results.[625]

In this same vein, testimony by an nonexamining coroner who testifies as to the contents of autopsy report made by an unavailable coroner and as to the cause of death is admissible. [626]

---

[624] *Crawford v. Washington*, 541 U.S. 36 (2004).

[625] State v. Crager, 116 Ohio St. 3d 369, 879 N.E. 2d 745 (2008).

[626] State v. Maxwell, 138 Ohio St. 3d 12, 2014-Ohio-1019 (2014). See also State v. Craig, 110 Ohio ST. 3d 306, 2006-Ohio-4571.

CHAPTER 68

Hearsay.

1. **Adoptive Admissions.**
2. **Unsworn Statements of out of Court Witnesses.**
3. **Cumulative Effect of Hearsay Testimony.**

Evid. Rule 801 defines hearsay as follows: "Hearsay is a statement, other than one made by the declarant while testifying at the trial or hearing, offered in evidence to prove the truth of the matter asserted."

1. Adoptive Admissions.

Evid. R. 801(D)(2) provides that a statement is not hearsay if the party against who it is offered has adopted or shown his belief in its truth. In *State v. Kidder*, the trial court erred in admitting the police officer's testimony as an adoptive admission of the defendant.

While interrogating the defendant, the sheriff told him the following: "He fully believes in his mind they were trying to kill him. * * * if he didn't think you tried to kill him, he wouldn't have called. * * *" 627

---

[627] *State v. Kidder* , 32 Ohio St. 3d 279, 513 N.E. 2d 311 (1987).

This statement made to the defendant was admitted into evidence under the theory that defendant's silent response was an admission by silence.

This court found the admission of this statement improper because there is no evidence that it was *adopted* by the defendant. "Given the context and circumstances surrounding the statements, it is not apparent that Kidder would have been able to deny the statements, and it was error to present them as adopted admissions." [628]

2. Unsworn Statements of out of Court Witnesses.

In *State v. Williams*, the trial court erred by admitting unsworn statements of an out-of-court witness. The witness refused to testify, and the court permitted the prosecutor to offer the statement made to police implicating the defendant. The trial court ruled that the statement was admissible for the limited purpose of proving the reluctant witness made the statement. The entire statement was read to the jury during closing argument. [629]

This court held, although a statement is not hearsay if it is admitted to prove it was made, not to prove the truth of the contents, here it was improperly used to prove the truth of the matter asserted. The judge's instruction made it clear that the statement was actually being used to judge the credibility of other witnesses. In other words, it was being used to prove the truth of

---

[628] *Kidder, supra.*

[629] *State v. Williams* , 38 Ohio St. 3d 346, 528 N.E. 2d 910 (1988).

the matter asserted. As a result, the defendant was denied his constitutional right to confront those who testify against him.

This statement was also not admissible under Evid. R.804(A)(2) which allows the introduction of a statement of an unavailable witness, although the witness did not testify, it still must be established that the statement qualifies as one of the exceptions of 804(B). Under the Ohio Rules "* * * a statement that would otherwise be excluded as hearsay may be admitted if the declarant is 'unavailable' as defined in Evid. R. 804(A) and the statement falls within one of the six exceptions of Evid. R. 804(B)." These exceptions are:

1. Former testimony.
2. Statement under belief of impending death.
3. Statement against interest.
4. Statement of personal or family history.
5. Statement by deceased or incompetent person.
6. Forfeiture by wrongdoing.

It should be noted that this admission of the statement did not require reversal. The remainder of the evidence presented was sufficient to convict the defendant. The statement was found to be harmless beyond a reasonable doubt.

The United States Supreme Court in *Crawford v. Washington* held that out of court statements that are testimonial in nature are not admissible unless the defendant has an opportunity to cross-examine the witness. [630] The statement is testimonial if it is being offered to prove the truth of the matter asserted.

---

[630] *Crawford v. Washington,* 124 S.Ct. 1354 (2004)

3. Cumulative Effect of Hearsay Testimony.

"Although violations of the Rules of Evidence during trial, singularly, may not rise to the level of prejudicial error, a conviction will be reversed where the cumulative effect of the errors deprives a defendant of a fair trial." Here three witnesses were permitted to testify at length as to hearsay information concerning the theft and investigation of automobiles. The court did not go into detail why it found the admission of the statements to be prejudicial cumulative error other than to say they were cumulative. [631]

---

[631] *State v. DeMarco*, 31 Ohio St. 3d 191, 509 N.E. 2d 1256 (1987).

CHAPTER 69

Hearsay Exceptions.

1. **Excited Utterancces.**
2. **State of Mind Evidence.**
3. **Medical Diagnosis or Treatment.**
4. **Declarant Unavailable.**
5. **Former Testimony.**
6. **Dying Declaration.**
7. **Attacking the Credibility of Hearsay Declarant.**
8. **Stipulations and Prejudicial Evidence (Evid.R. 403)**

Evid. R. 803 contains the exceptions to the hearsay rule that are admissible regardless whether the declarant is unavailable.

1. Excited Utterances.

Under Evid. R. 803(2) a statement is admissible as an excited utterance if it relates to a startling event or condition, and the statement was made while the declarant was under the stress of the event.

> A tape recording of the victim in an aggravated murder prosecution was properly admitted as an excited utterance pursuant to Evid. R. 803(2). The statement was

made forty-five minutes after the event while doctors were treating the victim for his wounds. The defendant was still in a state of nervous excitement, which could be determined by the testimony of the detective present, and the victim's voice on a tape recording. *State v. Huertas*, 51 Ohio St. 3d 22, 553 N.E. 2d 1058 (1990).

The court in *Huertas* quoted the following from the leading case on excited utterances: "To be admissible under Evid. R. 803(2) as an excited utterance, a statement must concern 'some occurrence startling enough to produce a nervous excitement in the declarant.' which occurrence the declarant had an opportunity to observe, and must be made 'before there had been time for such nervous excitement to lose a domination over his reflective facilities. * * *'" [632]

Where a child victim refused to testify at trial, it was proper for the trial court to admit testimony of a social worker who testified regarding the identity of the person whom the child said assaulted her. The statement was properly admitted as an excited utterance even though the competency of the child declarant was not established. This court held that Ohio Common Law has a four-part test in regard to the admission of excited utterances:

1. There was an occurrence to produce nervous excitement so the declarant does not have time to reflect.

2. The statement, even if not made at the time of the event, was made before the nervous excitement diminished.

3. The statement related to the startling circumstances.

---

[632] *Potter v. Baker*, 162 Ohio St. 488, 124 N.E. 2d 140 (1955).

4. The declarant had an opportunity to personally observe the matter of the statement.[633]

Here, fifteen hours passed between the event and the declaration, the declarant was in and out of consciousness and was subjected to questions. The court found that the questions did not negate the spontaneity of her utterance. The admission of her statement is not precluded if the question(s):

> "1. Is neither coercive nor leading.
> 2. Facilitates the declarant's expression of what is the natural focus of the declarant's thoughts
> 3. Does not destroy the domination of the nervous excitement over the declarant's reflective faculties.

In regard to admitting the excited utterance even though the declarant was not declared a competent witness, the common law of Ohio has long permitted this. "Tangy's ability to accurately perceive and relate facts was never shown to be deficient * * * Her refusal was not shown to be the result of inability. She was competent because of a presumption of competency not a demonstration of incompetency * * * competency is in large part, inherently satisfied by the elements required to establish an excited utterance." [634]

---

[633] *State v. Duncan*, 53 Ohio St. 2d 215, 373 N.E. 1234 (1978).

[634] *State v. Wallace*, 37 Ohio St. 3d 87, 524 N.E. 2d 466 (1988).

2. State of Mind Evidence.

It was proper to exclude a statement by a murder victim that he intended to kill someone. Appellant attempted to admit this under Evid. R. 803(3) as showing the state of mind of the victim so that it could be implied that, because the murder victim was afraid of someone other than the defendant, that maybe the defendant did not kill the victim. The statement was, "Rich is back in town. Lock your doors tonight, and if Rick comes over I'm going to have to kill him."

This statement was not admissible as a statement of the declarant's then existing mental, emotional, or physical condition, as an exception to the hearsay rule, because it does not state what the state of mind of the declarant was. Had the victim stated he was "afraid" of the person, it would be a statement of his state of mind; otherwise, it is merely inadmissible hearsay. In addition, the statement was irrelevant because the defense was not that "Rick killed the victim." [635]

The trial court properly admitted under Evid. R. 803(3) the victim's statement that she was fearful of the defendant, as a statement of the declarant's *state of mind*. This testimony must point to the future, "Accordingly, the testimony of a state-of-mind witness, that the victim was fearful and apprehensive was not inadmissible hearsay and was properly admitted. This court cited with approval, United States v. Cohen (C.A. 5, 1980), 631 F. 2d. 1223.[636]

---

[635] *State v. Greer*, 39 Ohio St. 3d 236, 530 N.E. 2d 382 (1988).

[636] *State v. Apanovich,* 33 Ohio St. 3d 19, 514 N.E. 2d 394 (1987).

The friends of a murder victim were properly allowed to testify as to her state of mind, which included her plans for the future, and her plans to break-up with the defendant. Such testimony would have been inconsistent with her contemplating suicide. The defense was that the victim killed herself. In addition, under 803(3) testimony that she was nervous and fidgety was properly admitted evidence of her emotional or mental condition.[637]

3. Medical Diagnosis or Treatment.

To admit statements made during medical diagnosis or treatment a person must be motivated to seek medical treatment.

In the past, in order to admit a statement a child made to a doctor, the child had to be motivated to seek treatment or diagnosis. *State v. Boston.*[638] Because of the problem of a child on its own seeking such treatment, the court modified this rule of *Boston* and held in *State v. Dever* that such statements are admissible.[639]

In *State v. Eastham*, 39 Ohio St. 3d 307, 530 N. E. 2d 409 (1988), statements a child made to a school counselor did not qualify under Evid. R. 803(4) as statements made for

---

[637] *State v. Sage*, 31 Ohio St. 3d 173, 510 N.E. 2d 343 (1987).

[638] *State v. Boston*, 46 Ohio St. 3d 108, 545 N.E. 2d 1220 (1989).

[639] *State v. Dever,* 64 Ohio St. 3d 401, 596 N.E. 2d 436 (1992).

medical diagnosis or treatment because it requires a physical condition, and as such did not have the same reliability since, inter alia, a person's "veracity, perception, memory or narrative ability may be impaired.

There is an interplay between the admission of statements made to a medical interviewer where that examiner plays a dual role. One role of a medical interviewer and the other role as a forensic interviewer. The medical interview can be admitted but the forensic interview involves confrontational clause issues which subject the admission of such statement dependent on whether the defendant has had an opportunity to cross-examine the declarant.[640]

4. Declarant Unavailable.

During defense counsel's attempt to introduce evidence that someone else killed the murder victim, the trial court erred by refusing to allow a defense witness to testify that a juvenile told the witness that he slit the throat of the victim. This court held that the juvenile was an unavailable witness, asserting his right against self-incrimination. Because the witness was unavailable, his statement should have been admitted as a statement against *penal interest* under Evid. R.804(B)(3).

Evid. R. 804(B)(3) requires corroborating circumstances to "clearly indicate" the trustworthiness of the statement. The determination of whether the corroborating circumstances are sufficient to admit the statements is left to the trial court's sound discretion as to the trustworthiness of the statement. This court seems to have adopted the criteria of *Chambers v. Mississippi*

[640] State v. Arnold, 126 Ohio St.3d 290, 2010-Ohio-2742

about evidence of sufficient corroboration that establishes a statement's trustworthiness:

"(a) the statements were made spontaneously shortly after the murder to a close acquaintance;

(b) Other evidence corroborated the statements;

(c) The statements were 'in a very real sense self-incriminatory and unquestionably against interest * * * and

(d) The declarant was available for cross-examination." [641]

It is not necessary for all of the above factors to be present to admit the statement. This court noted with approval that, in this case, it was significant that three of the four criteria were present.[642]

The court in *State v. Landrum* also discussed the principal that the credibility of a *person* as a witness does not affect the admission of the statement because the criteria of admission is whether the *statement is trustworthy, not whether the witness is necessary trustworthy*. The jury is always free to determine credibility of a witness. Even though in *Landrum* the trial court should have admitted this statement, however, because this was a death penalty case, this court independently weighed the evidence, as is required pursuant to R.C. 2929.05, and found the conviction proper.[643]

---

[641] *Chambers v. Mississippi,* 410 U.S. 284, S.Ct. 1038, 35 L.Ed.2d 297 (1973).

[642] *State v.Landrum*, 53 Ohio St. 3d 107, 559 N.E. 2d 710 (1990).

[643] See also *State v. Lott*, 51 Ohio St. 3d 160, 555 N.E. 2d 293 (1990).

In order to meet the hearsay exceptions of 804(B) as an unavailable witness the statement must further fall within the five exceptions of 804(B): it must be either:

> (1) former testimony; (2) statement under belief of impending death; (3) statement against interest; (4) statement of personal or family history; and (5) statement by deceased, deaf-mute or incompetent person." [644]

Here, the trial court permitted an unsworn out-of-court statement of a witness who refused to testify. The statement implicated the defendant in the crime. This court found that the admission of this statement, which did not fall within any of the above five exceptions, to be inadmissible hearsay used to prove the truth the matter asserted. [645]

As stated above, Evid. R. 804(B)(3) permits the exclusion of a statement made by a declarant against his penal interest unless "corroborating circumstances clearly indicate the trustworthiness of the statement. The constitutionally of this rule has been recently challenged where the trial court prevented the defendant from presenting evidence that another person admitted to four witnesses to shooting the victim in a felonious assault prosecution. While finding the rule constitutional, the court remanded the case to the court of appeals to determine whether the trial court abused its discretion in denying the testimony. It should be noted that two of the three court of appeals judges who heard the appeal tended

---

[644] *State v. Williams,* 38 Ohio St. 3d 346, 528 N.E. 2d 910 (1988).

[645] See Also Crawford v. Washinton , 124 S.Ct. 1354 (2004).

toward the admission of the statements. One ruled the exclusion unconstitutional and the other that the trial court erred in not finding sufficient corroborating evidence.[646]

The sixth amendment was violated where a police officer testified as to the statements of a non-testifying witness. Any attempt to justify the admission of such testimony as non-hearsay because it tends to show acts of the investigation is not justified especially where such testimony is clearly an attempt to use the hearsay to prove the matter asserted.

When a trial court is confronted with the choice of whether to admit hearsay testimony under the principle that it is not offered to prove the matter asserted but for other purposes this testimony must be assessed under Evid. R. 403(A) to determine whether it is outweighed by prejudice.

"Thus, if the testimony that is ostensibly offered to explain police conduct is more prejudicial than probative, the jury is more likely to rely on the testimony to prove the matter asserted, which tilts the particular testimony into hearsay."[647]

5. Former Testimony.

In *State v. Young*, [648] a young child abuse victim was found to be an unavailable witness where she refused to answer

---

[646] *State v. Swann*, 119 Ohio St. 3d 552, 895 NE. 2d 821 (2008).

[647] *State v. Ricks,* Slip Opinion No. 2013-Ohio-3712

[648] *State v. Young,* 5 Ohio St. 3d 221, 450 N.E. 2d 1143 (1983).

questions in a voir dire concerning her sexual abuse. The trial court was within its discretion to find her unavailable, pursuant to Evid. R. 804(4), because of her persistent refusal to testify.[649]

The trial court properly read her statement into evidence pursuant to Evid. R. 804(A)(2). Her refusal to testify satisfied the two-prong test established in *State v. Madison* [650] (prong one was satisfied when she refused to testify; prong two was satisfied because the defendant had an opportunity to cross-examine the witness but chose not to.[651]

Pursuant to Evid.R. 804(A)(1) concerning an unavailable witness, although Evid. R. 804(B)(1) allows for the introduction of statements of an unavailable witness, the prosecution has the burden, of showing a good faith attempt to secure the witness' attendance. In *State v. Keairns, w*here the prosecutor merely stated that subpoenas were issued and that he asked the Sheriff to continue to search for the witness. [652] The court held:

"A showing of unavailability under Evid. R. 804 must be based on *testimony* of a witness rather than hearsay not under oath unless the party against whom statement is being offered

---

[649] *State v. Boston*, 46 Ohio St. 3d l08, 545 N.E. 2d 1220 (1989).

[650] *State v. Madison,* 64 Ohio St. 2d 322, 415 N.E. 2d 272 (1980).

[651] See also *State v. Keairns*, 9 Ohio St. 3d 228, 460 N.E. 2d 245 (1984); and *State v. Jester*, 32 Ohio St. 3d 147, 512 N.E. 2d 962 (1987).

[652] Ibid.

concedes unavailability. * * * the mere statement that a 'continued search' had been made lacks sufficient particularity to enable the court to determine what steps had been taken and whether they were reasonable." The issuance of a subpoena or a bench warrant by itself is not sufficient. [653]

6. Dying Declaration.

Under Evid. R. 804 (B)(2), a dying declaration is admissible if made while the declarant believed his or her death was "imminent" if the statement concerns the cause or circumstances of his death. In *State v. Huertas*, a tape-recorded statement of the victim as to what happened was properly admitted into evidence as an excited utterance, but the statement could not have been admitted as a statement under belief of impending death because there was no evidence that the victim believed he was going to die. Although the victim was mortally injured, there is no evidence that he had a belief in his impending death because he told the treating physician he did not know the seriousness of his injuries. [654]

7. Attacking the Credibility of Hearsay Declarant.

Under Evid. R. 806, the credibility of a declarant whose hearsay statement is admitted into evidence may be attacked by any evidence that would have been admissible if the defendant had te~~stified. Thus, in *State v. Hei*~~*nish*, the state was permitted to

[653] See also, *State v. Young*, 5 Ohio St. 3d 221, 450 N.E. 2d 1143 (1983).

[654] *State v. Huertas* , 51 Ohio St. 3d 22, 553 N.E. 2d 1058 (1990).

ask the wife of the defendant if he had ever misled her about some "very material important matters since he has been married * * * to * * * her." [655]

Because it would have been permissible to ask the defendant this question if he had taken the stand, the question was proper.

8. Stipulations and Prejudicial Evidence (Evid.R. 403)

A trial court abuses its discretion when it admits into evidence a full record of the defendant's convictions when he was willing to stipulate as to the underlying convictions that are elements of the crime. The jury was influenced by improper considerations[656]

[655] *State v. Heinish,* 50 Ohio St. 3d 231, 553 N.E. 2d 1026 (1990).

[656] State v. Creech, Slip Opinion No. 2016-Ohio-8440

CHAPTER 70

Self-Identification.

Under Evid. R. 902(6), a document is admissible as a newspaper or a periodical if, on its face, it appears to be a newspaper or periodical.

In *State v. Greer*, a television schedule was admitted into evidence. There is no precondition for admissibility to establish the schedule's correctness. "When a document upon its face, purports to be a particular type of newspaper or periodical, its admission into evidence pursuant to Evid. R 902(6) is not dependent upon whether the material contained in the publication has been verified. If claimed to be unreliable, the document may be impeached after its admission." [657]

[657] *State v. Greer*, 39 Ohio St. 3d 236, 530 N E. 2d 382 (1988).

CHAPTER 71

Impeachment.

1. Impeachment with Evidence of a Crime.

Evid. R. 609 allows a witness's credibility to be attacked by evidence that the witness was convicted of a crime. The evidence of a prior conviction shall be admitted if the witness elicited it, or if it was established by public record during cross-examination. Further, evidence that the *accused* has been convicted of a crime is admissible if the crime was a felony.

The trial court has broad discretion in allowing such testimony. The policy behind allowing impeachment by use of evidence of other convictions is that it is used, not to prove the truth of the facts, but to challenge the credibility of the witness under the theory that if an inconsistency can be shown, it could be evidence that the witness is either unfamiliar with the reputation of

---

[658] *State v. Wright*, 48 Ohio St. 3d 5, 548 N.E. 2d 923 (1990)

the defendant or his standards as to a good reputation are lacking. This rule requires a determination by the trial court as to relevancy Under Evid. R. 403.[658]

Evid. R. 609 further allows for impeachment purposes a prior conviction even though the defendant has not been sentenced.[659]

Trial counsel, while impeaching a witness, does not have the right to expose the underlying facts of a conviction. Whether or not this exposure is permitted is left to the sound discretion of the trial court.

"The general rule is that it is within the sound discretion of the court to limit cross-examination to the name, date and place of conviction and the punishment imposed, when the conviction is admissible solely to impeach credibility." This rule exists to avoid undue prejudice as well as inquiries into irrelevant matters.[660]

2. Impeachment of Own Witness.

Under Evid R. 607, a witness may be impeached by any party. However, the credibility of a party's *own* witness may be impeached by a prior inconsistent statement *only where surprise and affirmative damage is shown.*

This does not apply to statements admitted pursuant to Evid. R. 801(D) (1), (D)(2), and Evid. R. 803 (hearsay and some hearsay exceptions).

---

[659] *State v. Cash*, 40 Ohio St. 3d 116, 532 N.E. 2d 111 (1988).

[660] *State v. Amburgey*, 33 Ohio St. 3d 115, 515 N.E. 2d 925 (1987).

If a witness does not remember, or if the answer is neutral, affirmative damage is not established. See the staff note to this rule.

In *State v. Holmes*, the court, in affirming a reversal by the court of appeals, held that the prosecution improperly impeached its own witness where the state never produced a prior inconsistent statement and was not surprised by the testimony of the witness. [661]

It was clear the prosecutor was not surprised because he talked to the witness two weeks before trial, and knew from the conversation how she was going to testify.

About a prior inconsistent statement, the prosecutor, without ever putting a prior inconsistent statement into evidence, attempted to impeach her by asking her if she said certain things to the police. The court of appeals properly held: "The prosecution herein * * * placed alleged prior inconsistent statements into evidence by way of impeachment, thus doing indirectly what it could not achieve directly." The prosecutor threatened the witness while cross-examining her to call other witnesses who would contradict her.

In *State v. Liberatore*, the prosecutor impermissibly was able to present substantial evidence through the impeachment of his own witness. It is impermissible for a party to attack the credibility of its witness by introducing an extra judicial statement through another witness. The prior inconsistent statement must be either recorded or under oath. The prosecutor was able to put into evidence inadmissible evidence where the purpose of his questions was clearly not to refresh the recollection of the witness, "but rather to encourage the jury to draw inferences from these questions." [662]

[661] *State v. Holmes,* 30 Ohio St. 3d 20, 506 N.E. 2d 204 (1987).

The determination as to whether a party is surprised is within the sound discretion of the trial court. A witness's grand jury testimony may be used to refresh the witness's recollection. *State v. Diehl.*[663]

This court found surprise was established simply because the state had no reason to believe the witness would contradict his grand jury testimony: "Where a witness has voluntarily made a statement, under oath, as to the existence of a state of facts, the party calling him may, in the absence of an express forewarning from the witness of an intention to repudiate it and notwithstanding knowledge of hostility, rely upon such statement and expect his testimony to be in accord therewith, and if the testimony is in direct contradiction thereto as concerning a material fact, such party will be deemed taken by surprise as a matter of law." [664]

3. Impeachment with a Parole Violation.

In *State v. Greer*, the trial court properly allowed the state to impeach the credibility of the defendant by evidence of a parole violation. Evid. R. 608(B) allows a witness' credibility to be attacked by the use of specific instances, if it is clearly probative of truthfulness. In order to be released on parole, pursuant to R.C. 2967.01(E), the parolee must promise to adhere to the terms and

---

[662] *State v. Liberatore* , 69 Ohio St. 2d 583, 433 N.E.2d 561 (1982).

[663] *State v. Diehl* , 67 Ohio St. 2d 389, 423 N.E. 2d 1112 (1981).

[664] *State v. Duffy,* 134 Ohio St. 16, 15 N.E. 2d 535 (1938).

conditions of parole. A violation of the terms and conditions of parole means the person has failed to keep his or her word, and hence evidence of a parole violation is probative of "truthfulness or untruthfulness." [665]

4. Improper use of Specific Instances of Conduct.

In *State v. Kamel*, the trial court improperly admitted specific instances of conduct by means of extrinsic evidence to attack the witness' credibility. In order to rebut the defendant's testimony that he never punished his children by pulling their ears, the state called a witness who stated he saw the defendant pull his children's ears at a store three or four days ago. [666]

Even if this evidence was probative, it was clearly inadmissible as a specific instance of conduct used to attack the credibility of the witness.

In *State v. Leuin*, a prosecution for gross sexual imposition, the trial court improperly permitted the state to attack the credibility of a defense witness with specific instances of conduct. The witness testified she and appellant never had sex and she was not his girlfriend. Several witnesses rebutted these facts. Evid. R. 608(B) prohibits the use of a specific instance of conduct to attack a witness' credibility. The specific instances may only be used on cross-examination of the witness in the *discretion of the trial court.* "The state's rebuttal testimony, by the state's own admission was

---

[665] *State v. Greer* , 39 Ohio St.3d 236, 530 N.E. 2d 382 (1988).

[666] *State v. Kamel* , 12 Ohio St. 3d 306, 466 N.E. 2d 860 (1984).

offered solely in an attempt to impeach the testimony of Williams. This is precisely the mischief that Evid. R. 608(B) was intended to prevent." [667]

5. Evidence Offered other than to Impeach Credibility.

The purpose of the prohibition of 608(B), that specific instances of conduct of a witness are not admissible to attack or support that witness' credibility, is to prohibit the admission of nonprobative evidence.

However, where the evidence is being offered for more than impeachment, it may be admissible. Evidence of a rape victim's reputation as having prior sex with a man was properly admissible since she claimed to be gay and would not consent to sex with a man (consent was the defense) "* * * the proffered testimony is directly probative of the issue of force, an element of the crime of rape. For this reason, Evid. R. 608(B) does not bar the introduction of the defense witness testimony." [668]

---

[667] *State v. Leuin* ,11 Ohio St. 3d 172, 464 N.E. 2d 552 (1984).

[668] *State v. Williams,* 21 Ohio St. 3d 33, 487 N.E. 2d 560 (1986).

CHAPTER 72

Motions in Limine.

Where a defendant's motion in limine to exclude evidence is overruled, the defendant is nevertheless required to object at trial prior to the admission of the contested evidence.

Where the state is granted a motion in limine preventing the defendant from introducing evidence, the defendant cannot claim that the granting of the motion to exclude is error unless a proffer is made specifying what evidence he or she intended to present. The nature of a motion in limine is interlocutory, and it does not ultimately determine the admissibility of the evidence, "Thus a motion in limine, if granted, is a tentative, interlocutory, precautionary ruling by the trial court reflecting its anticipatory treatment of the evidentiary issue."

Because the motion is interlocutory, "* * * appellant could have proffered the temporarily excluded evidence outside the presence of the jury when the issue arose during trial and if the proffered evidence was then excluded, he could have perfected an appeal as of right from the trial court's final judgment at the conclusion of the case."[669]

The above rule is not iron clad; it must be remembered that if the exclusion (1) affects a substantial right, and (2), the substance of the excluded evidence is apparent from the question

[669] *State v. Grubb*, 28 Ohio St. 3d 199, 503 N.E. 2d 142 (1986).

asked by counsel, the record may be interpreted as being preserved. In the case of *plain error* affecting substantial rights, Evid. R. 103(D) describes the power of the courts to take notice of the plain errors, and to implement appropriate remedies.

See *State v. Gilmore*, where the court held that a proffer of excluded evidence is not always necessary. As stated above, where a *substantial right* is affected, and where the substance of the evidence is apparent from the context, if not made by proffer, the issue may nevertheless be reviewable. [670]

In *Gilmore*, it was clear to the court from the context of the evidence that the defendant wanted to testify that the informant repeatedly asked him to sell drugs. This case shows the court's willingness to look at the context of the evidence to determine if there is sufficient record established, even though there was no *offer of proof*. However, the conviction was sustained because the appellant had not shown that the exclusion of the evidence affected a *substantial right*. "Moreover, we are convinced that even if the excluded testimony had been admitted, such evidence would not negate the overwhelming proof of defendant's guilt. See *State v. Williams* (1983), 6 Ohio St. 3d 281, 3d 281, paragraph six of the syllabus."

---

[670] *State v. Gilmore* , 28 Ohio St. 3d 190, 503 N.E. 2d 147 (1986).

CHAPTER 73

Out of Court Experiments.

"The admission of out-of-court experiments is left to the sound discretion of the trial court. A reviewing court is not to interfere with a trial court's ruling admitting such experiments absent an abuse of discretion. In any event, the question before us is not whether the trial court ruled as we would have ruled had we been confronted with such evidence, but whether the trial court abused its discretion so as to prejudice appellee." This court upheld the trial court's conclusion that the conditions of the breath-alcohol test the defendant wanted to admit could not be reliably duplicated. *Columbus v.* Taylor.[671]

1. Voice Prints.

Although the rules allow for adequate precautions for the admission of voice prints, the admission must nevertheless be made on a case-by-case basis as to their relevancy. *State v. Williams.*[672]

---

[671] *Columbus v.* Taylor, 39 Ohio St. 3d 162, 529 N.E. 2d 1382 (1988).

[672] *State v. Williams,* 4 Ohio St. 3d 53, 466 N.E. 2d 444 (1983). See also Evid. R. 402.

CHAPTER 74

Opinion Testimony of Lay Witnesses.

Evid R. 701 permits the testimony of a non-expert in the form of an opinion or inference if the testimony is rationally based on the witness' perception and helpful to the understanding of his or her testimony or a determination of a fact in issue.

In *State v. Jells*, a police officer was permitted to testify as to the similarity of two footprints attributed to the defendant. Appellant argued that such testimony was not admissible because the officer was giving unqualified expert testimony.

In finding the testimony admissible pursuant to Evid. R. 701 the court stated, "Thus a lay witness may be permitted to express his or her opinion as to the similarity of footprints if it can be shown that his or her conclusions are based on measurements or peculiarities in the prints that are readily recognizable and within the capabilities of a lay witness to observe." [673]

The officer's testimony was the result of personal observation. Because his testimony was not the result of a scientific test, the standard of a reasonable scientific certainty, as is the criteria for admission of expert scientific testimony, was not

---

[673] *State v. Jells* , 53 Ohio St. 3d 22, 559 N.E. 2d 464 (1990).

required. See also, *City of Urbana ex rel. Newlin v. Downing*, where the trial court properly admitted evidence of a non-expert's opinion concerning obscenity. [674]

In *State v. Duncan*, a statement by a witness that contained an appraisal of the event was properly admitted since her appraisal was relevant to a fact in issue. [675]

In the same vein, in *State v. Rohdes*, the court upheld the admission of the excited utterance of a witness that contained an appraisal. The witness had observed the murder of her boss. The issue was whether the statement could be admitted as an appraisal as well as an excited utterance. Although it could be argued that the statement was inadmissible under Evid. R. 701, as an improper opinion, the court focused on the fact that the declarant was the only witness to the murder and her view was highly relevant to a fact in issue. [676]

---

[674] *City of Urbana ex rel. Newlin v. Downing,* 43 Ohio St. 3d 109, 539 N.E. 2d 140 (1989).

[675] *State v. Duncan,* 53 Ohio St. 2d 215, 373 N.E. 2d 1234 (1978).

[676] *State v. Rohdes,* 23 Ohio St. 3d 225, 492 N.E. 2d 430 (1986).

CHAPTER 75

Pleas, Offers to Plead and Related Statements.

Evid. R. 410 governs the admissibility of evidence of pleas, offers to plead, and related statements. The following are inadmissible against the defendant

I. Pleas of guilt later withdrawn.

2. Pleas of no contest.

3. Pleas of guilty to a violation.

4. Statements made in the course of plea negotiations that did not result in a plea of guilty, or resulted in plea of guilty that was later withdrawn.

However, a statement is admissible if another statement made during the same course of plea bargaining was introduced. In addition, a statement is admissible in a prosecution for perjury or false statement if it was under oath, on the record, and in the presence of counsel.

1. Statements Made During Plea Negotiations.

Although Evid. R. 410 provides that statements made by the defendant in plea negotiations are not admissible at trial. Statements made to police officers by the defendant as to the possibility of dropping the charges against him were not technically plea negotiations and are admissible. "His statements do not contain an offer to plead guilty to any charge, nor do they indicate serious effort at negotiating such a plea." [677]

The prohibition, pursuant to Evid. R. 410(A)(2), of the admissibility of a no contest plea in any civil or criminal proceeding against the defendant, does not prevent the admission of a no contest plea to prove a prior murder conviction specification pursuant to R.C. 2929.04(A). Evid. R. 410 and Crim. R. 11(B)(2) only prohibits the admission of a no contest plea, "These rules do not prohibit the admission of a *conviction* entered upon that plea when such conviction is made relevant by statute." The purpose of Evid. R. 410 is to protect statements made in the course of plea bargaining and the admission of a conviction entered on a no contest plea does not contravene the policy of the rule.

Evid. R. 410 had been amended effective July 1, 1991, allowing the admission of a statement made in plea negotiations where another statement of the defendant has been admitted "and the statement should, in fairness, be considered contemporaneously with it." The new amendment however, prohibits the admission of statements made in the course of plea bargaining where defense counsel, or the prosecuting attorney, were participants.

---

[677] State v. Kidder, 32 Ohio St. 3d 279, 513 N.E. 2d 311 (1987).

CHAPTER 76

Relevancy.

Relevant evidence is evidence that has "* * * any tendency to make the existence of any fact that is of consequence to the determination of the action more probable or less probable than it would be without the evidence." Evid. R. 401. "Generally speaking, the question of whether evidence is relevant is ordinarily not one of law but rather one which the trial court can resolve based on common experience and logic.[678]

Where one is challenging the admission of evidence because it is not relevant, it must be shown that the court abused its discretion in admitting the evidence. To determine error, the context and the impact of the irrelevant evidence must be considered.

In Lyles, the admission of the evidence was harmless beyond a reasonable doubt because the remainder of the properly admitted evidence pointed overwhelmingly to the defendant's guilt. Further, even if the trial court had abused its discretion in admitting the evidence, it must be established that the defendant has been materially prejudiced as a result.[679]

---

[678] *State v. Lyles*, 42 Ohio St. 3d 98, 537 N.E. 2d 221 (1989).

[679] See also, *State v. Maurer*,15 Ohio St. 3d 239, 473 N.E. 2d 768 (1984).

1. Relevant Circumstantial Evidence.

It is not necessary that relevant evidence be direct evidence; circumstantial evidence is often relevant. In *State v. Moore*, the state failed to provide a tape recording of the defendant pursuant to Crim. R. 16(B), because it felt that the recording did not bear directly on the offense charged. This court found the statement to be relevant, and concluded if the defendant had known of its existence he would not have denied having the conversation that was later used to impeach him. Although the evidence was not direct evidence of guilt, it turned out to be relevant impeachment evidence. [680]

In *State v. Jells*, an aggravated murder case, the court approved the admission of the defendant's blood stained pants and shoes, even though it could not be determined if the blood stains were human blood. The court, without discussing why, ruled the evidence was relevant. The court probably found the evidence relevant because it tended to prove, "the existence of any fact that is of consequence to the determination of the action." Evid. R. 401. [681]

The *Jells* court was also aware that a three-judge panel, which is presumed to consider only relevant evidence, tried the case. See also *State v. Moreland.*[682]

---

[680] *State v. Moore*, 40 Ohio St, 3d 63, 531 N.E. 2d 691 (1988).

[681] *State v. Jells*, 53 Ohio St. 3d 22, 559 N.E. 2d 464 (1990).

[682] *State v. Moreland,* 50 Ohio St. 3d 58, 552 N.E. 2d 894 (1990).

It was proper for the trial court to admit evidence in an aggravated murder trial, that the victim was burned, even though the coroner could not determine the exact cause of death. The coroner testified there were three possible causes of death including burning, and even though the coroner testified the burning could have occurred before or after death, the testimony was relevant since it was established that the defendant had access to a type of kerosene that could have been used to burn the victim.

Further, the testimony concerning the burned body was relevant to the coroner's inability to pinpoint the cause of death; the burning of the body prevented him from determining the cause of death. If he would not have been able to testify to the burning, he would not have been able to state why he could not determine the cause of death. *State v. Heinish.* [683]

It was proper to admit evidence that a defendant had a list of the jurors in order to show that the cellmate that testified against the defendant did not get information about the case from defendant's legal papers where he testified that all he saw were the jury lists. This information was relevant to bolster the credibility of the cellmate. It also did not unduly prejudice the defendant since the trial court explained to the jury that the list is a public record. *State v. Roe.* [684] The trial court has broad discretion to determine whether a relevant declaration is admissible as a hearsay exception.

---

[683] *State v. Heinish*, 50 Ohio St. 3d 231, 553 N.E. 2d 1026 (1990).

[684] *State v. Roe,* 41 Ohio St.3d 18, 535 N.E. 2d 1351 (1989).

CHAPTER 77

Voice Analysis and Identification Testimony.

Voice analysis and identification testimony is permitted.[685] Ohio has not adopted the "Frye" test (1923), 54 U.S. App. D.C. 46, 47, 293 F 1013, requiring that such evidence to be admitted must be based on scientific principles that have been sufficiently established and to have gained general acceptance. This court relies on the rules of evidence:

"Like our counterpart in Maine, we refuse to engage in scientific nose counting for the purpose of deciding whether evidence based on newly ascertained or applied scientific principals is admissible. We believe the Rules of Evidence established adequate preconditions for admissibility of expert testimony, and we leave to the discretion of this state's judiciary, on a case by case basis, to decide whether the questioned testimony is relevant and will assist the trier of fact to understand the evidence or to determine a fact in issue."[686]

---

[685] *State v. Williams*, 4 Ohio St. 3d 53, 466 N.E. 2d 444 (1983).

[686] See also, *State v. Bressen* ,51 Ohio St. 3d 123, 554 N.E. 2d 1330 (1990).

CHAPTER 78

Flight as Evidence of Guilt.

Evidence of a defendant's flight from a crime scene may be admitted at trial as evidence of consciousness of guilt. In *State v.* Eaton the defendant asserted an accident defense. [687] The court, in finding evidence of flight from the scene admissible, quoted with approval the following from Wigmore: "Flight from justice and its analogous conduct have always been indicative of a consciousness of guilt * * * It is to-day universally conceded that the fact of an accused flight, escape, from custody, resistance to arrest, concealment, assumption of a false name, and related conduct, are admissible as evidence of consciousness of guilt, and thus guilt itself." [688]

Flight from the scene, therefore is relevant evidence to disprove a defense of accident.

---

[687] *State v. Eaton*, 19 Ohio St. 2d 145, 249 N.E. 2d 897 (1969). Judgment vacated, in part, in unrelated issue by Eaton v. Ohio 408 U.S. 935, 92 S. Ct. 2857, 33 L. Ed. 2d 750.

[688] 2 Wigmore on Evidence (3d Ed.), 111 Section 276.

CHAPTER 79

Gruesome Photographs.

Admission of photographs, even if gruesome, is left to the sound discretion of the trial court.

Unless it can be shown that the trial court *abused its discretion* in admitting the photographs or that *material prejudice* occurred, the admission of the photographs will be upheld.

"Properly authenticated photographs, even if gruesome, are admissible in a capital prosecution if relevant and of probative value in assisting the trier of fact to determine the issues or are illustrative of testimony and other evidence, as long as the danger of material prejudice to the defendant is outweighed by

their probative value and the photographs are not repetitive or cumulative in number."[689]

A trial court must balance the potential prejudice of gruesome photographs with the value of their admission. If the photographs are illustrative of testimony from a coroner, police officer, or other witness, it may generally be assumed that they are admissible (with the exception that they may be overly repetitive or cumulative.) Photographs of fatal wounds are admissible as being illustrative of intent to kill.

---

[689] *State v.Maurer,*15 Ohio St 3d 239, 473 N.E. 2d 768 (1984)

There is theoretically a potential for prejudice if the photographs are cumulative because repetitiveness has the potential to overwhelm the jury. There has been no clear- cut guidance from the court as to what number of photographs is cumulative.

In *Maurer*, five “gruesome” photographs were admitted, as they were "not so numerous so as to be repetitive or cumulative.[690]

In *State v. Morales*, the court held that in a capital case the test has changed concerning Evid. R. 403, "to be admissible is a capital case; the probative value of each photograph must outweigh the danger of prejudice to the defendant and, additionally, not be repetitive or cumulative in nature." [691]

This holding is contrary to the normal standard of Evid. R. 403, where probative value must be minimal and prejudice great before they are excluded. However, the court has nevertheless cautioned the use of numerous gruesome photographs.

The court made it clear in *Morales* that it does not condone the use of excessive photographs, and will determine their propriety on a case-by-case basis. "We strongly caution use of this type of evidence so that any question of probative value, as compared to cumulative, repetitious and prejudicial effects, will be avoided."

In *State v. Durr*, two photographs of the victim's body in an advanced state of decomposition were admitted. Their admission was upheld because they were illustrative of the testimony of the

---

[690] See also *State v. Jackson*, 57 Ohio St. 3d 29, 565 N.E. 549 (1991).

[691] *State v. Morales,* 32 Ohio St. 3d 252, 513 N. E. 2d 267 (1987), certiorari denied (1988), 484 U.S. 1047.

coroner; and they showed the personal articles found on the body, which was relevant to identification. [692]

In *State v. Wiles*, the court found the photographs were "clearly gruesome and repetitious" however since appellant failed to object to their admission at trial, there was no plain error in their admission. The photographs were nonetheless probative because they revealed the number and location of stab wounds on the victim. [693]

The court did address cumulativeness in *State v. Watson*. Although appellant moved to suppress the admission of the photographs, he failed to object to their admission at trial, which left review only for plain error. Nevertheless, the trial court erred in admitting all five photographs that depicted the victim's brain blown out of his skull. "Although one or two of these photos may have been admissible, the trial court erred by admitting all five." We are left with the fact that the admission of the photographs was not plain error. [694]

---

[692] *State v. Durr* , 58 Ohio 3d 86, 568 N.E. 2d 674 (1991).

[693] *State v. Wiles* , 59 Ohio St. 3d 71, 571 N. E. 2d 97 (1991).

[694] *State v. Watson* , 61 Ohio St. 3d 1,572 N.E. 2d 97 (1991) (reversed on other grounds).

CHAPTER 80

Hypnotically Refreshed Testimony.

The rules governing the admission of testimony of a hypnotically refreshed witness take three basic forms: (1) Testimony of a witness under hypnosis is inadmissible. (2) A witness will be permitted to testify to events recalled prior to being hypnotized if the trial court finds the testimony to be substantially in conformance with the pre-hypnotic recollection of the witness. (3) Where the witness has been refreshed by hypnosis his testimony is admissible if the trial court determines that under the totality of the circumstances the testimony is reliable. [695]

The court in footnote 4 of *Johnston* held that the party who wishes to offer testimony of events prior to hypnosis should conduct a pre-hypnosis interview that is recorded or at least in writing. The purpose of the interview is to give the trial court information as to what the witness recalled prior to being hypnotized.

If the events testified to by the witness were essentially the same as those from his pre-hypnotic interviews, this would be sufficient evidence that the witness was testifying from pre-hypnotic recollection. If the guidelines are not followed concerning a pre-hypnotic interview the trial court may, in its discretion, exclude the testimony.

---

[695] *State v. Johnston*, 39 Ohio St. 3d 48, 529 N.E. 2d 898 (1988).

An abuse of discretion was found where the trial court failed to determine whether the refreshed testimony was sufficiently reliable. "Upon retrial, the trial court should conduct a pretrial hearing placing the burden on appellant, as the offering party, to demonstrate by clear and convincing proof that, under the totality of the circumstances, Rine's hypnotically refreshed memory is sufficiently reliable to warrant admission." *Johnson I, supra.*

Admission Criteria.

It should be noted that concerning the admission of testimony that has been refreshed by hypnosis, the following criteria has been created by the court:

1) The hypnosis session should be conducted by a licensed psychiatrist or psychologist trained in the use of hypnosis, to ensure the most accurate recall possible.

2) The qualified professional conducting the hypnosis session should be independent from any of the parties to the case to avoid any biased procedures or questions.

3) Any information given to the hypnotist by any of the parties to the case prior to the hypnosis session should be recorded, at a minimum in writing, so that the trial court can determine the extent to which the subject may have received any information from the hypnotist.

4) The hypnosis session and all other contact between the hypnotist and the subject should be recorded preferably on video tape, so that a permanent record is available to reveal the presence of any suggestive procedures or questions.

5) Generally, only the hypnotist and subject should be present during the hypnosis session, in order to protect against inadvertent influence. However, other persons may be present if their attendance is necessary and steps are taken to prevent their influencing the results of the session.

The court further pointed out that the trial court may also consider the following in examining the totality of the circumstances:

The presence of conflicting or corroborating independent evidence, the appropriateness of using hypnosis to restore the witness's memory, any motivation the witness may have for remembering or forgetting the events to which he testified.

Finally, the court should give the opposing party wide latitude in cross-examination and should instruct the jury of the potential dangers of hypnosis.

See also, *State v. Maurer*, where the court allowed the testimony of a witness who, although he had been previously hypnotized, testified to the same events that he had related prior to being hypnotized. The court held that the issue of credibility of the witness could be resolved by the trier of fact as it would any other witness. [696]

---

[696] *State v. Maurer,* 15 Ohio St. 3d 239, 473 N. E. 2d 768 (1988).

CHAPTER 81

Testimony of Prior Identification.

R.C. 2945.55 provides "When identification of the defendant is an issue, a witness who has on previous occasion identified the defendant, such person may testify to such previous identification. Such identification may be proved by other witnesses."

In *State v. Breedlove*, two witnesses to a robbery were properly permitted to testify that they previously identified the defendant from a group of police photographs. However, the admission of the police photographs with police file numbers was prejudicial error "* * * [it was unjustifiable] to present police mug shots, bearing police identification numbers, from which a reasonable inference can be drawn that the defendant, at some indefinite time in the past had had trouble with the law." To admit evidence of prior criminal involvement, the evidence must comply with R.C. 2945.59, which provides for the admission of evidence of similar acts. [697]

The court in *Breedlove* further held that it was proper to admit the testimony of an identification witness who testified that she picked the picture of the defendant out of a police photo array, and that the photographs were "photographs of guys that have committed crimes." Similarly, the evidence was properly admitted where a police officer testified that he had shown another witness photographs "acquired through perhaps warrants that went out for wanted individuals * * *."

---

[697] *State v. Breedlove* , 26 Ohio St. 2d 178, 271 N.E. 2d 238 (1971).

A police officer is competent to testify that a witness prior to trial had made photographic and personal identification of the defendant, since R.C. 2945.55 allows identification to be proven by other witnesses. This court approved the admission of this evidence primarily because it showed the process by which the witness was identified because the process itself was under attack. This process allows the corroboration of the primary identification. *State v. Lancaster.*[698]

[698] *State v. Lancaster*, 25 Ohio St. 2d 83, 267 N.E. 2d 291 (1971).

CHAPTER 82

Medical Records.

Where a defendant had the opportunity to bring in the preparer of medical records and fails to do so, this opportunity is sufficient to satisfy his confrontational rights.[699]

---

[699] *State v. Spikes*, 67 Ohio St. 2d 405, 423 N.E. 2d 1122 (1981).

CHAPTER 83

Trial Court May Call its Own Witnesses.

Evid. R. 614 allows the trial court to call witnesses on its own motion, and to allow each party to cross-examine the witness. The calling of a witness by the trial court will not constitute error absent a clear abuse of discretion.[700]

[700] State v. Apanovitch, 33 Ohio St. 3d 19, 514 N.E. 2d 394 (1987).

PART SIX: HABEAS CORPUS

CHAPTER 84

Habeas Corpus.

1. Relief for Excessive Bail.
2. Excessive Bail in Pretrial Release
3. Reversed Conviction.
4. Denial of Appeal Bond.
5. Where Appeal is the Proper Remedy.
6. Post-Conviction Relief and Habeas Corpus.
7. Discretion of the Court of Appeals.
8. Habeas Jurisdiction According to Territory.
9. Application for the Writ.
10. Contempt of Court.
11. Court's Discretion and Mandatory Functions.
12. Parole Hearing Delays.
13. Adult Parole Authority.
14. Indefinite Commitment to a State Hospital.
15. Involuntary Plea.
16. Denial of Right to Speedy Trial.
17. Where Defendant is tried before petition is heard.
18. Lack of Jurisdiction and Particularity.
19. Challenge of the Indictment.

20. Commitment Papers required before review and petition.
21. Speedy Trial.
22. Revocation of Probation.
23. Ineffective Assistance of Counsel.
24. Review of Void Sentences.

R.C. 2725.01, the habeas corpus statute, permits anyone who is unlawfully restrained of his or her liberty, or is entitled to the custody of another to file a writ of habeas corpus "to inquire into the cause of imprisonment, restraint, or depravation."

1. Relief for Excessive Bail.

Habeas corpus is the proper remedy where excessive pretrial bail is set. In *State ex rel. Baker v. Troutman*, in order for the surety to post bail, the local rule required the surety to agree to pay whatever fine and court costs were assessed to the defendant from the cash or securities deposited to the court. [701]

This court found that local rule to be in effect a type of excessive bail that conditioned the defendant's right to bail on the surety's consent to forfeit the bail for fines and costs, "We view its operation as excessive bail under Section 9, Article I [of the Ohio Constitution] because it placed limiting conditions on bail that were unrelated to appearance of the accused."

The court concluded that respondent had a *clear duty* to release the defendant and the defendant had a *clear right* from

[701] *State ex rel. Baker v. Troutman,* 50 Ohio St. 3d 270, 553 N.E. 2d 1053 (1990).

relief to the unconstitutional bail requirement. Further there existed no adequate remedy at law in the ordinary course of law, primarily because even if this were appealed, it would take too long to aid Baker "* * *we find no merit in forcing [the bondsman] to appeal only to receive the same result." [702]

2. Excessive Bail in Pretrial Release.

Habeas corpus is the proper remedy in which to raise a claim that the court has imposed excessive bail in pretrial release. However here, as in any case, the petitioner must allege facts that illustrate an abuse of discretion in determining bail.[703]

"[W]hen a petition for a writ of habeas corpus is presented, if it appears that the writ ought to issue, a court of judge authorized to grant the writ must grant it forthwith." R.C. 2725.06.

A three-million-dollar bail was not excessive where the facts show that an unquestionable propensity on behalf of the defendant to violate the law and where he was a possible flight risk. Crim. R. 46(C) delineates a non-exhausted list of relevant factors to be considered in determining bail.[704]

3. Reversed Conviction.

Where a trial court fails to rule on a motion to vacate a sentence based on a conviction that was reversed, the motion to vacate would normally serve as an adequate

---

[702] *Troutman, supra.*

[703] *Jenkins v.Billy*, 43 Ohio St. 3d 84, 538 N.E. 2d 1045 (1989).

[704] *Ahmad v. Plummer*, 126 Ohio St.3d 262, 2010-Ohio-3757.

remedy at law. However, when the court does not render the decision for several months, a habeas corpus action is proper. [705]

The *Mallery* court found a duty on the part of the trial court to terminate the incarceration for a probation violation that was based on a conviction that was later reversed.

Mallery, however, was overruled in *Zanders v. Anderson.* Where the court held that a reversal of a conviction on which a probation violation is based does not make the probation violation a nullity because the facts of the violation, even though not sufficient for a conviction, can nevertheless be sufficient for a probation violation. [706]

4. Denial of Appeal Bond.

Habeas corpus is the proper remedy where a court of appeals denies an appeal bond or where excessive bail is set after a judgment of conviction where the petitioner is lawfully committed by a court of competent jurisdiction. [707]

---

[705] *In re Petition for Mallory*, 17 Ohio St. 3d 34, 476 N.E. 2d 1045 (1985).

[706] *Zanders v. Anderson,* 74 Ohio St. 3d 269, 658 N.E. 2d 300 (1996).

[707] *State ex rel. Pirman v. Money*, 69 Ohio St.3d 591, 635 N.E.2d 26 (1994).

5. Where Appeal is the Proper Remedy.

Habeas corpus does not lie where an appeal is the proper remedy. Where one is incarcerated because of a criminal conviction and properly sentenced, any alleged trial errors must be pursued by way of an appeal. [708]

6. Post-Conviction Relief and Habeas Corpus.

After enactment of Section R.C. 2953.21 to R.C. 2953.24 inclusive, the Post-Conviction statute, the right to relief in habeas corpus to collaterally attack judgments of conviction no longer exits.[709] Prior to this enactment there was no other adequate remedy other than habeas corpus to collaterally attack a conviction based on the alleged denial of a prisoner's rights under the Constitution.[710]

7. Discretion of the Court of Appeals.

Where appellant prosecutor challenges a court of appeal's modification of bond pursuant to a habeas corpus petition, the court of appeals is not required to find an abuse of discretion by

---

[708] *In re. Copley*, 29 Ohio St. 2d 35, 278 N.E. 2d 357 (1972).

[709] *Freeman v. Maxwell*, 4 Ohio St. 2d 4, 210 N. E. 2d 885 (1965).

[710] See also *Gerhart v. Tate*, 33 Ohio St. 3d 120, 515 N.E. 2d 917 (1987), and *Noble v.McMaken* 45 Ohio St. 2d 236, 344 N.E. 2d 129. (1976).

the trial court in setting the bond. Moreover, even though the court of appeals did not specifically state the bail was excessive, there was no error since these cases are considered original actions and not as appeals. The court of appeals may make an independent decision "* * * and exercise its own discretion under Crim. R. 46 in the same manner as would the trial judge."[711]

8. Habeas Jurisdiction According to Territory.

A court or judge in the county in which the institution is located must issue under R.C. 2725.03 a habeas corpus writ for a penal institution or state benevolent institution. R.C. 2725.03 allocates habeas corpus jurisdiction according to territory.[712]

9. Application for the Writ.

Where a writ of habeas corpus alleges: "he is unlawfully restrained of his liberty without legal authority, by the aforementioned respondents, in the Chillicothe Correctional institute * * * these allegations are not sufficient to maintain a habeas corpus action because the petitioner must attack the *jurisdiction* of the sentencing court." [713]

---

[711] *In re De Fronzo*, 49 Ohio St. 2d 271, 361 N.E. 2d 448 (1977).

[712] *Bridges v. McMacklin,* 44 Ohio St. 3d 135, 541 N.E. 2d 1035 (1989).

[713] *Lippert v. Engle*, 49 Ohio St. 2d 281, 361 N.E. 239 (1977).

10. Contempt of Court.

A person sentenced to jail because of contempt of court may not file a habeas corpus petition alleging denial of right to counsel because contempt proceedings are not criminal.[714] Appeal is the proper remedy in a contempt proceeding. The petition must comply with R.C. 2725.04, be "signed and verified," and must specify the officer, or name of the person by whom the prisoner is confined, or restrained.[715]

11. Court's Discretion and Mandatory Functions.

Mandamus will not issue to control a court's discretion; it will issue however, to direct a court to exercise jurisdiction or "mandatory functions per R.C. 2731.03. [716]

This principal can be seen in *State ex rel. Martin v. Corrigan*. Here the court was directed to pay assigned counsel fees, even though the judge had discretion in setting the amount of the fees. [717]

---

[714] *State v.Timson*, 38 Ohio St. 2d 122, 311 N.E. 2d 16 (1974).

[715] *In re Calhoun*, 47 Ohio St. 2d 15, 350 N.E. 2d 665 (1976).

[716] *State ex rel. Sawyer v. O'Connor*, 54 Ohio St. 2d 380, 377 N.E. 2d 494(1978).

[717] *State ex rel. Martin v. Corrigan* 25 Ohio St.3d 29, 494 N.E.2d 1128 (1986).

12. Parole Hearing Delays.

Where it is alleged that there is a delay by the Adult Parole Authority in having a final parole revocation hearing, the court is required to apply the following two-part test to determine if the alleged parole violator is entitled to a writ of habeas corpus:

(1) The court must determine if the delay was reasonable,

(2) If the delay was unreasonable, whether the alleged parole violator was prejudiced. Here the petitioner alleged the delay of the final parole revocation hearing violated his due process rights. The court held when determining whether the delay is unreasonable the following factors should be considered: (1) the length of the delay, (2) the reason for the delay, and (3) the alleged parole violator's assertion of his right to a hearing within a reasonable period of time.

In regard to whether the delay was unreasonable and if prejudice results thereby, "The court must weigh any prejudice to the alleged parole violator in light of the interests protected by the 'reasonable time' requirement of R.C. 2967.15 and Ohio Adm. Code 5120:1-1-19(A)" This court cites three factors

These factors are"(1) prevention of oppressive prehearing incarceration; (2) minimization of anxiety and concern of the alleged parole violator, and (3) limitation of the possibility that delay will impair the accused parole violator's defense at his final parole revocation hearing." [718]

13. Adult Parole Authority.

Habeas corpus is not available where a prisoner challenges the Ad~~ult Parole Authority. It is not~~ a "substitute for appeal or for a

[718] *Coleman Stubbs*, 23 Ohio St. 3d 137, 491 N.E. 2d 1126 (1986).

mandamus proceeding. Although the writ is available to parties who unlawfully are deprived of their liberty; it is not available to those deprived of their freedom pursuant to a lawful criminal sentence." [719]

14. Indefinite Commitment to a State Hospital.

A person is deprived of his due process rights where he is indefinitely committed because of incapacity to proceed to trial. Such a person must be committed civilly pursuant to R.C. 5122.01.

Although R.C. 5125.08 provides a procedure for an inmate serving an incorrect sentence, there is no corresponding procedure where the person has not been sentenced. The court, in assuming the original indictment was proper, held: "However, that commitment must by nature be limited to a reasonable time. If it is determined that a person committed pursuant to these sections is responding to treatment and care, and will in the foreseeable future, probably be able to stand trial, that time might be extended somewhat.

"However, as soon as it is reliably determined that this is not the case, then other procedures must be instituted to either release the person or civilly commit him indefinitely, in the same way in which any other person may be committed."[720]

At the time of the ruling, although the petitioner was not in custody, the issue was not moot because the respondent may

---

[719] *Stahl v. Shoemaker*, 50 Ohio St. 2d 351, 364 N.E. 2d 286 (1977).

[720] *Burton v. Reshetylo*, 38 Ohio St. 2d 35, 309 N.E. 2d 907 (1974).

appeal the granting of a writ of habeas corpus because otherwise "[t]o so hold destroys appellant review of the granting of the writ, a circumstance which is undesirable * * *" [721]

15. Involuntary Plea.

Habeas will not lie where the petitioner alleges he did not enter a knowingly and voluntary plea. Such a challenge can be made during post-conviction proceedings. Further if appellant alleges he was incompetent at the time of the plea; such allegation does not affect the jurisdiction of the trial court.[722]

16. Denial of Right to Speedy Trial.

Appellant should appeal from the judgment of conviction where he claims he was denied his right to a speedy trial. A writ of habeas corpus would be improper because delay in a trial or preliminary hearing cannot be the subject of habeas after the defendant has been convicted or has pleaded guilty because the delay no longer exists.[723]

---

[721] *Ibid.*

[722] *Pollock v. Morris*, 35 Ohio St. 3d 117, 518 N.E. 2d 1205 (1988).

[723] *Bulus v. Engle*, 48 Ohio St. 2d 3, 355 N.E. 2d 493 (1976).

17. Where Defendant is Tried before Petition is Heard.

Where the defendant is tried before his petition for habeas corpus is heard, the court may deny the petition because he should have proceeded pursuant to R.C. 2953.21 to R.C. 2953.24, via post-conviction relief. [724]

18. Lack of Jurisdiction and Particularity.

A petitioner must state with particularity why the court or magistrate lacked jurisdiction to enter the process, judgment or order "Otherwise, it will appear that the writ ought not to be granted, and the petition will be dismissed pursuant to R.C. 2725.06," *Hammond v. Dallman.* [725]

In *Hammond*, the court granted the writ, but denied relief and remanded the petitioner to custody. The writ was granted because pursuant to R.C. 2725.06, it appeared on its face that it ought to be granted because it alleged the court did not have jurisdiction. The court treated respondent's motion to dismiss as a return pursuant to R.C. 2725.12 and R.C. 2725.14, the return showed jurisdiction of the trial court.

Petitioner also filed a motion for summary judgment attacking the sufficiency of the indictment; such an attack is too late in the game. "* * * an indictment cannot be collaterally

---

[724] *Noble v.McMaken,* 45 Ohio St. 2d 236, 344 N.E. 2d 129 (1976), *Freeman v. Maxwell*, 4 Ohio St. 2d 4, 210 N.E. 2d 885 (1965).

[725] *Hammond v. Dallman* , 63 Ohio St. 3d 666, 590 N.E. 2d 744 (1992).

attacked after a judgment of conviction 'because the judgment of conviction necessarily finds a defendant, where the court rendering it had jurisdiction of the person of the defendant and also jurisdiction of the subject matter * * *' State v. Woziak (1961), 172 Ohio St. 517, 18 O.O. 2d 58, 178 N.E. 2d 800." [726] The *Hammond* court also made it clear that if the claim had been made with particularity, it would not have appeared from the petition that the writ should issue.

19. Challenge of the Indictment.

The sufficiency of an indictment cannot be challenged through habeas corpus. In *State ex rel Haddock v. McMacklin*, [727] appellant challenged the indictment alleging it was obtained fraudulently. A challenge of the sufficiency of the indictment may only be made by direct appeal. This type of challenge does not implicate the jurisdiction of the court and is not a proper a habeas corpus action.[728]

---

[726] *Hammond,supra.*

[727] *State ex rel Haddock v. McMacklin* , 61 Ohio 3d 433,575 N.E. 2d 184, (1991).

[728] See also, *State ex rel Justice v. McMacklin*, 53 Ohio St. 3d 72, 558 N.E. 2d 1183 (1990) where the petitioner claimed the indictment was fabricated by the prosecutor's office, and the grand jury foreman's signature was forged. The contention was not jurisdictional and the petition was properly denied. See, also Wireman *v. Adult Parole Auth.*, 38 Ohio St. 3d 322, 528 N.E. 2d 173 (1988).

Res judicata applies to successive writs of habeas corpus. R.C. 2725.26 allows appeals of habeas corpus cases. The petitioner had no appeal of right because "* * * he elected voluntarily to receive and did receive a decision from the state's highest court in the first instance, which limited his right to appeal to a discretionary appeal to the United States Supreme Court. By so choosing, he waived in effect, R.C. 2725.26's right to appeal and accordingly the doctrine of res judicata applies to him as well." [729]

20. Commitment Papers Required for Review and Petition.

A petition for habeas will be dismissed for failure to comply with R.C. 2725.04(D), which mandates that the commitment papers or the cause of detention be exhibited. The inclusion of the commitment papers is necessary to inform the court as to how the commitment came into effect otherwise the petition will contain naked allegations that cannot be acted upon.[730]

21. Speedy Trial.

A claimed denial of the right to a speedy trial cannot be brought in a habeas corpus action after the defendant has pleaded guilty or has been convicted. Although habeas may lie where there is a delay in bringing the defendant to trial,

---

[729] *Hindlin v. Alexander* 63 Ohio St. 3d 153, 586 N.E. 2d 86 (1992).

[730] *Bloss v. Rogers*, 65 Ohio St. 3d 145, 602 N.E. 2d 602 (1992).

habeas may not lie where the delay has terminated, such as where the defendant has been convicted.

"The right to a speedy trial must be claimed at the time one is being deprived thereof, and the failure to do so constitutes a waiver." [731]

22. Revocation of Probation.

Revocation of probation is a final appealable order and not an action appropriate for habeas corpus.[732]

23. Ineffective Assistance of Counsel.

Ineffective assistance of counsel is a non-jurisdictional claim that must be raised upon appeal.[733]

24. Review of Void Sentences.

A sentence that is void because it did not include post-relief control is reviewable and res judicata will not apply to the conviction and determination of guilt. Further a direct appeal from a resentencing is not a first appeal of right.[734]

---

[731] *Mack v.Maxwell,* 174 Ohio St. 275,189 N.E. 2d 156(1963), *State ex rel Dotson v.Rogers*, 66 Ohio St. 3d 25, 607 N.E. 2d 453 (1993).

[732] *In re Hunt*, 46 Ohio St. 2d 378, 348 N. E. 2d 727 (1976); *State ex rel. Tucker v. Rogers*, 66 Ohio St.3d 36, 607 N.E. 2d 461 (1993).

[733] *McConnaughy v. Alvis*, 165 Ohio St. 102, 133 N.E. 2d 133 (1956).

State v. Fischer, Slip Opinion No. 2010-Ohio-6238. See also *State v. Bezak*, 114 Ohio St.3d 94, 2007-Ohio-3250, 868 N.E.2d 961

PART SEVEN: POST TRIAL ISSUES

CHAPTER 85

Forfeitures, Forfeiture Requirement.

Where an enforcement agency attempts to acquire criminal contraband by the forfeiture process it must strictly comply with the requirements of R.C. 2933.43.

A forfeiture that fails to comply with the requirements of R.C. 2933.43(C) is invalid. In *Ohio Dept of Liquor Control v. Sons of Italy Lodge 0917,* the state failed to follow the notice requirements, resulting in an invalid forfeiture.

“Strenuous due process protections must be afforded in order to avoid unfair forfeitures where the property's status as contraband is unclear. As the connection between the illegal act and the alleged contraband associated with it becomes increasingly tenuous, the necessity for due process protection becomes increasingly important, and the observance of procedural requirements may not be summarily dispensed with." [735]

---

[735] *Ohio Dept of Liquor Control v. Sons of Italy Lodge 0917,* 65 Ohio St.3d 532, 605 N. E. 2d 368 (1992).

CHAPTER 86

Presentence Investigation.

A presentence report may include the defendant's arrest records, not only his convictions. Neither R.C. 2947.06 nor R.C. 2929.03 delineate what should be included in the presentence report; as such, the information included is left to the sound discretion of the trial court. Further, Crim. R. 32.2 requires in addition to the defendant's record, that his or her social history be included. A presentence report must be ordered before the offender can receive community control sanctions or probation.

Social history can include *alleged* wrongdoing, and arrests in addition to criminal history. [736]

A subsequently appointed counsel has a right to review a previous presentence report of the defendant.[737]

[736] *State v. Cooey*, 46 Ohio St. 3d 20, 544 N.E. 2d 895 (1989).

[737] State v. Johnson, 138 Ohio St. 3d 282, 2014-Ohio-770.

CHAPTER 87

Sentencing/Probation.

1. Loss of Jurisdiction by Trial Court.
2. Conditions of Probation, Discretion of Sentencing Court.
3. Violation of Probation while serving in a Rehabilitation Facility.
4. Probation Revocation Hearing.
5. Sentencing by a Substitute Judge.
6. Mandatory Sentences and Judicial Release
7. Constitutionality of Extreme Consecutive Sentences.
8. Credit for Time Served Prior to Sentencing.
9. Imposition of Sentence Consecutive with another Court's Sentence.
10. Resentencing and Modification of Original Sentence.
11. Judicial Discretion in Sentencing.
12. Appellate Review of Felony Sentences.
13. Voided Sentence for failure to Impose Post-Release Control.
14. Failure to Inform Defendant of Post-Release Control.
15. Appeal of Agreed Sentence that is contrary to law.
16. Failure to Impose Court Costs at Sentencing.
17. Hospitalization of Mentally Ill Defendant
18. Post-conviction DNA testing.
19. Restitution.

1. Loss of Jurisdiction by Trial Court.

A court loses jurisdiction to execute the original sentence for a probation violation if the period of the original probation expires before there has been an extension of the original terms. In *State v. Yates*, after the probationer was released, he was charged with absconding, which apparently occurred before his term of probation expired. However, since the charge was made after the probationary period expired the trial court no longer had jurisdiction, " * * * because the state failed to initiate probation violation proceedings during the original probation period, we conclude that the trial court lost its jurisdiction to impose the suspended sentence once the term of probation expired." [738]

2. Conditions of Probation, Discretion of Sentencing Court.

A trial court does not abuse its discretion in imposing, as a condition of probation, that the offender have "no association or

[738] *State v. Yates,*, 58 Ohio St. 3d 78, 567 N.E. 2d 1306 (1991).

communication, direct or indirect with anyone under the age of eighteen (18) years not a member of his immediate family."

R.C. 2951.02 gives the trial court *broad discretion* in imposing conditions of probation: "In the interest of justice * * * the court may impose additional requirements on the offender * * * compliance with the additional requirements shall also be a condition of the offender's probation. The only caveat is that the conditions should not unnecessary restrict the probationer's liberty." [739]

The court in *Jones* established the following criteria to be considered by a trial court in determining conditions of probation :

"Whether the conditions: are (1) reasonably related o rehabilitating the offender; (2) have some relationship to the crime of which the offender was convicted, and (3) relates to conduct which is criminal or reasonably related to future criminality and serves the statutory ends of probation."

In addition, the court, added a "common sense" factor to the conditions concluding that in the case of not associating with minors the "associating or communicating with minors should reasonably be interpreted as meaning illicit or potentially unlawful association or communication."

It is proper for a court to include restitution to the state reparations fund as part of a sentence. [740]

---

[739] *State v. Jones,* 49 Ohio St. 3d 51, 550 N.E. 2d 469 (1990).

[740] *State v. Bartholomew*, 119 Ohio St. 3d 359, 894 N.E. 2d 307 (2008).

3. Violation of Probation while serving in a Rehabilitation Facility.

Where a defendant has received a suspended sentence and is placed on probation on condition that he serve eighteen months at a rehabilitation facility and voluntarily leaves the facility after only 54 days, the trial court, after finding him to be a probation violator, is permitted to execute the original sentence without giving the offender credit for the time spent in the rehabilitation facility.[741] Ohio has no specific statutory authority for the trial court to credit the offender for time spent in a rehabilitation facility.

This scenario should be contrasted with the case of an offender who has already been delivered to a facility and is serving or is 'awaiting to serve his sentence, (by facility we do not mean a rehabilitation facility as in *Nagle* but a prison or reformatory)

Under R.C. 2949.08(C), the jailer, administrator, or keeper shall reduce the total days of his sentence "for any reason arising out of the offense for which the prisoner was convicted and sentenced including confinement in lieu of bail while awaiting trial * * *"

However, a person who fails to comply with the conditions of probation who is sent to a rehabilitation facility is to be dealt with "as in other cases of probation violation" R.C. 2951.04(F).

---

[741] *State v. Nagle*, 23 Ohio St. 3d 185, 492 N.E. 2d 158 (1986).

4. Probation Revocation Hearing.

A probation revocation hearing held without a preliminary hearing is not per se unconstitutional where counsel represented the defendant and there is no objection to the lack of a preliminary hearing until after the close of the state's case.

A probationer has no right to a writ of prohibition to prevent a probation violation hearing from going forward where the probation violation was based on a charge that was later dismissed.

In *State ex rel. Dowdy v. Baird,* the violation was found on the day of the hearing and the original sentence was reinstated. There was no showing that the probation violation charge was based exclusively on the dismissed charge of gross sexual imposition. There is similarly no double jeopardy or collateral estoppel issue where the criminal charge is dismissed after revocation of probation. However, an appeal is nevertheless possible. [742]

The prosecuting attorney is entitled to notice and an opportunity to be heard on a community control (probation) violation hearing.

The prosecution, "has the burden of proving that a violation occurred, because it maintains an interest in ensuring that the proper sentence is imposed to punish and rehabilitate the offender while protecting the safety of the public and because it is responsible for preserving error for appeal, the state, through the prosecuting attorney, is entitled to notice and an opportunity to be heard in all such hearings."

---

[742] *State ex rel. Dowdy v. Baird*, 3 Ohio St 3d 10, 444 N. E. 2d 1031 (1983).

Probation officers are not authorized to prosecute probation violations, only to supervise and to report to the court such violations.

Where such opportunity is denied the matter will be remanded to the trial court so that the prosecuting attorney can have an opportunity to be heard.[743]

5. Sentencing by a Substitute Judge.

Where a defendant was convicted in a misdemeanor trial and failed to appear for sentencing and was captured several months later and sentenced by another judge, the original judge may set aside the sentence and sentence the defendant himself. Crim. R. 25(B) infers that the trial judge must perform the sentence unless unable to do so.

Here "* * * Judge Fais was clearly available and able to sentence appellant. Therefore, the imposition of sentence on appellant by Judge Jenkins was a usurpation, although apparently inadvertent* * *" *Beatty v. Alston.* [744]

---

[743] State v. Heinz, 146 Ohio St. 3d 374, 2016-Ohio-2814.

[744] *Beatty v. Alston* , 43 Ohio St. 2d 126, 330 N.E. 921 (1975).

6. Mandatory Sentences and Judicial Release.

Where a statute requires a mandatory prison sentence, it does not imply that the sentence must be served consecutively with any other sentence unless by statute it is specifically required.

R.C. 2929.13 (F) specifies which crimes require mandatory sentences. R.C. 2929.14 and R.C. 2929.41 specify which sentences are to be served consecutively.

Because R.C. 2929.14 and 2929.41 specify which sentences are to be served consecutively, it is the only authority by which a trial court is *required* to impose mandatory consecutive sentences. If the crime is not specified in the above two statutes the trial court is not required to imposed consecutive sentences.

> The trial court erred in imposing consecutive sentences. The court erroneously believed that because the offense of rape requires a mandatory sentence that when there are multiple convictions of rape, the mandatory provisions would not be adhered to if some of the sentences were to be served concurrently.

A court is free to excise its discretion by imposing consecutive sentences, but it is not required to do so unless directed by statute. [745]

A defendant who is sentenced to a mandatory sentence is not eligible for judicial release under R.C. 2929.20.[746]

---

[745] *State v. Johnson,* 116 Ohio St. 3d 541, 880 N.E. 3d 896. (2008).

[746] State v. Ware, Slip Opinion No. 2014-Ohio-5201.

7. Constitutionality of Extreme Consecutive Sentences.

Where a defendant is sentenced to consecutive sentences of 134 years for a series of felonies, such a long sentence is not cruel and unusual punishment in violation of the Eight Amendment to the United States Constitution.

Without a showing that each individual sentence is grossly disproportionate, the fact of imposing consecutive sentences is not unconstitutional since it has been held by many courts that Eight Amendment proportionality review does not apply to consecutive sentences.[747]

It is improper however, to imposed consecutive sentences for felony and misdemeanor convictions under R.C. 929.41(B)(1).[748]

R.C. 2929.41 (B) permits consecutive sentences for only a narrow class of convictions where one is convicted of both a felony and a misdemeanor. Those are: R.C. 2907.322: pandering sexually oriented matter involving a minor, escape, and possession of a deadly weapon while under detention.

In the absence of the above convictions, concurrent sentences must be given for those convicted of both felonies and misdemeanors.[749]

Further, where there is a jointly recommended sentence, the trial court does not have to make consecutive sentence findings as required by State v. Bonnell[750]R.C. 2929.14(C) (4). Such a sentence is deemed "authorized by law."[751]

---

[747] State v. Hairston, 118 Ohio St. 3d 289, 888 N.E. 2d 1073 (2008).

[748] State v. Polus, 145 Ohio St. 3d 266, 2016-Ohio-655.

[749] State v. Polus, 145 Ohio St. 3d 266, 2016-Ohio-655.

8. Credit for Time Served Prior to Sentencing.

R.C. 2967.191 requires that a defendant who is sentenced to concurrent terms of imprisonment be given credit for any jail time served prior to conviction for each sentence. If the defendant receives consecutive sentences, he is to be given credit for only one of the sentences. See also Ohio Adm. Code 5120-2-04(F), (G).[752]

9. Imposition of Sentence Consecutive with another Court's Sentence.

A trial court may impose a sentence consecutive to a sentence from another court. Because R.C. 2929.14(E)(4) and R.C. 2929.41(A) were severed in State v. Foster, 109 Ohio St. 3d 1, 845 N.E. 2d 470 (2006), the former presumption of concurrent sentences has been abrogated. Hence, where the defendant had been previously sentenced to a ten-year sentence, a different Common Pleas Court properly sentenced the defendant to a term of imprisonment consecutive to the previous term of imprisonment.[753]

---

[750] 140 Ohio St. 3d 209, 2014-Ohio-3177, 16 N.E. 3d 659.

[751] Staet v. Sergent, Slip Opinion No. 2016-Ohio-2696.

[752] *State v. Fugate*, 117 Ohio St. 3d 261, 883 N.E. 2d 440 (2008).

[753] *State v. Bates*, 118 Ohio St. 3d 174, 887 N.E. 2d 328 (2008).

10. Resentencing and Modification of Original Sentence.

There is no violation of the Double Jeopardy Clause where a defendant is resentenced after his original sentence was modified by the court of appeals even though the defendant had been released from prison and was subject to post release control. Such modification is always subject to review by this court. This is true even though the modified prison term had expired. The defendant had no expectation of finality. There is a difference between an expectation of finality for an acquittal and one for a sentencing. [754]

R.C. 2929.191 delineates the procedure for a trial court to correct a sentence where it fails to inform the defendant that he will have post-release control and that the parole board may impose a term of up to ½ of the original sentence if there is a violation of post-release control or supervision.

For sentences imposed prior to the enactment of R.C. 2929.191 the de novo sentencing procedures as defined by case law are to be followed.[755]

At a resentencing hearing where the state is required to choose which allied offenses the defendant is to be sentenced on, a defendant is permitted to raise the issue of judicial bias even though it was not raised on the original sentencing hearing. The

---

[754] *State v. Roberts*, 119 Oho St. 3d 294, 893 N.E. 2d 818 (2008).

[755] *State v. Singleton*, 124 Ohio St.3d 173, 2009-Ohio-6434.

court must also hold a new resentencing hearing for the convictions that remain after the state has made its election.

"A defendant is not barred by res judicata from raising objections to issues that arise in a resentencing hearing even if similar issues arose and were not objected to at the original sentencing hearing. " [756]

A trial court cannot modify its sentence by reconsidering its own final judgment. A final order issued by the trial court causes the criminal sentence to be final. A final judgment of conviction occurs when; 1. The fact of the conviction is noted. 2, the sentence is imposed. 3. The judge has signed the order. 4. The order has been journalized by the clerk. Previously this court held in State v. Adams that a trial court could modify its sentence any time before it has been executed. However, by statute this authority has been repealed as part of the so-called shock probation statute of R.C. 22947.061(B).[757]

Where the trial court fails to include a mandatory driver's license suspension as required by the appropriate section that part of the sentence is void and upon resentencing the court is limited to only that portion of the sentence. Also, where a sentence includes a forfeiture that is nonmandatory it does not have to be a in a judgment order of conviction, but it does not have to comply with Crim. R. 32 [758]

---

[756] *State v. Wilson*, 129 Ohio St. 3d 214, 2011-Ohio-2669.

[757] *State v. Carlisle*, 131 Ohio St. 127, 2011-Ohio-6553.

[758] *State v. Harris*, 132 Ohio St.3d 318, 2012-Ohio-1908

11. Judicial Discretion in Sentencing.

Judges in Ohio have full discretion in sentencing a defendant to impose maximum, consecutive, or sentences that are beyond minimum but within the statutory range. The above statement is significant because it is a result of the United States Supreme Court's decisions in *Apprendi* and *Blakely*. Those cases dealt with sentence enhancements that by statue required judicial fact finding.

Judicial fact-finding wherein a judge's fact-finding increases a sentence beyond the "standard range" is a violation of the Sixth Amendment because a jury must find all of the facts that relate to punishment.

To remedy this situation in Ohio the Supreme Court of Ohio severed as unconstitutional R.C. 2929.14(B) and (C) and 2929.19.(B)(2) which required judicial fact-finding before imposing sentences within the ranges of 2929.14(A) as a result of jury verdict or plea. Also R.C. 2929. (E)(4) and 2929.41(A) were severed allowing a judge's discretion without a requirement of judicial fact-finding before consecutive sentences can be imposed. As well as, R.C. 929.14(D)(2)(b) and (3)(b) which contained sentence enhancements for certain offenders. [759]

In regard to resentencing, pursuant to *Foster,* a trial court has full discretion to sentence the defendant to consecutive sentences and has no duty to impose a minimum prison term.[760]

---

[759] *State v.Foster*, 109 Ohio St. 3d 1, 845 N.E. 2d 470 (2006). See also State v. Hodge, Slip Opinion No. 2010-Ohio-6320

Judge made finding of fact can implicate a violation of the 6th amendment right to a jury. Although judges are prohibited from finding facts that increase punishment they nevertheless are permitted to make a "legal" finding that may have the effect of increasing punishment. Hence statutory interpretation that increases a sentence is not judicial fact finding.

A conviction in a RICO prosecution in which the predicate crimes are not specified in the jury verdict form, but are found in the general verdict form is proper.[761]

In order to sustain a conviction under Ohio's RICO statue (R.C. 2923.32) It is not necessary for the state to establish a separate enterprise from the current activity ie. the crime. The same evidence may be used to establish both requirements i.e. 1. The enterprise, and 2. The underlying crime.

"Although the intention of the statute is to criminalize a pattern, there is no requirement that separate evidence be produced.

Here the defendant and an accomplice committed a series of burglaries and thefts. This series and their association, albeit a lose informal association is sufficient to establish the elements of a criminal enterprise.[762]

12. Appellate Review of Felony Sentences.

Standard of review for felony sentencing appeals.

Appellate Courts when reviewing felony sentences can only vacate a sentence where it finds clear and convincing evidence that the record does not support the trial courts findings or that the sentence is contrary to law.

---

[760] *State v. Elmore*, 122 Ohio St.3d 472, 2009-Ohio-3478.

[761] State v.Willan, 144 Ohio St. 3d 94, 2015-Ohio-1475.

[762] State v Beverly,

State v. Kalish, 2008-Ohio-4912, need not be applied since the passage of R.C. 2953.08(G). R.C. 2953.08(G) clearly states the ways in which a sentence can be modified or vacated and remanded for resentencing. An abuse of discretion standard is not to be used.[763]

Appellate courts must apply a two-step approach when reviewing felony sentences. First, they must examine the sentencing court's compliance with all applicable rules and statutes in imposing the sentence to determine whether the sentence is clearly and convincingly contrary to law. If this first prong is satisfied, the trial court's decision in imposing the term of imprisonment is reviewed under the abuse-of-discretion standard.[764]

If the trial court pursuant to R.C, 2947.23(A)(1) fails to inform the defendant at sentencing that if the court costs are not paid as ordered the court may impose community service. Such failure to inform can be appealed immediately and does not depend on whether the defendant has failed to pay the costs.[765]

13. Voided Sentence for failure to Impose Post-Release Control.

Where a sentence is voided because of the failure of the trial court to impose post-release control, the motion for withdrawal

[763] State v. Marcum, 146 Ohio St. 3d 516, 2016-Ohio-1002.

[764] *State v. Kalish,* 120 Ohio St. 3d 23 , 896 N.E.2d 124 (2008).

[765] State v. Smith, 131 Ohio St.3d 297, 2012-Ohio-781

of the plea should be treated as a *presentence* motion under Crim. R. 32.1 as was illustrated by the court in State v. Xie[766] which requires that such motions be freely and liberally granted. A *post-sentence* motion for withdrawal of a plea requires a showing of manifest injustice in order to prevail. [767] See also State v. Ketterer[768]

---

[766] State v. Xie (1992), 62 Ohio St.3d 521, 527, 584 N.E.2d 715.

[767] *State v. Boswell*, 121 Ohio St. 3d 575, 2009-Ohio-1577.

[768] *State v. Ketterer*, 126 Ohio St.3d 448, 2010-Ohio-3831

14. Failure to Inform Defendant of Post-Release Control.

Where a sentencing court fails to notify the defendant that he is subject to post release control at the time of sentencing, R.C. 2929.191 permits a subsequent judgment entry delineating the condition of post release control that should have been stated to defendant at the time of sentencing. [769]

However, the trial court's failure to impose mandatory post release control cannot be corrected after the defendant has served his sentence.[770]

Where a trial court has failed to impose post-release control for certain offenses pursuant to R.C. 2967.28, an action in mandamus is proper to compel the court to issue a proper sentencing entry. [771]

Where the trial court fails to include community control notice in the sentencing entry but did inform the defendant orally, a subsequent correction of the entry a nunc pro tunc, does not require a new sentencing hearing.[772]

---

[769] *State .v. Bloomer*, 122 Ohio St. 3d 200, 2009-Ohio-2462.

[770] *State v. Harrison*, 122 Ohio St. 3d 512, 2009-Ohio-3547. See also, *State v. Holdcroft,* Slip Opinion No. 2013-Ohio-5014.

[771] *State ex rel. Carnail v. McCormick*, 126 Ohio St. 3d 124, 2010-Ohio-2671

.

[772] *State v. Qualls*, 131 Ohio St.3d 499, 2012-Ohio-1111

A sentence that incorrectly imposes the wrong duration of post control is a void sentence that may be collaterally attacked. Therefore, where the defendant pleads to escape as a result of being in violation of post relief control that plea may be collaterally attacked.[773]

15. Appeal of Agreed Sentence that is contrary to law.

Where the defendant has agreed to a sentence that was found to be contrary to law, that sentence may be appealed. An agreement to a sentence that is contrary to law does not result in a waiver of the right to appeal.

Pursuant to R.C. 2953. (D)(1) a sentence may not be appealed if: 1. The parties agree to it; 2. The trial court in fact imposes the sentence; and 3. The sentence is authorized by law.

Under factor 3, if the sentence is not authorized by law the sanctions of R.C. 2953.08 (D)(1) do not apply and the defendant may appeal an unauthorized sentence.[774]

---

[773] *State v. Billiter*, Slip Opinion No. 2012-Ohio-5144.

[774] *State v. Underwood*, 124 Ohio St. 3d 365, 2010-Ohio-1

16. *Failure to Impose Court Costs at Sentencing.*

Where a trial court fails to impose court costs in open court it may upon remand impose those costs. The initial failure to impose costs does not invalidate the sentence. [775]

17. *Hospitalization of Mentally Ill Defendant*

Involuntary commitment under R.C. 2945.39 is constitutional it is civil in nature and the committed person does not have the same rights as a criminal defendant.

After the expiration of the one-year time for treatment and the defendant remains incompetent to stand trial, R.C. 2945.38(H)(3) provides the following determination that must occur pursuant to R.C. 2945.39, 2945.401, and 2945.402. R.C.

2945.39(A) provides two options civil commitment may be sought by the court or prosecuting attorney in probate court under R.C. Chapter 5122. R.C.

2945.39(A)(1).

Second, the court or prosecuting attorney may seek to have the common pleas court retain jurisdiction over the defendant. R.C. 2945.39(A)(2).

If after the defendant is committed to the maximum term the crime allows the prosecuting attorney can seek a civil commitment through probate court.[776]

---

[775] *State v, Joseph*, 125 Ohio St. 3d 76, 2010-Ohio-954.

[776] *State v. Williams*, 126 Ohio St. 3d 65, 2010-Ohio-2453.

18. Post-Conviction DNA Testing

R.C. 2953.72(A)(7) concerns the application for dna testing and R.C. 2953.71(U) defines a definitive test.

If a definitive test has been afforded a defendant any subsequent request for another dna test is not authorized. Hence, when considering an application for a post- conviction DNA test the court must determine whether a "definitive dna test has been afforded the defendant.

The defendant's prior dna test excluded him as the person whose dna was found on a cigarette at the crime scene.

However newly discovered evidence revealed the names of other possible perpetrators. This coupled with new dna technology which not only excludes but can identify caused the old test not to be definitive and the court should have granted defendant's request for a new test. [777]

19. Restitution

When court orders restitution the amount must be limited to the economic loss of the victim. Where the defendant disputes the amount of restitution, a hearing must be conducted.[778]

---

[777] *State v. Noling,* 136 Ohio St.3d 163, 2013-Ohio-1764

[778] *State v. Lalain,* Slip Opinion No. 2013-Ohio-3093

20. Sentencing of a Juvenile to Life Imprisonment.

The sentencing of a juvenile to life imprisonment without parole is not a violation fo the eight amendment as long as it is not a mandatory sentence. However, the sentencing court must separately consider the youth of the defendant as a mitigating factor.[779]

21. Where the law decreases the possible sentence after conviction but before sentencing.

R.C. 1.58(B) requires that when a penalty is reduced by law prior to sentencing, the reduced penalty is to be applied.[780]

22. Sealing of records (expungement)

A fourth-degree misdemeanor is a conviction that prevents the sealing of a criminal record. Under R.C.4503.11(A) Only minor misdemeanors pursuant to R.C. 4507, 4510, 4511, and 4549, are not to be counted when considering offenses that are sealable.[781] This is true even though since July 1, 2015 such an offense is a minor misdemeanor however there was no evidence that it was to be retroactive.

Sealing of criminal records and pardons,

---

[779] State v. Long , 138 Ohio St. 3d, 2014-Ohio-849.

[780] State v Taulor, 138 OhioST. 3d 194, 2014-Ohio-460.

[781] State v. J.M., Slip Opinion No. 2803.

A defendant who has been pardoned is not entitled to have his record of conviction sealed. There is no statute authorizing the sealing of a criminal record as the result of a pardon. R.C. 2953.32 allows for the sealing of a criminal case where the defendant has been found not guilty, for a dismissed indictment or a Grand Jury no bill. R.C. 2953.52 controls the sealing of criminal records for first offenders as defined therein.[782]

23. Diversion.

Where a noncitizen is admitted into a pretrial diversion program he must be advised pursuant to R.C. 2943.031(A) that his admission of guilt may result in deportation.

Under federal law, such admission pursuant to a diversion program can affect immigration status.[783] Even where after completing the program a dismissal of the charges are dismissed the defendant's admission constitutes a conviction under federal law which can only be remedied by an actual vacation of the plea due to substantive or procedure reasons.

Here an admission of guilt was required for admission into the program.[784]

24. No Contact Orders and Sentences

782 State v, Radcliff, 142 Ohio St. 3d 78, 2015-Ohio-235.

783 8 U.S.C. 1101(a)(48)(A).

784 State v, Kona, Slip Opinion No. 2016-Ohio-7796.

A community control sanction cannot be combined with a prison term. A defendant cannot be sentenced to prison and community control (probation) at the same time. A no contact order is a community control sanction. [785]

[785] State v. Anderson, 143 Ohio St. 3d 173, 2015-Ohio-2089.

PART EIGHT: APPEALS

CHAPTER 88

Appeals.

A Writ of Prohibition is proper to prevent the state from appealing were the court of appeals lacks jurisdiction. The ability of the state to appeal in a criminal case is established by R.C. 2945.67(A). The state may appeal as a matter of right:

1. A motion to dismiss all or part of an indictment.
2. A motion to suppress evidence,
3. Return of seized property,
4. The granting of post-conviction relief. The state may "appeal by leave of court to which the appeal is taken any other decision, except the final verdict, of the trial court in a criminal case."

Therefore, where the state seeks to appeal a trial court's grant of a motion for a new trial, the appeal must be made by leave of court. There is no right to appeal of the part of the state. And where the state has failed to file leave to appeal pursuant to App. R. 5 (C) within 30 days, the court of appeals lacks jurisdiction.[786]

1. All Assignments of Error must be Addressed.
2. Assignments of Error not raised at Trial.
3. Parties must be given an Opportunity to brief all Issues
4. Appellate Review of Consecutive Sentences.
5. No Constitutional Right to Bail on Appeal.
6. Bail, Factors to Consider in Deciding to Grant Bail.
7. Where Denial of Bail Appeal is an Abuse of Discretion.
8. Perfection of Appeal for Felony.
9. Statement of Evidence.
10. Record on Appeal.
11. Correction of the Record.
12. Transcript required before Courts of Appeal.
13. Filing of Notice of Appeal without a Formal Journal Entry
14. Procedure Where the Convicted Defendant Dies During the Pendency of the Appeal.
15. Abuse of Discretion in Dismissing Appeal.
16. Appeals by the Incarcerated, Where the Record is not Timely Filed.
17. Deliverance of Notice of Appeal to Prison Authorities.
18. Post-Conviction Relief and Delayed Appeal.

---

[786] *State ex rel. Steffe v. judges of the Court of Appeals , First Appellate Dist.*, 126 Ohio St. 3d 405, 2010-Ohio-2430.

19. Res Judicata and Delayed Appeal.
20. Final Appealable Order.
21. Reopening of Direct Appeal.
22. Ineffective Assistance of Counsel.
23. Dismissal of States Appeal for Failure to Serve Public Defender.
24. Appeal of Agreed Sentence that is Contrary to law.
25. Appeal of Sex Offender Registration.
26. Post-Conviction DNA Testing.
27. Removal of Retained Counsel.
28. Sufficiency and Merging of Multiple Offenses.

1. All Assignments of Error must be Addressed.

A Court of Appeals commits reversible error by not ruling on all of the assignments of error. The policy behind the rule that the court must rule on all assignments of errors has been stated by the court,"[r]easons for a decision are necessary - otherwise all parties concerned must speculate on the obstacles, legal or other, which need be overcome in an appeal to this court" [787]

2. Assignments of Error not raised at Trial

A court of appeals is not required to rule on assignments of error briefed, but not raised at trial.[788]

---

[787] *State v. Jennings*, 69 Ohio St. 2d 389, 433 N.E.2d 157 (1982)

[788] *State ex rel. Specht v. Bd. of Edn.*, 66 Ohio St. 2d 178, 420 N. E. 2d

3. *Parties must be given an Opportunity to brief all Issues.*

A court of appeals may not *sua sponte* raise an issue as to the constitutionality of a statute without affording the parties an opportunity to brief. Although a court of appeals may rule on issues that were not briefed by either party, out of fairness to the parties, the court should give notice or opportunity for briefing, *C. Miller Chevrolet, Inc. V. Willoughby Hills.* Although this case is not a criminal case, it deals with constitutional issues, which criminal cases often include. [789]

Where a constitutional issue was not raised at trial, it is waived. It is an abuse of discretion for the court of appeals to rule *sua sponte* on the constitutionality of a statute.[790]

A recent criminal case was decided on this same issue. Here the court of appeals inexplicably ruled that the verdict was against the manifest weight of the evidence without giving the parties an opportunity to brief the issue.[791]

1004 (1981).

[789] *C. Miller Chevrolet, Inc. V. Willoughby Hills,* 38 Ohio St. 2d 298, 313 N.E. 2d 400 (1974).

[790] *State v. 1981 Dodge Ram Van,* 36 Ohio St. 3d 168, 522 N.E.2d 524. (1988).

[791] State v. Tate, 140 Ohio St. 3d 140, 2014-Ohio-3667.

4. Appellate Review of Consecutive Sentences.

Where the general assembly grants a trial court authority to impose consecutive sentences, appellate review is limited to only to whether the trial court exceeded its authority. In reinstating defendant's conviction for aggravated burglary where he was sentenced consecutively with aggravated murder, the court quoted the following language from *Brown v. Ohio* (1977), 432 U.S. 161, "* * *[w]here consecutive sentences are imposed at a single trial, the role of the constitutional guarantee is limited to assuring that the court does not exceed its legislative authorization imposing multiple punishment for the same offense." [792]

[to be 5] An appellant court upon review of an appeal where the trial court has determined that certain offenses are allied must use a de novo review standard and is not to merely use an abuse of discretion standard even though there was a factual determination by the trial court. This is so because a review of allied offenses not only requires a factual finding but also requires an application of law.[793]

5. No Constitutional Right to Bail on Appeal.

There is no constitutional right to bail pending appeal. App. R. 8(B) outlines the procedure for bail on appeal. A

[792] *State v.Moss*, 69 Ohio St. 2d 515, 433 N.E. 2d 181 (1982).

[793] ***State v. Williams,* 134 Ohio St.3d 482, 2012-Ohio-5699.**

defendant may first apply for bail after conviction in the trial court and, if denied, may apply to the court of appeals, App.R. 8(A).[794]

Where the court of appeals denies the defendant bail, that denial will not be disturbed absent a showing of an abuse of discretion.[795]

---

[794] *State ex rel. Silcott v. Spahr*, 50 Ohio St. 3d 110, 552 N.E. 2d 926 (1990).

[795] *Jurek v. McFaul*, 39 Ohio St. 3d 42, 528 N.E. 2d 1260 (1988).

6. Bail, Factors to Consider in Deciding to Grant Bail.

Factors that should be considered by a court prior to granting or denying bail are, in addition to the nature and circumstances of the offense, the "petitioner's family ties, employment, financial resources, character and possible access to a foreign refuse." [796]

Accordingly, a three-million-dollar bail was not excessive where it the evidence showed that the defendant tried to hire a hit man to kill his wife, had substantial financial resources, and due to the possible lengthy sentence, it was very likely that he would leave the country. [797]

7. Where Denial of Bail is an Abuse of Discretion.

The Court of Appeals abused its discretion in denying bail where the risk factors, including appellant's age, length of residency in the community, home ownership, activity in community affairs, responsible employment, lack of a prior criminal record, and the fact that the minimum sentence was only six months would ordinarily support release on bond.

---

[796] *Burch v. Perini*, 66 Ohio St. 2d 174, 420 N.E. 2d 1001 (1981).

[797] *Ahmad v. Plummer*, 126 Ohio St.3d 262, 2010-Ohio-3757. See also *State v. Nields* (2001), 93 Ohio St.3d 6, 18, 752 N.E.2d 859.

The court of appeals further erred by denying the defendant's motion for bail without stating why the motion was denied. Although a court's failure to state why bail was denied does not necessarily indicate there were no grounds to deny bail, however, in examining what information was available to the court, an independent review of the facts and background by the court found both to be sufficient to comply with the requirements of Crim. R. 46(E)(1): that bail should be granted since there was no evidence that would support a belief in risk of flight or danger.[798]

8. Perfection of Appeal for Felony.

When a motion for leave to appeal to the Supreme Court is filed, the court of appeals does not lose its jurisdiction on an application for reconsideration until the Supreme Court exercises its discretion to hear the appeal pursuant to Section 2(B)(2)(b) Article IV of the Ohio Constitution.[799] In *Murphy*, it was argued that once a leave to appeal or certify the record is before the Court, a court of appeals does not have jurisdiction to grant an application for reconsideration.

An appeal in a felony case is not perfected before the Supreme Court until it is granted "on leave first obtained." "Once this court grants a motion for leave to appeal or to certify the record in such discretionary review cases, then and only then is

[798] *Liberatore v. McKeen*, 63 Ohio St. 2d 175 , 407 N.E. 2d 23 (1980). Overruled on unrelated matter; *Dapice v. Stickrath*, 40 Ohio St.3d 298, 533 N.E.2d 339 (1988).

[799] *State v. Murphy*, 49 Ohio St. 3d 293, 551 N.E. 2d 1292 (1990).

the court of appeals prevented from exercising any jurisdiction on the matter." *Murphy, supra*.

"We are asked to determine whether the mere filing of such a motion or notice of appeal before this court divests the court of appeals of jurisdiction in Toto. Since it is our view that the jurisdiction of the court of appeals does not end, in this context, until this court exercises and accepts exclusive jurisdiction in a case requesting invocation of the court's power of discretionary review"

9. Statement of Evidence.

A trial court has no duty to sign and settle a narrative statement presented by the appellant where it is not clear that there is no report of the evidence or proceedings, or that a transcript is not available. The court can properly refuse to sign or settle the statement, holding that a verbatim statement should have been submitted.[800]

Where the trial court files its own statement of the facts, that court's duty under App. R. 9(C) is satisfied because the trial court found appellant's statements as to the facts to be inaccurate. Appellant is free, pursuant to App. R. 9(E), to raise any question of the accuracy of the record to the court appeals. [801]

---

[800] *State ex rel. Corona v. Harris*, 63 Ohio St. 2d 95, 406 N.E. 2d 1120 (1980).

[801] *State ex rel. Fant v. Trumbo*, 22 Ohio St. 3d 207, 489 N.E. 2d 1316 (1986).

10. Record on Appeal.

Where the record does not indicate a written or oral waiver of the right to trial by jury, affidavits to that effect presented to the court of appeals do not comply with App. R. 9 as being part of the record on appeal.[802]

A reviewing court may only reverse the judgment of the trial court where it finds error in the trial below, "it follows that a reviewing court should be limited to what transpired in the trial court as reflected by the record made of the proceedings.[803] Here the court of appeals reviewed a transcript of the proceedings of a guilty plea that the trial court never reviewed. The transcript was not properly in the record of the proceedings below. "We conclude it was prejudicial error to the State of Ohio, appellant herein, for the Court of Appeals to add the transcript to the record before it and to render its decision based upon the contents of that transcript." *Ismail, supra.*

Where the trial court denies the defendant's motion for a new trial, a bill of exceptions must be filed with the court of appeals in order to "bring upon the record the evidence presented by affidavit or otherwise at the hearing on the issue. [804]

---

[802] *State v. Tate*, 59 Ohio St. 2d 50, 391 N.E. 2d 738 (1979).

[803] *State v. Ishmail*, 54 Ohio St. 2d 402, 377 N.E. 2d 500 (1978).

[804] *State v. Morris,* 42 Ohio St. 2d 307, 329 N.E. 2d 85. (1975).

11. Correction of the Record.

Pursuant to App. R. 9(E), the trial court, or the court of appeals may order the trial record supplemented or corrected. Where a party moves to have the record corrected, "It is within the province of the trial court to resolve disputes about the record on appeal." [805]

A court of appeals may authorize the correction or supplementation of the record where the accuracy is not in dispute (citations omitted) "but the court of appeals cannot resolve disputes about the trial court's record in the course of an appeal" *Schiebel, supra*. In *Schiebel*, the court of appeals improperly resolved the conflict that was contained in the motion to correct the record.

Such a conflict is in the realm of the trial court to resolve and where the trial court's ruling is accompanied with credible evidence, "* * *such ruling will not be disturbed absent an abuse of discretion." Here there was credible evidence with which the trial court ruled and the court of appeals improperly held that the trial court abused its discretion in correcting the record.

Where the defendant claims an electronic recording, device failed to accurately record the total proceedings, the defendant waived any claimed defects in the record where she failed to seek to modify the record pursuant to App.R.9 (E). This court reviewed the record, and could not find any prejudice because the record clearly inculpated the defendant. "We cannot imagine what detail important enough to be exculpatory could be absent from the record without an immediate, or at least an early outcry from appellant's counsel." [806]

---

[805] *State v. Osborn*, 49 Ohio St. 2d 135, 359 N.E. 2d 78 (1976).

A judgment entry of conviction is not required to display the manner of conviction. That is, whether the conviction was by a jury or bench trial, or whether there was a guilty or no contest plea. Where a trial court amends the judgment entry nunc pro tunc to include the manner of conviction, because of a clerical error, this does not cause the original order to be invalid and it is not a new final order wherein a defendant can institute a new appeal.[807]

12. Transcript required before Courts of Appeal.

Where a court of appeals reverses a judgment where no transcript was filed with that court,"* * * the judgment of reversal can stand only if it was based on errors apparent on the face of the record not requiring an examination of the transcript for determination. [808] In *Render*, the court of appeals reversed the judgment of the trial court on two grounds:

1. The trial court abused its discretion by not allowing the defendant to change his plea of guilty to former jeopardy.
2. There was no probable cause to issue a search warrant.

Although there was evidence that a former dismissed appeal did contain a transcript, that transcript and record was never filed in the appeal under consideration. The court of appeals heard oral argument and rendered its decision without the assistance of a transcript. On this issue, the court held: "The law

[806] *State v. Schiebel*, 55 Ohio St. 3d 71, 564 N.E. 2d 54 (1990).

[807] *State v. Lester,* 130 Ohio St.3d 303, 2011-Ohio-5204

[808] *State v. Render,* 43 Ohio St. 2d 17, 330 N.E. 2d 690 (1975).

in Ohio is clear that, where an authenticated transcript of proceedings in a trial court is necessary to exemplify the facts which determined the issues presented there, its absence requires a reviewing court, upon appeal, to dismiss the appeal or affirm the judgment of the court from which the appeal is taken." (Citations omitted)

Accordingly, the court of appeals erred in finding the trial court abused its discretion in not allowing a change of plea from not guilty to former jeopardy.

There was no transcript nor a journal entry or docket available to show that an alleged oral motion was made or the disposition of the motion, the same is true of the motion to suppress,

"In the absence of any record of proceedings on the trial court upon which to predicate reversal in the Court of Appeals, the judgment of the Court of Appeals is reversed." *Render, supra.*

13. Filing of Notice of Appeal without a Formal Journal Entry.

A sentencing in open court after conviction is sufficient for an appellant to file a notice of appeal even though no formal journal entry has been made.[809]

---

[809] *State v. Boyd,* 30 Ohio St. 2d 64, 282 N.E. 366 (1972).

14. Procedure Where the Convicted Defendant Dies During the Pendency of the Appeal.

Where a convicted defendant dies during the pendency of his appeal, App. R. 29(A) provides that a "personal representative of the deceased party may be substituted as a party on motion filed by the representatives, or any party * * *"

If the motion is not filed, "the court of appeals may dismiss the appeal as moot, vacate the original judgment of conviction and dismiss all related criminal proceedings, including the original indictment."

Since the rule provides that "any party" may suggest the death on the record, if the state suggests the death, the court of appeals should substitute any party including the decedent's attorney of record.

Where the death is suggested on the record by the dead defendant's attorney for dismissing the appeal and the original indictment, the state is given an opportunity to suggest the death on the record and move subsequently or simultaneously for a party defendant so that the appeal should continue.

If a convicted defendant dies before the notice of appeal is filed, the notice of appeal may be filed by his personal representative or, if none, his attorney within the time as the rules require (App. R. 4(B) states the time in which to file).

After the notice of appeal is filed, the appropriate person may then file a motion for substitution of a party, and then the court of appeals should substitute the proper party including the attorney of record. If the notice of appeal is not filed, "the original judgment of conviction shall stand with full force and effect as a valid subsisting judgment of the trial court." [810]

[810] *State v. McGettrick*, 31 Ohio St. 3d 138, 509 N.E. 2d 378 (1978).

15. Abuse of Discretion in Dismissing Appeal.

A court of appeals abuses its discretion in dismissing an appeal where the brief was filed 3 days late due to a good faith error by appellant's counsel in calculating the time in which to file the brief. Although App. R. 18 (C) permits a court of appeals to dismiss the appeal if the brief is not filed on time, in this regard, the court held:

"A court of appeals abuses its discretion when, after dismissing a case, *sua sponte* for a minor, technical, correctable, inadvertent violation of a local rule, it refused to reinstate the case when: (1) the mistake was made in good faith and is not part of a continuing course of conduct for the purpose of delay, (2) neither the opposing party nor the court is prejudiced by the error, (3) dismissal is a sanction that is disproportionate to the nature of the mistake, (4) the client will be unfairly punished for the fault of his counsel, and (5) dismissal frustrates the prevailing policy of deciding cases on the merits.[811]

In line with the principal that the courts of appeal should decide cases on the merits, the court held that the court of appeals improperly dismissed appellant's brief where he failed serve his brief to appellee within the time period of App. R. 18(A)," * * * nothing in the rule condones or sets forth an available sanction to the court of appeals should an appellant fail to serve his brief in a *tim*ely fashion, or for any defect in the mode of service caused by appellant." [812]

---

[811] *DeHart v. Aetna Life Ins.Co.*,69 Ohio St. 2d 189, 431 N.E. 2d 644 (1982); *Hawkins v. Correctional Institute*, 28 Ohio St. 3d 4, 501 N.E. 2d 1195 (1986).

If appellant fails to file the brief at all, the courts of appeal may dismiss the appeal pursuant App. R. 18 (C).

16. Appeals by the Incarcerated, Where the Record is not Timely Filed.

Where an indigent defendant files a timely notice of appeal, but does not file the record and brief within the prescribed time limit, the appeal is nevertheless valid. App. R. 3 (A) provides: "Failure of an appellant to take any step other than a timely filing of a notice of appeal does not affect the validity of the appeal."

Because App. R. 3(A) gives the court of appeals the option of either accepting or dismissing the appeal, or to take any other action it deems appropriate, the court in considering the discretion of a court of appeals in dismissing appeals by those incarcerated, held in *State v. Jones*,[813] "this laxity could well be ascribed to causes over which he should not be penalized."

Because appellant was in prison at the time the notice of appeal was filed, the court has given him the benefit of the doubt regarding why the brief and record was not filed.

Accordingly, even though appellate courts have discretion to dismiss such appeals, they should not automatically dismiss appeals from incarcerated appellants

---

[812] *State v. Herzing,* 11 Ohio St. 3d 337, 481 N.E. 2d 593 (1985).

[813] *State v. Jones* , 50 Ohio St. 2d 5, 361 N.E. 2d 453 (1977).

17. Deliverance of Notice of Appeal to Prison Authorities.

The Court of Appeals improperly dismissed an incarcerated defendant's appeal where, due to a clerical error, the notice of appeal was sent to the wrong county. The Court of Appeals for the proper county received the notice of appeal five days past the thirty-day period after the trial court filed the entry of sentence.

Because appellant delivered his notice of appeal with the Legal Officer of the prison within time of the rule, this delivery pursuant to prison procedure constituted a timely filing.[814]

18. Post-Conviction Relief and Delayed Appeal.

An appellant does not have a right to a delayed appeal, pursuant to App. R. 5(A), for post-conviction relief. Because post-conviction relief is quasi-civil, res judicata can apply.[815]

Where appellant files a motion for relief from judgment pursuant to Civ. R. 60(B) the trial court properly treated it as a petition for post-conviction relief and dismissed it as being untimely filed. Crim. R. 57(B) permits a court to look to the Civil Rules if no applicable rule of procedure exists. Here appellant was past time to file for post-conviction relief and attempted to use the civil rules to file f~~or relief from judgment und~~er Civ. R. 60(B). *State v. Schlee* [816]

[814] *State v. Wistful*, 46 Ohio St. 2d 31, 346 N. E. 2d 282 (1976). See also, *State v. Williamson*, 10 Ohio St. 2d 195, 226 N.E. 2d 735 (1967) where the court held the notice of appeal was timely filed when "he [the prisoner] delivers such notice to the proper prison authorities for forwarding to the court.

[815] *State v. Perry*, 10 Ohio St. 2d 175, 226 N.E. 2d 104 (1967).

On a subsequent post-conviction petition pursuant to R.C. 2953.23(A) (1) where the petitioner alleges he was prevented from preventing evidence due to a Brady violation, he must show he was "unavoidably prevented from presenting evidence. Where petitioner had a prior opportunity to present the evidence and delayed, he was not unavoidably prevented.[817]

The 180 period for filing a post-conviction relief period starts to run when the written transcript has been made available to the defendant. The filing of a videotape recording does not cause the period to run. Only the written transcript qualifies under App. R. 9 and R.C. 2953.21(A)(2).[818]

19. Res Judicata and Delayed Appeal.

Res judicata may be a vehicle to dismiss post-conviction petitions where the issue was not raised on direct appeal. [819]

Post-conviction relief is not available to a convicted defendant until normal relief has been pursued, "* * * a delayed appeal pursuant to App. R. 5 is not available in the appeal of a post-conviction relief determination pursuant to R.C. 2953.23(B). Additionally, we hold that post-conviction relief proceedings will

---

[816] *State v. Schlee*, 117 Ohio St. 3d 153, 882 N.E. 2d 431 (2008).

[817] *State v. Broom*, 122 Ohio St.3d 114, 2009-Ohio-4778

[818] *State v. Everette*, 129 Ohio St. 3d, 2011-Ohio-2856.

[819] *State v. Cole*, 2 Ohio St. 3d 112, 443 N.E. 2d 169 (1982).

be governed by the Ohio Rules of Appellant Procedure as applicable to civil actions." [820]

A court of appeals may not dismiss an appeal by an indigent defendant without first ascertaining whether his allegations that he was not notified of his right to appeal and his right to court appointed counsel for appeal are true. "If one's right to direct appeal and his right to court-appointed counsel for such an appeal are to be viable, it is imperative that there be such a determination of such rights by the appellate court." [821] In Sims, there was insufficient evidence in the record to determine whether the defendant knowingly and intelligently waived his right to counsel and appeal. The court of appeals erred by dismissing the motion without first making a factual determination.

Concerning indigency, the court of appeals must determine if the appellant is indigent. In the case of a delayed appeal, the transcript need not be furnished unless in the interests of justice, it is necessary and the delayed appeal is allowed. *Sims, supra*.

20. Final Appealable Order.

In regard to a final appealable order, although the language of Crim. R. 32 (C) states that the judgment of conviction must include the "Plea," a strict reading of this rule is not required. The judgment of conviction does not have to include the plea, it only has to include the sentence and the means of conviction.[822]

---

[820] *State v. Nichols*,11 Ohio St. 3d 40, 463 N.E. 2d 375 (1984).

[821] *State v. Sims*, 27 Ohio St. 2d 79, 272 N.E. 2d 87 (1971).

The final appealable order requirement Under R.C. 2929.03 (F) in a capital case is satisfied if "either the judgment of conviction or the sentencing opinion includes the guilty plea, jury verdict, or finding of the court upon which the conviction is based." [823] The judgment of conviction and the sentencing opinion can combine to form a final appealable order.

A denial of a motion to dismiss alleging a double jeopardy violation is a final appealable order.[824]

21. Reopening of Direct Appeal.

An application to reopen direct appeal must be filed within 90 days of journalization of the judgment of the Court of Appeals. Only with a showing of good cause can this appeal be allowed after the 90-day period. Lack of counsel is not good cause since defendant could have filed the application himself.[825]

22. Ineffective Assistance of Counsel.

Where a defendant files a timely application to reopen an appeal due to ineffective assistance of appellate counsel, he is not

[822] *State v. Baker*, 119 Ohio St. 3d 197, 893 N.E. 2d 163 (2008).

[823] *State v. Ketterer*, 126 Ohio St.3d 448, 2010-Ohio-3831.

[824] State v. Anderson, 138 Ohio St. 3d 264, 2014-Ohio-542.

[825] *State v. Keith*, 119 Ohio St. 3d 161, 892 N.E. 2d 912 (2008). See also, *State v. Williams*, 129 Ohio St. 3d 19, 2011-Ohio-232.

barred from review after his initial appeal is overruled. The appellate court must consider the application to determine whether a genuine issue exists as to whether the defendant was deprived of effective assistance of counsel. App.R. 26(B).[826]

23. Dismissal of State's Appeal for Failure to Serve Public Defender.

S.Ct.Proc. R. XIV (2)(A)(3) requires the prosecutor to serve on the Ohio Public Defender a notice of appeal. Failure to do so will result in the court sustaining a motion to strike.[827]

---

[826] *State v. Davis*, 119 Ohio St. 3d 422, 894 N.E.2d 1221 (2006).

[827] *State v. Owens* 122 Ohio St. 3d 1204, 2009-Ohio-4086.

24. Appeal of Agreed Sentence that is Contrary to Law.

Where the defendant has agreed to a sentence that was found to be contrary to law, that sentence may be appealed. An agreement to a sentence that is contrary to law does not result in a waiver of the right to appeal.

Pursuant to R.C. 2953. (D)(1) a sentence may not be appealed if: 1) The parties agree to it; 2) The trial court in fact imposes the sentence; and 3) The sentence is authorized by law.

Under factor 3, if the sentence is not authorized by law the sanctions of R.C. 2953.08 (D)(1) do not apply and the defendant may appeal an unauthorized sentence.[828]

25. Appeal of Sex Offender Registration.

An appeal of the sex offender registration requirement is a criminal appeal and is subject to the 30-day deadline of App.R. 4(A). This is true even though only the registration requirements are appealed and not the sentence. A delayed appeal, however, under App.R. 5(A) is still available to defendant.[829]

---

[828] *State v. Underwood,* 124 Ohio St. 3d 365, 2010-Ohio-1.

[829] *State v. Clayborn*, 125 Ohio St.3d 450, 2010-Ohio-2123.

A convicted sexual offender classified under Megan's law is required to verify his address every year. The subsequent enactment of the Adam Walsh Act which requires a Tier III offender to verify his address every 90 days does not apply retroactively.[830]

The addition reporting requirements and other obligations contained in S.B. 10 which amended R.C. 2950 cannot be applied retroactively because it would be a violation of Section 28, Article II of the Ohio Constitution which prohibits the enactment of retroactive laws. Therefore, when the crime is committed before the enactment of the amended R.C. 2950, but where the sentence occurs after the enactment. The defendant must be sentenced under the law in effect at the time the crime was committed. [831]

Although this court has invalidated portions of the Adams Walsh act the petition portion has remained in effect. "To remedy the violation, in Bodyke we declared unenforceable "the unconstitutional component" of the Adam Walsh Act's reclassification provisions. However, we held that the component could be severed from the rest of the act, and accordingly, we "left in place * * * the remainder of the AWA, 'which is capable of being read and of standing alone.'"

Id. at ¶ 66, quoting State v. Foster, 109 Ohio St.3d 1, 2006-Ohio-856, 845 N.E.2d 470, ¶ 98."

Therefore, where a person has been convicted under the Adams Walsh act and because not all provisions of the act were

[830] *State v. Gingell*, 128 Ohio St. 3d 444, 2011-Ohio-1481

[831] *State v. Williams*129 Ohio St.3d 344, 2011-Ohio-3374

declared unconstitutional the remaining aspects of the act are still in effect including the right to petition for reclassification.[832]

Where a person is convicted of a sexually oriented offense in another state, it must be determined: 1. Whether that offense is substantially equivalent to an Ohio offense and, 2. when the offender moved to Ohio whether he was required to register in that other state before it can be said that he is a violator because of a failure to register.[833]

---

[832] *State v. Palmer*, 131 Ohio St.3d 278, 2012-Ohio-580

[833] *State v. Lloyd*, 132 Ohio St.3d 135, 2012-Ohio-2015

The registration requirements of R.C. 2950 for defendants convicted of certain sexual offenses do not result in cruel and unusual punishment in violation of the Eighth Amendment or Article I Section 9 of the Ohio Constitution.

If a defendant is found guilty of an offense for which the above statue requires sex offender registration, the registration requirements are "automatic."[834] It makes no difference if in a presentence investigation a mental health profession concludes that the defendant is not a sexual offender.

Here, although the defendant pled guilty to having sex with a fifteen-year-old girl nevertheless the defendant challenged the registration requirements based on the opinion of his psychologist that the is not a sexual offender. The court made it clear that the registration requirements are "automatic."

26. Post-Conviction DNA Testing.

R.C. 2953.71 precludes after verdict dna testing if a previous dna test was performed and was outcome determinative. A new test can be granted if under the facts, it would be outcome determinative. Where, for example, at the time of the first test there was dna present that could not be separated from the dna of the victim and where later a new method of testing became available which could determine whether the dna present was the defendant's, such a test is outcome determinative. [835]

---

[834] State v. Blankenship, slip Opinion. 2015-Ohio-4624.

[835] *State v. Prade*, 126 Ohio St. 3d 27, 2010-Ohio-1842.

A capital defendant has the same appeal of right in a DNA application as does a non-capital defendant. The portions of R.C. 2953.73 that limit this appeal are unconstitutional as violative of the Equal Protection Clause of the U.S. and Ohio Constitutions. [836]

27. Removal of Retained Counsel.

The removal of retained counsel is a final appealable order. Although this court has previously determined that such an order is not a final appealable order.[837] Two factors cause that holding to be no longer valid. First, R.C. 2505.02 has since been enacted. Second, the United States Supreme Court in United States v. Gonzalez-Lopez (2006), 548 U.S. 140, held that such a dismissal of retained counsel can constitute structural error and a reversal of the conviction. [838] The availability of a post-conviction appeal must be contrasted with the result of the ruling on the rights of the defendant. The third prong of the test to be used when considering this issue is whether a post-conviction appeal would be "effective and meaningful". Because such a deprivation of counsel is now a structural error it would be automatically reversible rendering a post-conviction motion to be effective and meaningful.[839]

---

[836] State v. Noling,

[837] *State ex rel. Keenan v. Calabrese* (1994), 69 Ohio St. 3d 176.

[838] *State v. Chambliss*, 128 Ohio St. 3d 507, 2011-Ohio-1785.

[839] See also, *State v. Muncie* (2001), 91 Ohio St. 3d 440, 446 N.E. 2d

28. Sufficiency and Merging of Multiple Offenses.

It is improper for an appellant court to rely on improperly established judicial notice by the trial court to determine whether a new trial at the state's request is warranted. "We hold that the fact that was judicially noticed in error in this case should not have been considered evidence as part of the appellate court's sufficiency analysis."[840]

Where an appellate court is considering whether to merge multiple offenses that court should not limit its review to the state's theory of the case, but must consider the entire record: "We hold that when deciding whether to merge multiple offenses at sentencing pursuant to R.C. 2941.25, a court must review the entire record, including arguments and information presented at the sentencing hearing, to determine whether the offenses were committed separately or with a separate animus. The court of appeals erred by looking solely to what it perceived as the state's theory of the case at trial and by refusing to consider the information presented at the sentencing hearing. The analysis is not limited to the states theory that was presented at trial.[841]

1092, for an analysis of the factors that determine a 'final order."

840 *State v. Kareski,* Slip Opinion No. 2013-Ohio-4008

841 *State v. Washington*, Slip Opinion No. 2013-Ohio-4982

CHAPTER 89

Plain Error.

1. Plain Error
2. Structural Errors Contrasted with Plain Errors.

1. Plain Error

Crim. R. 52(B) provides, "Plain errors or defects affecting substantial rights may be noticed although they were not brought to the attention of the court."

The context in which plain error occurs at trial is usually the result of an omission on the part of defense counsel to object to the admission of evidence, the argument of the prosecutor, or an erroneous jury charge.

Plain error is the standard that must be applied since the court cannot properly review the error because the failure to object waives normal review. Plain error, although rarely found, may appear in any part of the trial. Accordingly, the entire proceeding must be examined.

The plain error rule is an exceptional means that should be used only to avoid a *miscarriage of justice*. See *Eaton v. United States.*[842]

---

[842] *Eaton v. United States*, 398 F. 2d 485, certiorari denied, 393 U.S. 937 (C.A. 5, 1968).

The rationale for resorting to plain error only in extraordinary circumstances is as follows: "Any other rule would relieve counsel from any duty or responsibility to the court and place the entire responsibility upon the trial court to give faultless instructions upon every possible feature of the case, thereby disregarding entirely the true relationship of court and counsel which enjoins upon counsel the duty to exercise diligence and to aid the court." [843]

Where defense counsel failed to object to a jury instruction, the court held in *State v. Long*,[844] "a jury instruction * * * does not constitute plain error under Crim. R. 52 (B) unless, but for the error, the outcome of the trial clearly would have been otherwise."

If the error does not affect the outcome of the trial, it will be found to be harmless error. A trial court cannot amend the indictment in a prosecution for possession of controlled substances where the amendment changes the identity of the crime.in *State v. Davis*, the court amended the indictment from a charge alleging the defendant possessed less than the bulk amount to possession of five times but less than fifty times the bulk amount of OxyContin. This amendment changed the identity of the crime and had the effect of convicting the defendant of a crime of which the grand jury did indict him. Not only was this a violation Crim. R. 7(D), it was also plain error.[845]

---

[843] *State v.Driscoll*, 106 Ohio St. 33, 138 N.E. 2d 376 (1922).

[844] *State v. Long,* 53 Ohio St. 2d 91, 372 N.E. 2d 804 (1978).

[845] *State v. Davis*, 121 Ohio St. 3d 239, 903 N.E. 2d 609 (2008).

2. Structural Errors Contrasted with Plain Errors.

There is a difference between a structural error and a trial error. A structural error requires automatic reversal while a trial error requires further analysis to determine if a substantial right has been affected.

Hence, in a prosecution for aggravated burglary where the trial court's instruction does not include the required culpable mental state for trespass, and where defense counsel did not object to this omission, it was necessary on appeal for this court to determine if the omission of the culpable mental state charge constituted a "trial error" which can be examined in the context of the whole of the trial to determine if the omission was harmless beyond a reasonable doubt or if a "structural error" was committed which is per se prejudicial. A failure to instruct on all of the necessary elements that constitute a crime is not necessarily error, as this court held in State v. Adams, 62 Ohio St. 3d 151, 404 N.E. 2d 144. Structural errors are rare and have been found is such cases where there was a denial of counsel, biased trial judge, racial discrimination, denial of public trial, incorrect reasonable doubt instruction, etc.

If the defendant had counsel and was tried by an impartial fact-finder, as was the case here, a plain error analysis is to be used to determine if any error was harmless.

Accordingly, the court found no structural error and remanded the case to the court of appeals for a plain error analysis.[846]

[846] *State v. Wamsley*, 117 Ohio St. 3d 388, N.E. 2d 45 (2008).

CHAPTER 90

Rules of Construction.

Under R.C. 2901.04, all offenses shall be "strictly construed against the state and liberally construed in favor of the accused." The rules are to be "construed so as to effect the fair and impartial, speedy, and sure administration of justice." Strictly construing the statute does not, however, confer authority for a court to construe the statute in favor of the accused when the statute is clear and unambiguous.

Courts do not have the authority to ignore the plain and unambiguous language of a statute under the guise of either statutory interpretation or liberal construction; in such situations, the courts must give effect to the words utilized.

1. Where Statutes must be read in Pari Materia.

In some instances, statutes must be read *in pari materia,* such as where they appear to overlap in culpability or in punishment.

For example, where identical conduct is violative of two or more statutes as in *State v. Kurtz,* where the defendant, a public official committed a theft offense. The issue was should the theft be prosecuted under one count as the theft statute requires, or as

---

[847] *State v. Kurtz* , 28 Ohio St. 3d 36, 502 N.E. 2d 210 (1986).

a series of separate offenses under the theft in office statute, which is silent as to multiple counts. [847]

The theft statute and the theft in office statute must be read in pari materia, the Court held: "the *in pari materia* rule of law of statutory construction applies only where the statue to be considered is ambiguous or the significance of its terms doubtful." Citing, *Morris v. Kaiser Engineers.* [848]

There was no ambiguity in this instance because theft in office, being a specific statute, controls over the general theft statute.

---

[848] *Morris v. Kaiser Engineers,* 14 Ohio St. 3d 45, 471 N.E. 2d 471 (1984).

CHAPTER 91

Juvenile Issues

R.C. 2901.08(A). It is an unconstitutional violation of the Due Process Clause of the Ohio Constitution and the Fourteen Amendment where a juvenile adjudication is treated as a previous conviction to enhance penalty or exposure for an adult conviction as permitted per. R.C. 2901.08(A).

Here a prior juvenile adjudication for aggravated robbery. R.C. 2929.13(F) required the trial court to impose an additional three-year sentence.

"Quite simply, a juvenile adjudication is not a conviction of a crime and should not be treated as one."[849]

It is a violation of due process for a mandatory transfer of a juvenile to adult court as required by R.C. 2152.10(A)in which certain crimes as well as some delinquent histories of behavior require such transfers.

This court found the above statute to be a due process violation for the following reasons:

1. 16 or 17 year olds are children and are to be treated as children until a transfer has occurred. They should be afforded full constitutional protections
2. Age should not be a determinative for transfer for adult prosecution.
3. Mandatory transfer precludes the juvenile court from treating the child individually.
4. Every child has the right to an amenability hearing prior to transfer.[850]

---

[849] State v. Hand, Slip Opinion No. 2016-Ohio-5504.

5. A juvenile in a non-homicide prosecution shall not be sentence for a term of years that has the effect of a sentence of life as being a cruel and unusual punishment in violation of the Eight Amendment. For the same reasoning of the United States Supreme Court in Graham v, Florida, 560 U.S. 48 which prohibited life without parole for nonhomicidal offenders, this court held that the effect of consecutive sentence here has the same effect of a term of life.
6. The salient aspect of Graham and this holding is that a juvenile at some time must be given a chance to reenter society

---

[850] State v. Aalim, Slip Opinion No. 2016-Ohio-8278.